Praise for *Lifelines*

"In the pages of *Lifelines*, I learned about Wen's remarkable background, and the searing experiences that drove her into public health. . . . Eventually the country will get past this virus, but Wen is right: Actually getting well is going to be a much longer project."

—Karen Tumulty, *The Washington Post*

"A provocative exploration of public health from an immigrant physician and expert's point of view [and] a moving account of an impressively fruitful life."

—*Kirkus Reviews*

"A stirring call for greater investment in public health programs to combat racism, poverty, gun violence, and other social ills . . . Readers will be inspired by Wen's belief in the power of public health to make America better."

—*Publishers Weekly*

"Our best doctors aren't created in medical school, they are born through remarkable life experiences with a desire and capacity to end the injustices others accept. Dr. Leana Wen is a public health superhero, destined to make profound changes in our world. This is her origin story."

—Dr. Sanjay Gupta, CNN chief medical correspondent

"Captivating, inspiring, and refreshingly honest, *Lifelines* takes you on an unforgettable journey to understand the power of public health to transform society. Dr. Wen's hopeful and wise account is a reminder of why she has quickly become one of America's most important physician leaders."

—Dr. Vivek Murthy, 19th surgeon general of the United States

"In this powerful book, Dr. Wen tells the compelling story of her journey to a career in medicine while giving a crash course in the nuts and bolts of policy and politics. Along the way, her writing will turn any reader into a believer in the power of public health and an advocate for getting off the benches and into the trenches."

—Senator Barbara Mikulski

"With its brave candor and clarity, this book is for people who might not know all the ways in which public health has saved their lives, but they will once they've read *Lifelines*. It is also for all the people who do know the importance of investing in public health, of prevention and treating everyone with dignity, and who want to learn how Leana Wen has accomplished this throughout her career as a doctor, public servant, and writer."

—**Chelsea Clinton, author, advocate, and vice chair of the Clinton Foundation**

"*Lifelines* is a truly special book. Dr. Wen takes us with her not just on her remarkable life journey but also into an exploration of the life-and-death implications of a system that too consistently leaves people behind. Here Dr. Wen shows that she is not only one of our great medical minds—she is also one of our great storytellers and changemakers."

—**Wes Moore, author of *The Other Wes Moore* and *Five Days*, CEO of the Robin Hood Foundation**

"During the pandemic, I came to count on Dr. Leana Wen's calm presence, tempered advice, and explanation of the science. Now that I've read her captivating and important *Lifelines*, I cannot begin to express how inspired I am by her personal journey. Many people are ambitious and smart, but few among them seek to improve life for others. Leana Wen's empathy and concern for the world around her shines through with every word."

—**Lisa See, author of *The Island of Sea Women* and *Shanghai Girls***

Lifelines

ALSO BY LEANA WEN

When Doctors Don't Listen:
How to Avoid Misdiagnoses and Unnecessary Tests
(with Joshua Kosowsky)

Lifelines

A DOCTOR'S JOURNEY IN
THE FIGHT FOR PUBLIC HEALTH

Leana Wen

A Metropolitan Paperback
Henry Holt and Company
New York

Metropolitan Books
Henry Holt and Company
Publishers since 1866
120 Broadway
New York, New York 10271
www.henryholt.com

Metropolitan Books® and ◼® are registered trademarks of
Macmillan Publishing Group, LLC.

Names and identifying details of all patients discussed have
been changed and some are composites.

The Library of Congress has cataloged the hardcover edition as follows:

Names: Wen, Leana S., author.
Title: Lifelines : a doctor's journey in the fight for public health / Leana Wen.
Description: First edition. | New York : Metropolitan Books, Henry Holt
    and Company, 2021. | Includes index.
Identifiers: LCCN 2021002382 (print) | LCCN 2021002383 (ebook) |
    ISBN 9781250186232 (hardcover) | ISBN 9781250186249 (ebook)
Subjects: LCSH: Wen, Leana S.,—Health. | Medical care. | Health policy. |
    Health promotion. | Opioid abuse. | COVID-19 (Disease)
Classification: LCC RA410.5 .W455 2021 (print) | LCC RA410.5 (ebook) |
    DDC 362.1—dc23
LC record available at https://lccn.loc.gov/2021002382
LC ebook record available at https://lccn.loc.gov/2021002383

ISBN 9781250839350 (trade paperback)

Our books may be purchased in bulk for promotional, educational, or
business use. Please contact your local bookseller or the Macmillan Corporate and
Premium Sales Department at (800) 221-7945, extension 5442, or by
e-mail at MacmillanSpecialMarkets@macmillan.com.

Originally published in hardcover in 2021 by Metropolitan Books

First Metropolitan Paperbacks Edition 2022

Designed by Kelly S. Too

Printed in the United States of America

1 3 5 7 9 10 8 6 4 2

To Sebastian, my partner in this life journey,
and to Eli and Isabelle. You are our everything.

"Our children are living messengers to a future we will never see. The question is how we will send them. Will we send them strong? Will we send them hopeful? Or will we rob them of their destiny, their dignity, and their dreams? Will we take from them their health and their ability to succeed before they even have a chance to get started?

No, we cannot do that. We will not do that. We must not do that."

—Representative Elijah E. Cummings (1951–2019)

CONTENTS

Prologue   1

PART I: LEARNING

1. *Chi Ku*   11
2. Belonging   29
3. White Coat, Clenched Fist   43
4. Opening Pandora's Box   61
5. When Doctors Don't Listen   73

PART II: LEADING

6. Doctor for the City   93
7. Saving Lives Today   108
8. Treating Addiction as the Disease It Is   124
9. Unrest and Recovery   143
10. Putting the Face on Public Health   160
11. Hurt People Hurt People   175
12. Going Upstream   190
13. New Beginnings   209

PART III: TRANSFORMING

14. Decisions   227
15. The Courage to Try   237
16. Preventable Harm   255
17. A Pandemic of Misinformation   271
18. The Invisible Hand of Public Health   287
19. COVID-19 Comes Home   299

Epilogue: Life Lessons   313

Acknowledgments   319
Index   323

Lifelines

Prologue

The first sign of something wrong was the sound of a high-pitched squeak.

"What's that?" Christine whispered. I had just opened the door of the apartment complex my family shared with hers and two others. We looked at each other as the noises continued. It was a wet rattle and wheeze.

Then we heard someone shouting in rapid-fire Spanish. I grabbed Christine's hand, and we ran toward the noise.

It was the apartment next to Christine's. The door was open and we saw that the noise was coming from Tony. He was in the third grade, two behind me and Christine. Tony was sitting upright, straight as a board, clutching the sides of a rocking chair. His cheeks were streaked with red. His breathing was short and shallow. Each exhale ended in a wheeze and a squeak, each shorter than the one before.

His eyes were wide and beads of sweat ran down his face. He looked terrified.

I knew that feeling well. Asthma.

Tony's grandmother was yelling and begging us to help. There was an inhaler on the floor. I grabbed it and held up it up to Tony's mouth. I pressed it, but nothing happened.

I got my own inhaler out of my backpack and pulled his lips open. I pressed twice. I took it out and tried again.

The medication dribbled out of his mouth. His eyes were starting to close. His breathing was slowing and I could barely hear the wheezing. His lips were turning purple and blue.

Christine's mother had heard the noise. She held the phone in her hand. "We need to call 911!"

"No, no, no!" The grandmother yelled. "Policia, no! No policia!"

"Not police, ambulance. Medical. Doctor. 911!"

I was holding Tony up, and he felt heavy in my arms. His grandmother shook him and begged him to wake up. She thumped him on his back. She grabbed him by his hair.

Christine's mother had been a nurse back in her home country. She lifted Tony and laid him flat on the floor. She pressed on his chest and breathed into his mouth.

Eventually, she stepped back and shook her head. The grandmother began to wail.

We listened to her scream and cry all night.

"Do you think Tony would have lived if we'd brought him to a hospital?" I whispered to my mother as we lay in bed. In Shanghai, where I was born, I'd had such severe asthma that I ended up in the hospital nearly every month. It was terrifying to fight for air, but I always knew that once I got to the hospital, the doctors would make me better.

"Maybe he was so sick that nobody could have helped him," my mother said.

"What about 911? In school, they always say to call 911 and an ambulance will come."

"Who knows who else would come? Maybe the police. They could all be deported and sent back to Mexico."

"So if something happens to you, I shouldn't call 911 because you'll be sent back to China? What about Father—what if his ulcer bleeds and he's very sick?"

"Think about what happened to your father in China. Going back is not better than death."

"But that's not right," I remember saying. "How come other people can call the ambulance and go to the doctor? Why is it different for us?"

My mother's answer fixed my future. "Life is like this for some people. Maybe one day you can change things for people like Tony and your father."

That night cemented my decision to become a doctor so that when I encountered another Tony, his life would not have to end in a preventable death.

Fifteen years later, I did meet another Tony. He, too, was a third grader with severe asthma. I got to know him because he and his mother would come to the emergency department every week, sometimes multiple times. He always had the same symptoms: wheezing, coughing, and gasping for breath. When it was particularly bad, he'd get that familiar frightened look in his eyes, the look of not knowing whether the next breath would come.

Each time, I had every medical tool at my disposal. I'd put a mask on him to administer oxygen and nebulizers. I'd give him steroid medications. I'd monitor his breathing. Most of the time, he'd get better within a couple of hours and go back home.

But he kept on returning, week after week. He and his mother were homeless. They shuttled between shelters and the homes of different relatives and friends. His clothes always reeked of cigarettes because his mother's boyfriend and her family smoked. At some point, they moved into a home of their own, but his asthma didn't improve—they were in a row house where all the units were vacant and harbored mold and other allergens. Two blocks away, an incinerator pumped out toxins.

This Tony was being treated at one of the best hospitals in America. Every time he got sick, we'd make him better. But medicine could not treat the poor air quality he breathed. Medicine could not change the poverty, instability, stress, and powerlessness of his and his mother's lives. This Tony, too, was a testament to the notion that the currency of inequality is years of life.

This is a reality I knew all too well from my childhood. My family and

I came to the United States from China with less than $40 to our name. We lived paycheck-to-paycheck and worried every month about making the rent. Inequality left a mark on everyone I knew: my classmates, who became victims of gun violence; their families, who were decimated by drug addiction; our neighbors, who died young from preventable diseases.

I became a doctor to save Tony. I chose emergency medicine so that I could treat everyone and turn no one away, not immigrants afraid of deportation or people who couldn't pay. But working in the ER was also where I saw the limitations of health care. I could resuscitate a young man dying from gunshot wounds, but what could I do about the violence on the street, violence so consuming that elementary schools didn't have recess outdoors? I could stitch up a child's laceration, but what could I do about the ache in her belly because the last meal she ate was her school lunch two days before? I could prescribe drugs for diabetes and heart disease, but how could I recommend healthy eating knowing that the corner store my patient depended on for food sold no fruits or vegetables?

It wasn't just health care that my patients needed: it was public health. Public health is housing. It's food. It's clean air. It's education. It's the ability to level the unequal playing field. It's the social supports that give everyone their best chance to survive. For so many people— indeed, for all of us—public health is our lifeline.

There is a saying that public health saved your life today—you just don't know it. Public health works when it's invisible, because it prevented something from happening. It is the forgotten subject that no one thinks about. Politicians don't campaign on a platform of public health. Budgets don't prioritize public health. Even the U.S. health-care system treats public health as the forgotten stepchild, with less than 3 percent of America's total health-care spending going toward it.

The late congressman Elijah Cummings often said that "the cost of doing nothing isn't nothing." The cost of neglecting public health is people's livelihoods and their lives. Now as never before, we have seen the tragic consequences of that neglect. The United States—and the world—has lived through the greatest public health catastrophe of our lifetimes: a pandemic in the form of COVID-19, which has killed hundreds of thousands of Americans and triggered an economic crisis, made all the worse by decades of disinvestment in public health and fueled by science denialism.

My life is a journey into public health. In this book, I tell that story with the goal of making this crucial but invisible work visible. When I was named health commissioner for the city of Baltimore in 2014, a position I held for nearly four years, I saw the immediate and far-reaching impact of public health—and of its neglect—every day. Like many other cities, Baltimore has its share of economic challenges that are directly reflected in poor health outcomes and vast disparities. A child born in one neighborhood has an average life expectancy of sixty-five years, while another born just a few miles away can expect to live eighty-five years—a twenty-year gap. The same neighborhood that has lower life expectancy also has higher infant mortality, more drug overdose deaths, higher homicide rates, lower educational achievement, and—not coincidentally—a larger concentration of poverty.

If the currency of inequality is years of life, then the opposite of poverty is health.

As the doctor for the city, I worked every day to improve the health and well-being of Baltimore's residents. These were not random people, but my neighbors and fellow community members. Every problem was deeply personal, yet they were all potentially solvable with the tools of public health: providing direct services like care for uninsured patients and services in senior centers and schools; implementing public education campaigns; and shaping health policies as a means to effect change on the city and state levels.

My role allowed me to be a vocal advocate and translate the community's needs into policy reform and programs that targeted the greatest sources of harm, such as combating the opioid epidemic, reducing infant mortality, and treating gun violence as a public health issue. My team and I were unafraid to call out racism as a public health concern and to tackle systemic injustices like childhood trauma and mass incarceration. There was always more to be done, more programs to start or expand, more policies to improve the public's health, and more people we could serve. And although the work was deeply immersed in the crushing reality of poverty and trauma, in Baltimore I witnessed the resiliency and dedication of people who gave everything of themselves to their communities.

Public health is unusual in that it straddles the worlds of science, advocacy, medicine, and politics. Through my experience, I learned how policies that improve health advance the goal of equity and how they translate into direct services on the ground. Public health ties to every aspect of society, and all sectors of our society are needed to strive together for better health.

My time in Baltimore forged my approach to patient advocacy, improving access to care, and responding to national public health crises. It was an approach that I brought to the leadership of a national organization, Planned Parenthood, that at the time was threatened with funding cuts that could have left millions of low-income women and families without cancer screenings, HIV testing, and other preventive care. Leading Planned Parenthood offered an opportunity to work for a world in which health care will finally be regarded as a fundamental right guaranteed to all, not a privilege available only to some. In that fight, I learned a great deal about the growing schisms in the country and saw access to health care threatened by escalating ideological battles in Washington.

These lessons proved invaluable when, in December 2019, a novel coronavirus quickly spread around the world and swept through the United States. Day by day, the public health catastrophe worsened, accelerated by the federal government's bungled response of deliberate obfuscation, rigid partisan ideology, and muzzling of top public health officials.

Those most affected were, once again, the most vulnerable populations, the people I had always been drawn to serve. With a background in emergency preparedness and public health expertise, I joined the battle against the pandemic, analyzing and guiding policies, advising businesses and schools as they navigated the challenge of keeping employees and students safe, and educating the public through the media. In many ways, responding to COVID-19 was my life's calling, the culmination of everything I prepared for.

There is a second story that I tell here, too: my own, which is at once a personal journey and an improbable and uniquely American story. Just before I turned eight, my parents brought me to the United States, seeking political asylum. They left their families and their lives in China to wash dishes, clean hotel rooms, and deliver newspapers so that I and, eventually, my younger sister would have the chance of a better life. We depended on Medicaid and food stamps. Living paycheck-to-paycheck, we went through times when we were homeless.

My life is a testament to public health. I was able to rise from my humble beginnings because of my parents' hard work and extraordinary sacrifice, as well as the fortuitous interventions of supportive mentors at critical moments. The social safety net played a no less crucial role, providing housing and food, education and health when we most needed it. This is all public health. It's what saves your life from infectious disease. It's what can change the reality of your zip code determining your life expectancy, or the place of your birth or the color of your skin determining your destiny. Public health is a powerful tool for wellness, advancement, and social justice. Housing, education, poverty, and violence—these are all public health issues. And, as we saw with COVID-19, the census, voting, and even the post office, are inextricably linked to public health issues, too.

I also want to share my story so that young people growing up in difficult circumstances know that that they too can dream big dreams and strive for them. Not every chapter that I tell is a tale of success; this book is also about resilience, grit, and the courage to persist.

A final reason for this book is a call to action. We generally understand getting involved to mean voting or running for elected office. These are not the only ways to make a difference in civic life. So much is done by people on the front lines, in community organizations, local government, and civic volunteering. In my work, I have met the most inspiring people—the formerly incarcerated, individuals overcoming the disease of addiction, and those who survived unimaginable horrors—who have succeeded in channeling their disillusionment and pain into their purpose and calling.

Those who are deeply embedded in their communities have a duty to speak up and be heard. They are the ones who know what works and what doesn't, who understand the hopes and dreams of fellow community members. It's they who must be represented so that the national discourse reflects the needs of the people on the ground. In my work and travels, I've encountered so many who feel alienated by the divisiveness of our times, yet there are those who seek common ground and have devised practical approaches that improve health and well-being for all.

We are at a critical point in our history, when we have the chance to channel uncertainty and anxiety into a sustained groundswell for equity and health. How will we ensure that our fellow citizens will no longer be robbed of decades of life, that *where* children live will not determine *whether* they live? How can we leave future generations a world where all aspects of health are understood as fundamental human rights, where no one is denied access to health care because of an inability to pay or someone else's political ideology? How can we bend the arc of the universe back toward justice, so that health is no longer defined as the opposite of poverty?

PART ONE

Learning

1

Chi Ku

Chi ku. In Mandarin, it means "to eat bitter"—to sacrifice and go through great hardships. My grandparents always added a second part: that one eats bitter in order to taste sweet.

I was born in Shanghai, China. My early memories were happy ones. I lived with my Nai Nai and Ye Ye, my grandmother and grandfather on my father's side. They had a one-room apartment in the heart of the bustling Huangpu District that was the gathering place for all their grandchildren. I was the youngest and spent my days helping Nai Nai wrap delicate dumplings and watching Ye Ye read books until my cousins finished school and came home to play.

We lived in very tight quarters. My grandparents' apartment barely fit a bed, a dresser, a small table, and a bamboo mat. Kitchen and washroom facilities were in the hallway and shared among a dozen families. When my parents first got married, they lived in the same room as Ye Ye and Nai Nai, their beds separated by only a curtain. When I was born, they moved out, to another apartment down the hall.

For most of my childhood in Shanghai, my mother lived away from home. She was a student at the same university where my Ye Ye taught, studying for a bachelor's and then a master's degree in English language and literature. Our neighbors spoke of my mother with awe. Going to college was exceptionally rare in those days. My mother had been in elementary school when the Cultural Revolution started and all schools ceased operation. Her mother—my other grandmother, Wai Po—smuggled books and taught my mother and her sister by candlelight.

It was a testament to Wai Po's persistence that both of her daughters tested into university just after the Cultural Revolution ended, despite their having no formal schooling beyond elementary school. They each had to beat out millions of others who vied for a small number of coveted college openings.

It was expected that university students lived on campus. So I saw my mother every other weekend.

Once, she'd been away for longer. When she came home, I didn't know what to say to her.

Nai Nai urged me to give her a hug. "Ask your mother how her studies are," she whispered to me.

"How are your studies?" I said.

My mother was not one for hugs or small talk. She held me at arm's length.

"Duo Duo's hair is so long," she said to Nai Nai, using my nickname, which was conceived out of irony. "Duo Duo" means "too many" and was a common moniker for children in families that had many off-spring. I was born shortly after the start of China's one-child policy, so I was destined to be the only child. "Duo Duo" didn't mean that I was one too many, but that I was the only one to embody the many ambitions everyone had for me.

"I'm going to cut it tonight. She looks better with short hair." My mother turned to me. I had a cold and was trying to suppress a cough. "Stop coughing. It will make your asthma flare up."

That night, we were eating Nai Nai's steamed fish when my chest started tightening. I started coughing and soon couldn't catch my breath. Nai Nai grabbed my inhaler and told me to take two puffs.

This was the routine. We tried the inhaler first, then she turned on a machine and put a mask over my face. If the attack was very bad, I'd swallow three pills, then put on the mask again.

"Isn't that too much medication?" my mother called out. "Shouldn't we go to the doctor?"

"No, we try this first," Nai Nai said. "Most of the time, we don't need to go."

Nai Nai put the mask over my face. I took a few breaths, then pulled it off so that I could cough.

My mother was grabbing my hand. "She can't breathe! We have to go get her help."

"She's fine!" Nai Nai insisted.

They both looked at me.

"I don't want to go to the hospital," I said. Tears were running down my face.

"Don't cry," my mother said. "The sniffing is not good for your asthma."

"I'm not crying. It's the mist from the breathing mask," I said. Each word took a breath to get out, and I was panting. My chest felt tight. Any tighter, and I was afraid that I wouldn't be able to take the next breath.

I was terrified. I turned to Nai Nai.

"It's OK," she said. She took me into her arms and started singing the song from my preschool about monkeys and ducklings.

My breathing didn't get better. With the next coughing spell, my mother began yelling that I was turning red and blue.

"Duo Duo is sick," she said. "I have to take her to the hospital now."

"I'll go," I said, "but I want to go with Nai Nai."

There was a story Nai Nai would tell me that always gave me nightmares. It was about a beautiful woman who made many men fall in love with her. They would do anything for her. They all wanted to marry her and so bestowed her with flattery and gifts. What they didn't know was that she was actually a monster who would kill them when she grew tired of them, which inevitably happened. When it became time, she would peel off her face, which was a mask all along, and reveal a horrific pale-faced ghoul.

Nai Nai told me the story so that I would be careful of strangers—they were not always who they said they were. Sometimes I had dreams about this woman being my mother, and I'd wake up soaked in sweat as I imagined her peeling off her face.

That night, when my mother stared at me, her face was as white as the pale-faced ghoul from Nai Nai's stories. Nai Nai carried me in her arms, and my mother followed us out the door. Tears were running down my cheek, and also down hers.

IN THOSE DAYS, I DIDN'T understand why my mother and my father were gone all the time. Ye Ye and Nai Nai would tell me that it was *chi ku*: their lives were hard so that my life could be better.

Chi ku was the same answer my grandparents gave when I asked them about their early days. From my aunt and my cousins, I'd pieced together some details, though most of their story remained unclear. I know that they had grown up in a poor village near Guangzhou in southern China and got married in their teens. Somehow, Ye Ye was able to go to school and defied all the odds to attend university and become a renowned linguistics scholar in Shanghai.

During the Cultural Revolution, he and other academics were deemed elitists and targeted for persecution. Ye Ye was tied up and beaten in front of his students and then imprisoned. Nai Nai was forced to leave her children, who were sent to labor camps. Their home was burned and every possession confiscated by the government. My father, then in his twenties, ran away and became a revolutionary against the Communist regime. He was caught, jailed, and suffered innumerable abuses that I would only learn about many years later.

The one story that Nai Nai liked to tell was how my parents met. The Cultural Revolution had ended, and she and Ye Ye had rebuilt their lives in Shanghai. Nai Nai's concern was her only surviving son, who was approaching forty and still didn't have a wife or child.

She asked Ye Ye, who by then had been restored to his faculty position at the university, to set my father up with one of his students. In those days, unmarried men and women were not supposed to go out by themselves. This woman brought her roommate as a chaperone on their first date.

That roommate was my mother, and it was love at first sight for her and my father. My father was eleven years older, handsome, and a rebel. They were married within months.

People told different versions of their courtship. I knew that Wai Po didn't approve of the relationship, but nobody explained why. Did they have a wedding? I was always told no, but then my aunt showed me a photo of my mother in a wedding dress. I asked Nai Nai about it. She immediately put the picture away and said that we shouldn't talk about it anymore.

My father was absent for long periods of time. When he was home, he had many friends who came to visit. I didn't know any of their names; I was told to call all of them "uncle." One day I asked one of the uncles whether he was an engineer like my father. Nai Nai was so upset that she took me outside to the hallway and slapped me, the only time she'd ever hit me. "Never say anything to anyone about your father," she said.

When he was at home, my father reentered our daily lives as if he were never gone. He went to work during the day and spent time with the family at night. Nai Nai and my aunts—his sisters—would fawn over him, and someone would always make his favorite meal of spare ribs and sticky rice.

One day, my father took me to the park. There was a lily pond, and I reached in to try to touch the fish. I lost my balance and fell in the water. It was winter and I was freezing. The pond was probably no more than a few feet deep, but I was terrified. The next thing I remember, my father was in the pond with me. He lifted me out and, as I proudly reported to Nai Nai and Ye Ye, he saved my life.

For months after that, every time Nai Nai would take me to the park, I'd peer into the lily pond in the hope that I would see my father's reflection. Once, I deliberately stepped into the water, certain that my father would materialize and rescue me. I had either grown taller or the pond was shallower, because the water only came up to my chest. My father did not appear, and after a moment I climbed out, wet and disappointed.

————

I WAS SEVEN WHEN MY mother told me that she was leaving.

It was the first warm day of the new year. We were walking along the Huangpu River. I remember my mother buying two ice cream sandwiches from the sidewalk vendor. Mine was melting and my mother took out a tissue to wipe my hands. Hers had melted, too, and she also had ice cream all over her face. We pointed to each other and laughed.

"Duo Duo, now I'm going to tell something," she said. "Ever since your father and I met, we've been looking for a way out of China." She explained that because of my father's rebellious activities during the Cultural Revolution, he was labeled a political dissident. Whenever foreign dignitaries came to visit, and whenever the government perceived an internal threat, he would be taken in for questioning. Sometimes he was imprisoned.

"He lives in constant fear. We all do," she said. "You must have seen that our family has different circumstances than other people."

I nodded. Virtually everyone in my parents' and grandparents' generations had experienced great suffering during the Cultural Revolution, but I saw that there was something unusual about my family. Although they behaved as if nothing was wrong when my father went away, they would never speak of him, and in their silence I would feel their anxiety. When he'd come back, he would always be thin and gaunt, with dark shadows under his eyes. Nai Nai and my aunts would fuss over him, but our neighbors stayed away. Classmates who would stop by after school to play would stop coming.

"I knew when I married your father that our lives will always be like this while we're in China," my mother went on. "This is not a good life for us, and it will not be a good future for you. One needs to look forward, not always behind, because one is always afraid of the shadows. That's why I study so hard, so that I can get into an American university."

Later, I'd learn that this was one of the few ways out of China at the time, and that this had been my parents' plan from the time they first met. My mother must have known that this was what she had to do, and how much my father and our entire family were counting on her.

It took a year to apply, and another full year for my parents to borrow enough money from relatives to supplement their savings for the visa and plane fare. The plans were finally coming together. They had enough to buy her ticket (and tickets for my father and me to follow afterward), her visa was approved, and she was about to start a PhD program.

In fact, she'd been accepted to two PhD programs. One was at the University of Illinois in Chicago, to continue her work in English literature. The other was at Utah State University, in educational psychology. Her professors didn't know much about Illinois, but someone had a colleague who knew someone who had studied in Utah. In addition, my mother thought that psychology was a more useful degree than English. "English is useful in China, but in America, who wants a Chinese person who specializes in English?"

So, Utah it was. In less than a week my mother would be leaving for a place called Logan.

"Duo Duo, we are going to America," she said. "You are going to be an American."

Soon, she was gone. No one could tell me when I'd see her again. My grandparents showed me a letter that said she had arrived safely. They acted as if it was just like when she went away to study at the Shanghai university, but I knew this was different. There was a plan that my father and I would join her, but no time line. It depended on when my father was home again, and whether our visas would come through.

The days went by as we waited, and the magnolia trees grew delicate blossoms and then turned a golden brown.

AS THE WEEKS STRETCHED INTO months, I became more and more convinced that I didn't want to leave the life I knew. My girlfriends and I read sad poems aloud to each other about eternal friendship. We vowed that we would keep in touch. I told my cousins that I wanted to live with them. My journal entries from those days had long treatises on why I didn't want to go to America.

I begged Ye Ye and Nai Nai to let me stay. Ye Ye tried to console me, but Nai Nai was unyielding.

"Do you know why your mother is in America?" she asked, her thick eyebrows furrowing as her lips pursed together. "She doesn't know one person there. It is frightening for her, but she is doing it because she wants you to have a better life." She handed me a dish towel. "Dry your tears and never speak of your selfish desire again. From now on, you are living for something bigger than yourself."

If my parents were eating bitter for me, I needed to learn to eat bitter for them, too.

I have only two more memories of my life in China. One was in the hospital. I was being led to see my father. A nurse pulled back the curtain, and I didn't recognize the man in the bed. His eyes were yellow and there were two tubes down his throat, one through his mouth and one through his nose. I watched the nurses change his sheets, and they were stained with black tar that smelled like week-old chicken liver. In my clinical work later, I'd recognize this distinct scent of gastrointestinal bleeding. Every time I smelled it, I'd see my father lying in that bed, prone and helpless, and me staring at him just as helplessly.

The second memory was of our last hours in China. The day after my father was released from the hospital, we headed to the airport. As we walked through the terminal, my father leaned on my aunt on one side and Nai Nai on the other.

It would soon be my job to watch out for him. In the months since my mother had left, Ye Ye had been trying to teach me basic English phrases. I didn't learn nearly enough to communicate, so we came up with a plan. Ye Ye gave me twenty slips of paper. Each had Chinese on one side and English on the other.

"My father has a bleeding ulcer. He just had an operation and blood transfusions. Please call a doctor," was one. I also had slips of paper to explain that we had visas and that my mother was waiting for us. Ye Ye and I practiced each situation, and he gave me his English-Chinese dictionary in case I needed to translate something that wasn't on the paper.

At the gate, we said our goodbyes. Nai Nai had warned me not to cry. I lasted until I saw that she herself couldn't hold back her tears. I hugged her and Ye Ye. We knew we might never see one another again.

Thankfully, I didn't need to use the slips of paper during the flight. My father and I landed at Los Angeles International Airport on December 12, 1990, and went through immigration without incident. The immigration officer asked me for my name, and I told him "Linda"—Ye Ye and I had decided that it was the English name closest to my Chinese name, Linyan. The officer wrote down "Leana" and pronounced it as I do now, "Lee-na." That was my new name. My father, Xiaolu, became "Louis." My mother, previously Ying, was "Sandy."

We still had one more flight, a much shorter one. When "Louis" and I arrived in Salt Lake City, there was a tall white man with my mother, whom she introduced as her professor. He was her thesis adviser and the person who had sponsored her visa. Only much later did I recognize how unusual it was for a professor to offer to drive nearly three hours each way, in heavy snow and sleet, to pick up the family of a student. This was the first of many acts of kindness we would experience in America.

OUR NEW HOME WAS IN the graduate student accommodations of Utah State University, on the second floor of a set of low-rise buildings. The one-bedroom apartment was easily five times the size of Ye Ye and Nai Nai's room in Shanghai. My mother showed me how the kitchen and bathrooms were actually inside the apartment and that they were our own. Everyone kept their doors closed, and I didn't hear the neighbors except when they came out into the courtyard area.

All I could think about was how cold it was! After the flights and visas, my parents had only forty American dollars. That was all they came to the United States with. It was a lot for them—it was what they had earned in China in a year. Heat was a luxury we could not afford.

Because electricity was included but not heating or hot water, I helped my mother boil water on the electric stove and used that for everything: to cook, to wash our hands, and to fill the bathtub.

We washed our clothes by hand and hung them to dry on the balcony. The next day, there were icicles covering everything. When I tried to take down the clothes, my father's shirt broke in my hand. To go out, I wore five layers of pants and even more sweaters. When I walked through the snow, my sneakers and pants quickly became soaked. At night, we slept huddled together to keep warm.

A week after we arrived, someone knocked on the door. There was no one there when we answered, but there was a huge brown bag just outside. In it were several pairs of boots, winter coats, mittens, hats, and a thick down blanket.

There was also a note: *Welcome home.*

Apparently, the local church had held a clothing drive for our family. This was the same church that would host us for every holiday meal, enlist volunteers to teach me English, and raise money for my father's hospital stay when his ulcer bled again.

"Americans are so nice!" my parents said often. "We are so lucky." My father speculated that Utahans must be kind to outsiders because they needed more people to live there. In comparison to Shanghai, a city of twenty-four million people, Logan was minuscule, with a population of thirty thousand who were nearly all white and Mormon. But there was just a handful of us immigrant families—all tied to the university—and welcoming us could not be the solution to increasing the population.

My mother thought it was because America is a land of immigrants, that everyone had relatives who were once strangers in a strange land. She also attributed the warm welcome we received to the church, which was a new experience for us. We were not allowed to have religion in China. Everyone around us went to church every Sunday, and I started going, too. The values I was taught, of tolerance, respect, and compassion, were the values exemplified by my mother's professor, our neighbors, and everyone else in our community. I didn't understand the intricacies of Mormonism versus other forms of Christianity (or other religions, for that matter), but I did appreciate the early grounding I received in a community of faith and fellowship.

A FEW WEEKS AFTER WE arrived, I started school at Hillcrest, the local public elementary school. I was entering the third grade midway through the school year. That morning, I practiced saying, "Hello, my name is Lee-Na" in front of the mirror, dressed in my newly donated winter coat over three sweaters and four pairs of pants.

My mother walked with me to my new school and introduced me to the teacher.

"Hello, my name is Lee-Na!" I said. I bowed to her. She said something to me that I didn't understand. She saw my puzzled expression and said it again, slower, but I still didn't understand.

This continued throughout the day. I wondered if the words Ye Ye taught me were really English. Everyone spoke at what seemed like fifty times the speed of what I'd learned. I also got very hot, and by the end of the day I was carrying around a pile of sweaters and pants.

I was also hungry. In my school in China, every student would get a bowl with rice and vegetables, sometimes some pork shavings, and we'd go to assigned tables. In America, I had no idea where to start once I walked into the cafeteria. Students looked like they were picking and choosing different foods, but they were all nothing I'd seen before.

I tried to mimic what others were getting. When I got to the line, I saw that there was a cash register. I didn't have any money. I left my lunch on the counter and hid in the bathroom until the bell rang.

After two weeks of hungry afternoons, a teacher found me in the bathroom. She helped me sign up for a free lunch program and showed me how to put food on my tray. I learned that in America, people like to eat their food separately, green beans separated from the chicken and potatoes instead of all mixed together in one bowl. I learned that in America, milk came in a little paper container and that there was a way to peel it open without splashing the contents everywhere.

I also learned that in America, it wasn't just adults who are kind. On my first day of eating school lunch, four students sat down next to me.

"Hello, my name is Becky," one of them said. "Want to play together at recess?"

I wasn't sure what that meant. She pantomimed skipping rope, something I loved. I nodded eagerly. "Oh! Yes!"

"That's jump rope," she said.

"I like jump rope!" And I was thrilled to be having my first conversation with real Americans.

Every recess, I played with Becky and her friends. She invited me to her home after school. Becky had several brothers and sisters, and they also brought over their friends. Her mother gave us cut-up apple slices and the occasional Oreo cookie. We'd sit on her bunk bed in the room she shared with her sister. From school and from my new friends, I picked up conversational English quickly and soon was able to talk to Becky about our families. I was fascinated by how her family could trace their roots to Joseph Smith and the mass exodus to Utah. She was just as transfixed by my stories of Ye Ye, Nai Nai, and a land that seemed so far away.

Just as I did in China, I enjoyed going to school in America. My teachers prepared extra homework for me, and I used Ye Ye's dictionary to memorize twenty new words every night. I went to church with Becky's family, and our Bible study teacher would stay after Sunday service to tutor me. Older children and adults would make a point of speaking to me and helping me learn English. Their efforts paid off. Within two years, I would win my grade's spelling bee.

So many people helped me in those early days. As with my friends in China, I've long lost contact with Becky, our Bible study group, and my other teachers. I wish I could find them to tell them how much their generosity and kindness made all the difference in my life.

I also didn't appreciate at the time how much my family relied on public services to help us in those difficult days. My mother went to a public university that granted her free tuition and subsidized our housing. I took part in a school lunch program and attended public schools from elementary school through college. We had Medicaid and relied on reduced-cost clinics for our health care. Later on, we would need food stamps and housing assistance during particularly difficult times.

For us, these public assistance programs were not "entitlements." My parents weren't using them to game the system; they were trying their best to make it on their own, and these programs ensured that our basic needs were met. My parents certainly had no plans to depend on the government in perpetuity. In fact, my mother spoke constantly about how she was ashamed to be "taking advantage." In her mind, public assistance was reserved for the neediest, and since there was a finite amount of services, she strove to get us out of this category so that the services could be used by others.

"Always remember how good this country has been to us," she'd tell me. "China may be where we were born, but America is where we have chosen to make our home. America is our country now, and we must give to our country and its citizens." It was this spirit that would lead her, in time, to retrain as a public school teacher and to choose to work in some of the most challenging areas in Los Angeles.

Though my parents and I were now living together, I still almost never saw them. My mother was studying during the day and then went to her job of cleaning rooms in a guesthouse across town. I was usually asleep by the time she came home, and she was always gone by the time I got up to go to school.

My father, too, was laser-focused on getting work. Unlike my mother, who spoke fluent if heavily accented English, my father didn't know the language and didn't have the benefit I did of immersion at a young age. He was a very proud man who hated to admit that he had a major deficit that held him back in our new home. There were no "English as a second language" classes for him to take, and even if there were, I'm certain that he would have prioritized earning an income. He'd learned enough English to get his driver's license, but he turned red when people addressed him. "Sorry, I don't speak English," he'd respond.

Every day my father would leave in the morning to look for work. There was nowhere that would make use of his engineering background, but he was quick with his hands and eager to do anything. He did some handyman work for our neighbors until the local plumber asked him to stop. A couple of downtown businesses gave him odd jobs like cleaning and restocking shelves. At some point, he went to another town to work in a cheese factory. He never talked about what happened there, but after a month or two, he came home and told us that he couldn't set foot there again—and to this day, he cannot bear the smell of cheese.

There were many nights when I'd wake up to my parents' raised voices as they argued over money and work. My father would talk about how unhappy he was and why he needed to move to another city so that he could make use of his skills and earn money. He had a friend from Shanghai living in Los Angeles, which is where he wanted to go because L.A. had many more opportunities. My mother would counter that she was doing fine in Logan and she needed to complete her degree. Also, our family had been apart for so long and was finally together. *Stay for Duo Duo*, she'd plead. *Eat bitter for her.*

One day, my father left for Los Angeles. I wrote in my diary that they must have had a fight, because we didn't say goodbye—he just left. We had lived together for such a short time. I worried about him and when we'd see him again. We had no money for long-distance calls, so we communicated by mail. I'd send him updates about my school, and he'd write back to tell us about L.A. I pictured it to be just like Logan, only bigger. The people would be just as nice, only there would be more jobs for my parents.

When my mother finished her PhD, my father came back to pick us up. By now I was ten years old, and it was time for a new adventure. We packed all our belongings into a car and drove west, with a detour along the way to Yellowstone National Park.

Our stay at Yellowstone was brief—we spent two nights in a motel before the long drive south—but I associate it with some of our happiest times as a family. Someone took a photo of me feeding a squirrel. My right hand is raised as I watch the squirrel cautiously. My parents are standing behind me, just out of focus, holding hands and smiling. This is my lasting snapshot of our time at Yellowstone, the two of them enjoying each other's company and mine.

It would be the first and only road trip, and the first and only vacation, that we ever took together.

Life in L.A. was not at all what I expected. For the first couple of months, we stayed with my father's friend. My father was delivering newspapers for a Chinese company, and my mother found work for a translation business that promised to sponsor her work visa. Soon, they saved up enough money and we moved into a two-bedroom duplex that housed three families.

It wasn't long before we had to leave. My father's van was stolen, and he got fired. The company my mother worked for closed so suddenly that one morning she went into work only to find that all the office furniture had been taken away. She couldn't get the wages owed to her.

My mother tried to plead with the landlord that we needed a few more weeks. Couldn't he spare us and give us more time to find the rent? He gave us a week but increased the rent. We couldn't make the payment. Neither could one of the other families, who were evicted along with us.

This time, there was no one to help us when we were out of options. My father's friend would have tried, but he and his family were going through hard times, too. There were no church communities, no kind professors, no school friends, and no acts of lenience and compassion. We weren't in Logan anymore.

We found another place to stay. It was affordable for a reason: most of the other houses on the block were boarded up. In our apartment complex, there were condoms and needles in the staircases. It was right next to the railroad tracks, and every night we could feel the rumbling of the trains as we heard sirens all around us. One day, we had a break-in. We came home to find drawers emptied and belongings all over the ground. What cash we had was gone, and all the windows were smashed. The burglars left a note: Go away Chinks.

In those first several months in L.A., we would move at least four more times. It always had to do with money that we didn't have.

At some point, my mother and I ended up in a shelter that only accommodated women and children. (My father found a place that housed migrant male workers.) My mother and I would look for a bed at this shelter every night. There was one day when my mother came back late, and we were told that our beds were no longer available. My mother pleaded with them, but they couldn't make an exception.

We spent the last of our savings on a motel room. The owner, who was Vietnamese and had young kids herself, took pity on us and let us stay the rest of the month there. We paid her what we could. My mother did some cleaning and I helped out at the front desk.

We moved into our own place again when my mother found a job in a video store. It was a store that rented adult videos. I knew my mother was ashamed. She never told me what this video store did, but I heard my father shouting at her about how indecent it was. She'd yell back that at least she had work and it was supporting our family.

I also knew that my mother was suffering abuse from her boss. She'd often come home crying, and I'd see bruises around her wrists. She wouldn't talk about exactly what he did, but I could feel her powerlessness and humiliation. I knew that she had to put up with it for us—for me.

The more tenuous our financial situation, the worse my parents fought. I'd curl up against the wall and pretend to be asleep while they shouted at each other. She blamed him for not being able to find a job because he didn't know English; he asked what was the point of her years of education if she couldn't find better work.

There was another worry that was just as existential as our financial problems: our immigration status. My parents talked about it constantly. Going back to China was not an option, but neither was overstaying our visa. The one thing my mother feared more than anything was the prospect of us losing our immigration status.

"We cannot ever become illegal," she'd say virtually every day. We knew of so many families who had become undocumented, and it prevented their work opportunities and limited their children's educational potential.

I was optimistic that my mother would figure out a situation through work. She had several employers who brought her on with the agreement that they would sponsor a work visa for her. Every time, though, they'd end up reneging once they saw how expensive and onerous the process was.

As always, my mother had a backup plan. One day, I came back from school to find her folding my clothes.

"You and I are moving to Canada," she said.

Canada? This was the first I'd heard of it. My mother explained that Canada had more welcoming immigration policies than the United States, and they'd given my mother and me a visa to enter the country.

This was Plan B. Plan A was through my father, but it was much riskier and unlikely to succeed. Years ago, he had applied for political asylum. It was a long process. We hadn't heard anything, and our visas were running out.

"If he gets it, then all of us can stay," my mother told me. "But I don't think it's going to work. We don't have enough time. Then we have to go with the other plan. Your father and I will get divorced. That way, he can marry someone who has visa status. It's called a paper marriage, and people do this all the time."

I could not fathom what she was saying. All I knew was that I couldn't start all over again.

I started pleading with my mother. I told her that I missed Nai Nai and Ye Ye but had finally got used to America. That I missed my friends in Logan and was finally figuring it out in L.A. I was doing well in school again. "Why do you have to ruin my life?" I said.

"This is not just about you," she replied. She finally turned to look at me. I saw from her face that she was going to tell me something very serious. "Duo Duo, can you keep a secret?"

"If I do, can I stay here?"

She sighed. She sat down on the bed and gestured for me to sit next to her. She took my hand and put it on her belly.

"This is my secret," she said. "Meet your little sister. You cannot tell your father. If you tell him, he won't go through with the plan. He won't want to divorce or for us to be apart."

I had no idea what to say.

"Look, Duo Duo, I don't want to leave and start over, either," she continued. "I've tried so hard to make a new life for us in this country. This is a setback, that's all. Can you help me so we get through this together?"

That night, we packed up everything we could fit into four suitcases. My mother told me about our new home: Calgary, Alberta. I checked out a French dictionary from the library and began to drill myself in

French vocabulary words, thinking that everyone in Canada spoke French. I started saying goodbye to my friends.

A few days before we were to board the plane to Canada, my father was called to his immigration hearing. At the last minute, a friend convinced him to bring a lawyer with him.

This turned out to be key. They were in with the immigration officer for under an hour when they were told that our asylum status was granted.

It's over, I thought. *We can stay in America. Our family can stay together. We don't have to start all over again.*

Most of that turned out to be true, but there was one outcome I could not have fathomed. In April 1994, my little sister was born. I was eleven and so excited to have a little companion. I'd picked her name, Angela, because to me, she was an angel, a gift from heaven. I had big plans for her. She wouldn't have all the family around as I did growing up, so I had to make up for that with my own love and attention. And I needed to shield her from all the trouble I'd gone through so that she didn't have to *chi ku*.

My parents had a different plan. They decided that it would be best for Angela to be raised in China by my grandparents. When she was just three weeks old, she was gone.

I was heartsick and furious. I couldn't understand how my parents could send away our own flesh and blood. I wrote in my diary that my mother must not have wanted either of us. If she did, how could she stand to send my baby sister away?

It would take me many years to understand the difficulty of my parents' choice and the depth of their sacrifice.

2

Belonging

In L.A., one of the places we lived in was the duplex that we shared with three other families. The walls were so thin that we could hear every conversation, though we didn't understand what was being said because all the neighbor families spoke different languages. My friend Christine's family shared our floor; the duplex also housed an elderly Vietnamese couple and the family who'd fled from Mexico only to lose their young son, Tony, in an asthma attack that did not have to be fatal.

Even before Tony died, I understood that society did not value everyone the same way. People like us who were poor and came from other countries weren't treated like others. We didn't belong; in many ways, we didn't matter. I was conscious of those around me who were struggling just to survive. One of my father's coworkers had a heart attack but didn't have the money to pay for a hospital stay. A woman in our neighborhood became sick with pneumonia but never sought medical care. They both died. Their families mourned their deaths, and I remembered wondering whether they, and Tony, could have been saved if they had the means, or if they weren't immigrants.

When I grow up, I thought, *could I be that person who would care for*

everyone, especially those who had nowhere else to go? Could I become
a doctor, a healer, and work to change the reality of my neighbors and all
those whom society cast aside?

WHEN PEOPLE LEARN THAT I started college at age thirteen, they make
a lot of assumptions. They think I must have been very smart, that high
school must have been terribly boring, and that I probably really struggled to fit in with my classmates.

Only one of those things is true. How I came to college so young
was neither about my smarts nor about my experience in high school.

It was mainly because of money, which was a daily concern. About a
year after my sister was sent back to China, our family's living situation
started to stabilize. My mother was tutoring a wealthy family during the
day while getting her teaching certification at night. My father found
a Chinese boss who appreciated his ability to fix just about anything. I
was finally able to complete a year at the same school without transfer-
ring. I made friends and even played in the school orchestra.

Health care was a luxury that we could ill afford. When my father's
stomach ulcer flared up, he couldn't miss work to see a doctor, so he
relied on pills he'd brought from China that had long expired. When
those ran out, he found an herbalist who gave him a concoction in
exchange for household repairs. I had problems with my teeth from years
of taking steroids for asthma. Going to a dentist would cost too much,
so my mother found a cheaper alternative. We went to the apartment of
a man who claimed to have been a dentist back in China. His kitchen
was an illegal clinic that served other poor immigrants at $10 a visit.
There was no anesthesia. I remember sobbing when I got my cavities
filled, then the blinding pain when I had to return for a root canal. It
would take me until my thirties to get over my fear of dentistry.

My parents had terrible fights about our finances. Around the time
my sister was sent away, I started down a path to make money for my
family. I couldn't legally earn an income, but there were other ways I
could bring money home. There was a church nearby that paid me $5
to play the piano at their Saturday and Sunday service. If I left a basket

on the piano, congregants would chip in, and I'd end up with $20 on an average day or $30 on a good one.

One day, a woman whispered to me that I could make better money standing outside the supermarket. I'd seen people asking for money there. I decided that I could try that, too.

After school, I walked to the supermarket and stood in the parking lot. "My parents and I just moved here," I said to people as they came out. "My father lost his job and we need money for rent. Can you help us?"

Most people turned away, but a few of them actually gave me something. A Chinese couple handed me all the spare coins they were going to deposit in the supermarket's change machine—a total of nearly $10. An older white woman gave me the extraordinary sum of $50. "Take this. You need this more than me," she said.

That first day, I made $100. I thought I'd figured out the solution to our money problems. When people at the supermarket started asking questions about why I was always there, I tried another market and then a row of restaurants. I used different story lines. Sometimes my father needed money for an operation. Other times, it was my mother who was sick and couldn't work.

I learned that there was a mall where wealthy white people shopped. It took over an hour's bus ride to get there. I began to skip school to go, and I hid the money in an old backpack in our closet, waiting for the right moment to give it to my parents.

A couple of weeks into this, my parents were having another argument about money. As usual, there wasn't enough for rent, and the accusations were flying as to whose fault it was.

This time, I was ready. "Please don't fight," I said. "We have enough. Look!" I took out the bundle of cash I had saved up. "And I have a lot more coins, too!"

My parents stared at me.

"Where did you get this money?" my mother asked.

"Working," I said.

"What do you mean, working?"

"Playing the piano."

"Don't lie. You can't make that much playing the piano," my mother said. "Where did it really come from?"

"It doesn't matter. We have the money to pay for rent. So please don't argue anymore."

"But how did you get it? Did you steal it?" My mother was becoming more agitated. "How did you get it if you're in school? Or have you been skipping school?"

I told her that I didn't steal anything. Other people gave me the money. I did miss some school, but I could catch up.

By this point, my mother was yelling not just at me but also at my father. "I cannot believe this. We have given up everything for her and now she doesn't go to school. What an ungrateful daughter!"

"I did this for you!" I shouted. "I don't want to do this, but it's to help our family!"

"Nobody asked you to do this! Can you imagine what Ye Ye and Nai Nai would say? We came to America so that you can be a common beggar?"

"I just wanted to help you." Tears were running down my face. My mother took a step forward as if she was going to slap me. She stopped as my father put his hand on her shoulder.

"Look, Duo Duo," he said. "It's not your fault. But you can't do this. Other people work hard for their money, too. We need to make money the right way. You can't lie and bring shame to our entire family like this. And you need to go to school."

"Do you know how much I wanted to go to school when I was your age?" my mother said. "Your grandmother risked going to jail if the government found out she was helping me to learn. She bought books on the black market. I taught myself English because it's what I had to do. Your father and I found jobs because it's what we have to do. We didn't go the easy way and beg for money. You cannot, either."

I went back to school and never missed a single day again. But I didn't stop thinking about how I could help my parents with their finances. Even as my mother found stable work as an elementary school teacher and we moved to a solidly middle-class community in the San Gabriel Valley, she and my father fought over money every day. There was no sign that they'd bring Angela back. When I asked, my mother would say that their responsibility was first to me, and I wasn't "settled" until I had a job or was in college.

There was a solution that offered both of these possibilities. When I was in eighth grade, I had a classmate who had an older sister at California State University, Los Angeles, one of our local public universities. She was part of a work-study program that paid for her education and some of her expenses. I found out that the college accepted young students my age, as long as they passed a series of exams.

This was nothing like the difficulty of the exams my mother had taken; studying for them was also nothing compared to the pressure that she must have felt. I took the studying very seriously, though, because my mother impressed upon me that this was the ticket our family needed. I didn't want to skip high school—I was finally in a good school and had found a group of friends I liked. I had a glimpse of what a "normal" life was like.

When I found out that I had passed the test and had been accepted to the Early Entrance Program, I had conflicting emotions. This was my goal and I was glad to have met it, but I also realized that "normal" was not in the cards. Instead of starting high school that fall, I'd enter college. I could earn enough money to support myself through work-study, and my parents could focus on bringing my sister back.

Soon after I started college in the fall of 1996, my sister returned to the United States, brought by a family friend who was traveling from China. My parents and I went to the airport to pick her up. My mother began crying as she spotted a tiny toddler sitting on top of a pile of suitcases. We ran toward her. My mother picked her up and then handed her to me. Then we were all crying. Angela was finally here to stay.

I have a letter from Ye Ye during this period in which he told me about his childhood. There was no school in his village, and he'd had to walk five miles each way, barefoot, to get an education. There was only one pair of pants among the entire family, so although he sometimes wore the pants, often he went dressed in old dishcloths knotted together. Yet he always made it to school, no matter how hard the wind was blowing or how high a fever he had. From an early age, he knew that education was the ticket to a better life, for him and for his family.

Ye Ye reminded me of the Chinese saying: *bai shan xiao wei xian*: of all the hundreds of important behaviors, filial piety is the most important. Filial piety, or *xiao xun*, directly translates into "respect and obedience."

"You are showing your parents your *xiao xun*," he wrote, "that you are a respectful and obedient child."

I didn't think of my actions as respectful or obedient. I fought a lot with my parents in those days, particularly with my mother. I look back and I regret so much of what I said to her, how angry I was at her, and the many things I chose not to see about her. But I knew even then that I would be forever bound by duty to honor my family's sacrifices.

I WENT TO COLLEGE WITH the sole intention of earning a degree and making money to help my parents. I wasn't there to make friends or socialize. I was so much younger than my classmates that I knew I wasn't going to fit in. Rather than be rejected, I didn't make the effort to try.

There were a few dozen other students around my age who were part of the Early Entrance Program. I never tried becoming friends with them, either. I figured they must all have wanted to be there. They were probably child geniuses from privileged backgrounds who were at college because they wanted an intellectual challenge. Years later, I'd learn that some of them had circumstances more in common with mine than I'd thought. It was a missed opportunity not to seek them out as friends; perhaps I could have found a community to belong to instead of feeling entirely on my own.

As it turned out, Cal State L.A. was a good place to go if you just wanted to put your head down and study. It was a commuter school of thirty thousand, where the majority were nontraditional students. Most of us were minorities for whom English was a second language. Many students were older, some with children of their own, and nearly all had other jobs. They were also there just to get through their classes, obtain a degree, and strive toward a future that was better than that of their parents.

I was alone, but I didn't have much time to feel lonely. I went to my classes and I studied. In between, I went to my work-study placement—a laboratory.

By this time, I was certain that I wanted to be a doctor. I wanted to treat the Tonys of this world and work in the kind of community I grew up in. It was well and good to have this grand aspiration, but I had no idea how to actually get there. No one in my family was a doctor. My parents had a friend who had been a doctor in China, but who, like them, struggled just to obtain menial jobs in America. When I first started college, I thought that even verbalizing that I wanted to be a doctor would be ludicrous—who was I to think I could do this, when the only doctor I'd really gotten to know was the pediatrician who had treated my asthma in China?

During my interview for the work-study program, the director of the program, a biochemistry professor named Raymond Garcia, asked me what I wanted to do. Dr. Garcia was a military veteran and a bigger-than-life presence, with a swaggering walk and resonant voice. I was ter-rified of him, and even more terrified that he would laugh if I told him my dream.

"I want to be a lab tech," I said. This sounded like a realistic goal. My parents had a friend who got a science degree and became a lab techni-cian. I thought this made sense; after all, I was interviewing for a job to work in a laboratory.

I figured that Dr. Garcia accepted my reply at face value, because I was accepted to the program and placed in a lab with his colleague, Donald Paulson. Dr. Paulson's research was in inorganic chemistry, something I knew nothing about. He and his graduate students would show me a great deal of patience and kindness, teaching me every-thing from washing beakers and using pipettes to eventually running my own experiments.

Both Dr. Paulson and Dr. Garcia would press me on what I really wanted to do. They weren't persuaded that my great ambition was to be a lab tech. It took me well over a year of working closely with them to admit that I longed to become a doctor. I think they suspected as much, and they began to introduce me to their former mentees who had gone on to medical school. They were all nontraditional students who had had a tough path: most got in only after their second or third applications, and everyone emphasized how critical it was get top grades and test scores on the Medical College Admissions Test (MCAT).

"When I got to medical school, I saw that everyone else knew the rules of the game. But nobody taught me," one of them said. I'd hear this theme over and over again. Our college had a premed advising program that was much smaller than those of other universities. Of the many thousands of students who aspired to be doctors when they first started college, only a handful would be accepted to medical school. The premed office seemed to spend most of its time talking students out of medicine and into other health professions like nursing and pharmacy. No doubt this was the right decision for many students who ended up in stable and meaningful jobs, but I wondered how many students could have become doctors if they had had the support to follow through with their original aspirations.

The graduates I met through Dr. Paulson and Dr. Garcia emphasized that I needed to stick with it. Some of them had been told by the premed office to change paths, but they pursued their dream and eventually they succeeded. And they were clear on one point: "You need to know that we are at a disadvantage because of our backgrounds and the school we came from. We have to do that much more to get anywhere close to an even playing field."

Through these former mentees, I got connected with a program to shadow physicians in a nearby emergency department. This turned out to be a critical but unwritten requirement of the application process, and I wouldn't have known about it but for the advice from these graduates. I saved up to enroll in an MCAT test prep program, also something I wouldn't have considered doing until they stressed how important it was for learning specific test-taking skills. (In medical school, I would become a teacher for Kaplan and see for myself how different these skills are. Students with means didn't hesitate to spend thousands of dollars on these courses, placing them at a much higher starting point than those for whom these courses were a significant financial burden.) After a friend's sister was diagnosed with a rare leukemia, I organized a bone marrow drive for her that drew hundreds of donors. I'd seen this as something that I did in my spare time, but I learned from the med students that this kind of activity was what I needed to highlight in my application.

I was extremely grateful for the crash course on the rules of the road, but it didn't seem fair that I was the only recipient of this advice while all the thousands of other premeds had to figure it out on their own. And so, in my third year, I enlisted a few other classmates to start a chapter of the American Medical Student Association (AMSA) at Cal State L.A. We organized a monthly speaker series where we brought in admissions committee members from nearby medical schools to talk about what they looked for in applicants. Knowing that most of our members worked and had significant family responsibilities, we provided opportunities for them to participate in service activities by having designated volunteer spots at campus blood drives and student health wellness fairs.

As I got to know the other members of the AMSA chapter, I was so impressed by their backgrounds and their various motivations for practicing medicine. Most of them were also immigrants; many were first-generation college students. Like me, none of them had grown up in families of doctors, but they all had seen what it meant to go without health care. While I was fortunate to have arrived at college with a solid grounding in math and English, many of these students did not. They struggled with their first courses, and even if they were able to improve over the years, their GPAs were too low to make the cutoff for medical school.

Dr. Garcia was concerned about this phenomenon, too. He began a program to identify and assist minority pre–health professional students in that critical first year. I became a tutor and peer mentor to these students, many of whom thrived once they received that initial personalized assistance.

"You can do anything you put your mind to," Dr. Garcia used to say to the students. I believed in this wholeheartedly. I also saw for myself that while opportunity is not universal, talent is. Whatever I achieved was possible only because others allowed me to have an opportunity, one to which many other students did not have access. I will forever be indebted to Dr. Garcia, Dr. Paulson, and the alumni from whom I received information, support, and guidance. In return, I felt it was my obligation to provide similar resources to those who came after me and to help level the playing field for them.

WHEN IT CAME TIME TO apply to medical school, I was far from certain that I'd get in. I had good grades and a solid record of extracurricular activities, including an elected position on the student government board. Thanks to test prep, I also had MCAT scores that were easily above the admission threshold. Still, I saw the statistics from my school. The previous year, there were students with similar test scores and commendable activities who did not get accepted to a single medical school.

My premed adviser cautioned me to prepare for rejections everywhere, even if I applied to forty schools. When Dr. Garcia heard that, he said, "Then you just have to apply to forty-one!"

I took his advice as I steeled myself to apply again the following year if I got rejected from them all. There was one major barrier: the cost of all of these applications. There was a central application fee, plus fees for every school that were, at the time, up to $100 per school. If I made it through the first round, there was then a mandatory in-person interview that would incur additional travel costs. If I applied to forty-one schools and then interviewed at a dozen, it would cost about $10,000.

This was an unthinkable amount of money to me. Many of my classmates felt the same way. This was just one more expense added to the cost of medical school tuition that dissuades so many people from seeking careers in medicine. Even at that time, more than twenty years ago when I was applying, tuition cost around $30,000 per year. Students who needed support for tuition and living expenses could easily incur debt of over $200,000. This was an astronomical sum of money that so many families just could not fathom.

I had already decided that the only way I could go to medical school was through the MD/PhD combined program. These programs were very competitive to get into, but most of them offered full tuition and coverage for living expenses. I had enjoyed my experience working in Dr. Paulson's lab, and though I wasn't sure that I felt passionate about lab work, I knew that I couldn't start medical school and rack up $200,000 worth of debt. In retrospect, this was not great reasoning to enter a PhD program, but it was one that I'd see over and over again for students who came from less advantaged backgrounds: our educational and career choices were driven by financial considerations because they had to be.

In order to pay for my many applications, I cut the number of courses I was taking and doubled my hours in the lab and with tutoring. This ended up delaying my graduation for a year, but I was still very young, and it was necessary to save up the money I needed. Another professor, Carlos Gutierrez, recommended that I apply for two scholarships, which also helped with costs. Once I received offers for interviews, I borrowed a suit from a professor's daughter and found a handbag at the Goodwill store. I always chose the cheapest travel option and stayed with students, which turned out to be a great way to get to know the school environment.

In the end, I was accepted to thirteen medical schools. Most were MD/PhD programs with full tuition and a living stipend. I chose the school that I felt was the best match for me: Washington University in St. Louis, Missouri. Wash U had a tight-knit student body and a supportive faculty. On my interview, I'd met John Atkinson, a physician and the head of a lab whom I admired and hoped would be my research supervisor. There was also something about St. Louis that really drew me. I felt at home there in a way that I never did in Los Angeles. To this day, I still love St. Louis; the only city I feel more at home in than St. Louis is my beloved Baltimore.

I was also eager to leave Los Angeles and be far away from my family. My relationship with my mother had hit a new low. We fought constantly. She'd make disparaging comments about my college achievements. She'd tell me that getting into med school was a fluke, that I'd just gotten lucky and now needed to focus on not failing. I'd accuse her of some terrible things in return, like not caring about me and my sister and trying to drive our father away.

One day, my mother was so upset, she threw all my belongings onto the street. I stormed out and didn't see her for almost a year. I didn't invite my family to my graduation until a few days before, and by then, my mother refused to go.

Still, I was on my way. In 2001, at age eighteen, I began medical school at Washington University. After years of hard work, I could finally see the path to becoming a doctor.

THE FIRST YEAR OF MEDICAL school was nothing if not challenging. I struggled to keep up with my classmates. I wasn't used to studying so hard and still being near the bottom of my class. Many of my classmates had taken some version of our preclinical classes (anatomy, histology, immunology) in their undergraduate or graduate programs. These courses hadn't been available to me, and I felt like I was learning everything for the first time.

Wash U had a pass-fail grading system in the first year that was supposed to acclimate students and allow those who came from less rigorous schools to catch up. I was passing, but just barely. I really worried that I wasn't going to make it and would let down Dr. Garcia, Dr. Paulson, and all those professors who had put their faith in me. I began thinking that my mother was right. Maybe it was a fluke that I had gotten in, and everyone would know it soon. I didn't know the term at the time, but I was suffering from impostor syndrome. Not a day went by when I didn't question whether I should really be there. Maybe I shouldn't have gone to a top-tier school; clearly, I wasn't up to the task. I didn't belong.

My doubts were so severe that when the premed club at Cal State L.A. invited me to speak with the current students, I almost didn't show up. I had already returned to campus but couldn't make myself walk up the stairs into the classroom.

I was about to turn back and leave when a young woman stopped me. I recognized her as one of the new AMSA leaders who'd taken over for me.

"All the students are so excited to hear from you," she said. "You're someone who made it, and we all want to be where you are."

Struggling and likely to be failing—is that what they meant? But she kept on talking as she explained how much she saw herself in me. She, too, was a first-generation immigrant. She also didn't know any doctors growing up. Now she was applying to medical school because she saw people like me who came from where she did and were doing what she aspired to do.

I recalled something that my mother used to say. She always talked about how as much as we were *chi ku*, as much as we were sacrificing, there were always other people who needed help even more than we did.

"You need to make a difference wherever you can," she'd say, "because there will be someone out there you can help."

In Logan, she took new Chinese graduate students under her wing and helped to settle them and their families. In L.A., she always made sure to give something—money when we could afford it, food or donated clothes when we couldn't—to our church and the local homeless shelter. These are the places that helped us in our time of need, and it was our obligation to give back.

Becoming a public schoolteacher was the perfect job for her. It combined the two things she loved most—education and helping others. She chose to teach elementary school in Compton and then East Los Angeles, areas where many of the children came from extremely disadvantaged backgrounds. She adored her students. They reminded her of herself, young people with endless potential but many barriers in the way. Her job was to do all she could to help them overcome the obstacles and set them up for their lives ahead—as she did with me and Angela.

"There is always someone out there looking up to you," she'd tell her students.

In that moment, this young woman was looking up to me. I may have been doubting myself as a medical student, but there were all these premeds who wanted the opportunity that I'd been given, and I needed to be there to help them in the way that others helped me.

I went to speak to the club, then I went back to St. Louis, where I studied even harder. It took me most of that first year to get used to the cadence of medical school and to catch up with my classmates. Whenever I had doubts, I thought about the Cal State L.A. students who were looking up to me.

And I thought about my mother. As much as our relationship was strained, I admired her more than anyone else in the world. Giving up was never an option for her, and it wasn't for me, either.

3

White Coat, Clenched Fist

By the end of my first year, I'd started working in John Atkinson's lab. This was the lab I had wanted to join for my PhD research. As I was on the "clinician-scientist" track, I wanted to learn from someone who had the career that I was working toward, a practicing physician who saw patients with particular diseases and did research that could directly help them.

Dr. Atkinson had a reputation for being both a compassionate doctor and a renowned scientist. As I shadowed him in his rheumatology practice to treat patients with rare immunological diseases called complement-deficiency disorders, I'd see his expert clinical skills in action. His patients adored him. Many of them had moved away from the St. Louis area but traveled hundreds of miles for their appointments. Like Dr. Paulson, he was also an experienced educator and led a laboratory that produced top-quality scientific articles and drew young scientists from around the world.

My own clinical work would soon start in earnest. One of my first rotations was neurology. I was called for an emergency consult in the ER. Paramedics were about to bring in a man in his thirties who was having a seizure. A coworker had found him—his name was Eric—on the bathroom floor, unconscious.

When I arrived with the neurology resident, the ER team was in full action. A nurse was holding Eric down while another tried to secure an oxygen mask over his face. His eyes fluttered open and closed. His teeth were clenched. White foam bubbled out his mouth. Both arms were bent at the elbow and shook as his legs thrashed rhythmically on the stretcher. There was matted blood in his dark blond hair.

The emergency physician was directing the rest of the team on what to do: "He's still seizing. We need vitals and a D-stick. Push another dose of Ativan."

As the nurses and techs followed what I knew to be the standard seizure protocol, the neurology resident asked the paramedics for more information. How long had he been in this state? It was now more than twenty minutes since he'd been found, but his colleagues hadn't seen him since the staff meeting that morning.

The time line was very concerning. Just five minutes of a continuous seizure is status epilepticus, a life-threatening emergency. Based on the dried blood, he could have been seizing for hours. A seizure of that length would almost certainly result in brain damage.

Had he been sick, with a fever? This was important to know, because meningitis—an infection of the brain—could be contagious. No, he'd been fine that morning. There was no foreign travel and no known sick contacts. The blood was likely from hitting his head after his seizure started.

What kind of work did Eric do? He was a paralegal with a desk job. There was no exposure to dangerous chemicals.

Other medical history? No history of diabetes, and his glucose was normal. No history of drug use. His colleagues didn't know if he had had seizures before, but there was a medication card in his wallet that listed the names of seizure medications.

Eric had been given two doses of an anticonvulsant en route and one more in the ER. They weren't working. He needed something stronger.

The additional medications would cause his breathing to stop. The emergency physician was already putting a breathing tube down his throat. Soon, he was connected to a ventilator, which began breathing for him.

One of the nurses was speaking to a young woman just outside the door. She was wearing pink scrubs. I learned that she was Eric's wife, who was a respiratory tech in our hospital. She told us that her husband had a history of epilepsy. His last seizure was several years ago. Their twin girls were three years old, and he hadn't had a seizure since they were born.

"What medications is he taking?" I asked.

"There are two of them, but I don't think he's been taking them." She told us that Eric had gotten laid off when his company downsized. He was working a temp job that didn't offer health insurance. She looked into getting him onto her health plan, but it would cost over $1,000 a month more. Those were the rules of her insurance company because of his "preexisting condition"—his epilepsy. Without insurance, the seizure medications cost hundreds of dollars a month.

"I think he's been stringing them out. Maybe he's out of them, I'm not sure," she said. "He said it would be fine, that he's done this before . . ." She trailed off. She took his hand, which, like the rest of him, was no longer shaking.

"Is my husband going to be OK?"

Nowhere in the seizure protocol was there an answer for this woman—an answer that would soon upend her life.

An hour later, Eric was transferred to the ICU. His lab work came back with undetectable levels of the two medications, meaning that he hadn't been taking them. His wife later confirmed that the pill bottles at home were empty and hadn't been refilled for months. Neurology specialists saw him and conducted many tests, but they could not detect brain activity.

He never regained consciousness. Later that week, his wife decided to withdraw life support. Eric died with her and their daughters at his bedside.

Eric's death haunted me just as Tony's did. Both died not because medicine per se had failed them but because our health-care system did. Tony would almost certainly be alive now if he had gotten prompt medical care. Eric might never even have had a seizure in the first place if he had been able to afford his medications. Both are terrible tragedies, made worse by the fact that they were preventable. Two lives were ended far too early, their families forever devastated.

My medical education was teaching me exactly what I came to learn: how to alleviate suffering and to save lives. I was at one of the top medical schools, learning from some of the most skilled doctors in the world who had at their fingertips the most advanced technology and state-of-the-art treatments. Every day, Wash U's hospitals delivered exceptional care to thousands of patients, and I was training to provide this care myself.

But what if I encountered problems that medicine alone could not solve? If what was making my patients sick was the health-care system itself, wasn't it my obligation to also fix the system? And how would I go about learning the skills to do so?

THERE MUST HAVE BEEN OTHER students in my class who were wrestling with these questions, but it was hard to find them. Medicine is a conservative profession, and medical education is steeped in tradition and hierarchy. Medical training has a clearly defined cadence. The first two years of medical school are preclinical classroom-based instruction; the next two years are clinical, with learning on the hospital wards. After graduation, there come three to seven years of internship and residency, and possibly additional fellowship training. Those pursuing PhDs or other advanced degrees typically did so in between the preclinical and clinical years.

Early in our training, it was made clear that we were there to learn to be excellent clinicians and scientists. We understood that our job was to function within the system that was already in place, not to look for problems with it or, God forbid, try to change it. To be fair, there is an endless amount of information to learn, and it should be a medical school's top priority to ensure that its students have a solid grounding in medicine and science. But we were actively discouraged from anything approaching advocacy. Many of our professors believed that activism wasn't something doctors should do at all, and medical students should keep their heads down and focus on studying.

I quickly learned that bringing up issues like affordability of health insurance—much less the right to universal health care—was too "political" a topic for our professors. I was becoming more engaged by issues like this, not only because of my family's experience with economic hardships but also because of a growing awareness that broader social change was necessary to fit my view of what medicine can and should accomplish. When several classmates and I tried to start a chapter of Medical Students for Choice, we were told that "choice" was too controversial: the name had to be something more neutral. Our chapter took on the name of Reproductive Options Education, which conveniently spelled out *Roe*.

Some of the more advocacy-inclined students were involved in the Wash U chapter of AMSA, the same organization I'd worked with at Cal State. Our med school sponsored a few students every year to attend the AMSA national convention, and because of my involvement as an undergraduate, I was selected to attend.

It would not be an exaggeration to say that this convention changed the entire trajectory of my career. For four days, I heard talks from medical students, residents, and practicing physicians who not only verbalized the systemic problems I encountered but were actively doing something about it. Along with over a thousand physicians-in-training, I listened in awe to Victor Sidel and Jack Geiger, two of the cofounders of Physicians for Social Responsibility, which won a Nobel Prize for its work to halt nuclear proliferation during the Cold War. I met Quentin Young, one of the most vocal doctors to advocate for a single-payer health system, under which the government is the sole funder of a country's medical services, distributing money collected through taxes and individual premiums. "Health care must be a human right," he proclaimed, to raucous applause.

After the most rousing keynote of the conference, I introduced myself to the speaker, Fitzhugh Mullan. Dr. Mullan, or Fitz, as I would later call him, was a former assistant U.S. surgeon general who had headed the state health department in New Mexico and then the National Health Service Corps. Attending medical school in the 1960s, he was shocked by the lack of physician engagement in the social justice issues of his time, like the civil rights struggle and conditions of poverty affecting his patients. He and others founded the Student Health Organization, which was instrumental in the formation of AMSA.

I had read his book, *White Coat, Clenched Fist: The Political Education of an American Physician*, and I told Fitz that I wanted to grow up to be just like him, with the "fire in the belly" that he exemplified in fighting for his patients. He agreed right there and then to my working with him. I'd do so remotely throughout medical school and residency; after residency, I'd move to Washington, D.C., and join him at George Washington University.

The most high-impact part of the conference was the breakout sessions led by medical students, where they presented what they were doing to advocate for universal, affordable health care and to bring additional diversity and tolerance to the medical profession. As I participated in workshops to learn how to bring these programs to my med school, I felt, for the first time, that I had found my tribe. These were all people who had been drawn to medicine for the same reason I was. They wanted to learn how to be great doctors, but they were also disillusioned because a traditional medical education was not sufficient to equip us with the skills we needed to bring about the systemic change that our patients needed.

Indeed, AMSA's motto is "It takes more than medical school to make a physician." Medical school may teach the necessary technical and scientific skills, but being a doctor is also about advocating and fighting for our patients.

ONE OF THE THINGS I appreciated most about AMSA was its focus on leadership development. AMSA was proudly a student-run and student-led organization. There was a terrific professional staff of about thirty people who managed membership, conference planning, grants, and other operational duties, but the board was made up entirely of students elected by their peers. The national president and board chair was a student who took a year off from their medical training to lead the organization.

At that first national convention, I was so inspired that I ran for a national board position. To my surprise, I won, and began representing my region in the Midwest. I'd travel to other medical schools and talk about AMSA's work and the importance of physician advocacy in Missouri, Kansas, Nebraska, Iowa, Minnesota, South Dakota, and other neighboring states. One of my favorite experiences was leading a contingent during the 2004 presidential primaries to "bird-dog" in Iowa. Several other medical students and I would show up at pancake breakfasts and town halls to ask the various Democratic candidates to commit to HIV/AIDS funding and expanding health-care access to the uninsured. Several candidates made these commitments, and we students received a lot of encouragement from Iowans to continue our advocacy.

The following year, I was elected to the Trustee-at-Large position and served a two-year term to be vice-chair and then chair of the House of Delegates. The House of Delegates was where chapter leaders debated policy positions and passed resolutions. AMSA already had policies that were far ahead of the rest of the medical profession: we were the first mainstream medical organization to endorse universal health care, and our major legislative priority was to improve patient safety and reduce medical error.

I wanted to lead the House of Delegates to set policies that embraced a broader social justice agenda. Our national leadership included strong advocates for LGBTQ rights and reproductive health, who presented compelling data on how stigma and misunderstanding among medical professionals contributed to undiagnosed cervical cancer, higher rates of HIV, and unmet health needs particularly among low-income women, women of color, and LGBTQ people. We passed resolutions that called attention to these disparities, which paved the way for medical education reform that included culturally competent and inclusive care.

A topic that drew significant internal debate was the relationship between the pharmaceutical industry and the medical profession. When I first started medical school, sales representatives from drug companies were everywhere. They sponsored lunches and came to grand rounds, where they distributed promotional materials that were indistinguishable from the scientific articles that we studied. They also supplied free pens and stethoscopes that prominently displayed the names of medications. Med students and doctors alike were more than happy to use these "free" devices, which turned them into walking billboards. Some of our professors were paid to be experts and received all-expenses-paid vacations to exotic locations. Students talked about these perks as something to look forward to one day.

I, too, didn't question the omnipresent role of "drug reps" (as they are commonly known) until an AMSA event in 2002, where two respected physicians—Bob Goodman, the founder of an organization called No Free Lunch, and Marcia Angell, the former editor of the *New England Journal of Medicine*—presented studies that showed the influence of drug companies' advertising on physicians' prescribing behavior. Doctors who received pharmaceutical promotions, which was called "detailing," were more likely to prescribe brand-name medications that were far more expensive—and often no more effective—than generic medications. Drug companies knew this and in fact were spending twice as much on marketing as they were on research and development of new drugs.

What was most interesting from the studies was a phenomenon described as "you but not me." When asked if physicians were influenced by drug companies' advertising, doctors would answer that yes, of course, doctors are influenced. It's human nature. But when they were asked whether they themselves would be influenced by these ads, the same doctors said no. This was the problem—if we believe that others are influenced but we are not, that justifies our own behavior, even if there is a clearly established conflict of interest.

When Dr. Goodman and Dr. Angell presented these findings, they were met with stony silence and quite a few angry questions. Understandably, there was reluctance to admit our own culpability. Our members were also defensive. Several attendees pointed out that we were only students so we couldn't even prescribe anything. Others observed that many med students struggled with student loans, and the free lunches and stethoscopes helped defray costs. Anyway, they said, the problem was that our schools needed to change their practices; there was nothing we could do as students.

Despite the vocal opposition from a sizable portion of the membership, our national board took a bold step to become the first major medical organization to adopt a "PharmFree" position. AMSA would no longer allow pharmaceutical companies to advertise specific medications at our conferences or in our publications. We would not permit drug reps to attend our events and have unfettered access to our members. We would start a national PharmFree campaign to educate physicians-in-training about conflicts of interest. Many members signed a "no free lunch" pledge for themselves and some even began to do "counter-detailing," visiting practicing physicians to encourage them to eschew industry-sponsored promotions.

The AMSA board made it clear that our goal was not to demonize drug companies, which had an essential role to play in our health-care system. The problem wasn't with pharmaceutical companies funding research or sponsoring programs where their interests were clearly disclosed. Our goal was also not to shame doctors, who were functioning in a status quo system and doing what everyone else did. Rather, we were heeding the new evidence and doing what was best for our patients, so many of whom were struggling with the cost of prescription medicines and being priced out of lifesaving care. Patients expected that we would have only their best interests at heart. We saw ourselves as restoring the trust and integrity that defined the profession we were entering.

Over the next several years, our grassroots campaign turned what was initially dismissed as a fringe issue among kooky activists into a set of new standards that guided interactions between drug companies and the medical profession. As more and more students refused to attend drug rep–sponsored lunches and urged their peers to turn to unbiased sources for information, medical schools began to examine their own policies.

Within a few years, we achieved a tipping point in medical students' views. When Dr. Angell was invited back to address the AMSA convention in 2006, her talk was standing-room-only, and long lines of students gathered to thank her afterward. By the time I graduated from medical school, in 2007, several other national medical organizations had joined us with new conflict-of-interest policies. Big Pharma began changing its marketing practices, and in 2012 Congress would pass the Physician Sunshine Act that codified drug company payment disclosures into law.

I learned some key lessons from our work in the PharmFree movement. First, going against the orthodoxy was hard. It was particularly difficult in the early days, when many students expressed that as much as they might agree, they didn't want to stick their necks out and create trouble. I sympathized with those students who had already struggled so much to get where they were; they had a lot to lose if they were labeled by their school administrations as troublemakers. What kept us going was the knowledge that we were on the right side of history, and we were always guided by serving in our patients' best interests.

Second, the movement was headed by many national leaders at AMSA, but it was powered by grassroots activism. We on the national level provided direction and garnered resources, but none of the work would have been possible without thousands of activists in dozens of schools around the country who propelled local efforts. Without their work on the front lines, our message would have never caught on and spread.

Third, those who did not agree with us were not bad people, and getting them on board required incremental steps. When they heard our message for the first time, it was natural that their initial reactions were suspicion and defensiveness. To change their minds, we needed to show them evidence, but just as important, we needed to understand where they were coming from and to meet them where they were.

That required reining in those advocates who had more extreme views and saw any engagement with corporate entities as "selling out." A lot of our time was spent negotiating with these folks to come up with commonsense compromises. After all, our goal was measured by how many people we could bring to our side, not how many we could alienate.

Success also required tolerance of incremental change. There were many on the progressive flank who harbored an "all or nothing" mentality: they had one definition of success, and anything short of that was compromising their values and therefore could not be tolerated. But success does not occur overnight, and each small success should be celebrated as a step in the right direction. We were training to be doctors, so we had to be practical in our approaches as we aimed to be revolutionary in our vision.

My fellow AMSA leaders and I would have similar spirited debates regarding approaches to universal health care. At that time, the United States had over forty-five million uninsured people. Many more were underinsured and had limited access to health care. These were the patients we treated every day, and every day we could see that our system was broken and patients were dying because of it. I could understand why those in the progressive wing believed that we needed a total overhaul of our broken system. Intellectually, I could see the appeal of a single-payer system that Canada and some other countries have; it saved administrative costs and ensured that everyone had access to a basic level of health care.

At the same time, single-payer was just one of many possible ways to get to universal health care. It might have been the most efficient option, but it also required a complete overhaul of the health-care system, which seemed unlikely in the near future. I saw the needs that my patients had at that moment. Those who were suffering now could not wait for wholesale change years down the line.

Many AMSA leaders thought as I did. We were in the camp that believed getting to a single-payer system would take too long and therefore was impractical. We urged incremental reform in the meantime so that at least we could help some patients get insured and have access to better care. As an organization, we ended up embracing both positions. Overall, we aligned with single-payer advocates as the "ideal" strategy, but our everyday work was focused on supporting more practical reforms that could occur in the meantime. We kept our eyes on the prize, which was quality, affordable, and accessible health care—and didn't get hung up on a single strategy to get there. In the years to come,

AMSA would become an early and vocal supporter of the Obama administration's Affordable Care Act as a method to achieve universal health care through improving the existing system rather than a total overhaul.

After three years on the national board, I ran for and was elected national president of AMSA in 2005. I took a year off, moved to the organization's headquarters in Washington, D.C., and devoted myself fully to health policy and advocacy. I represented our membership of sixty-five thousand physicians-in-training in dealings with Congress, and I also oversaw the national office operations and traveled throughout the country to visit our chapters. PharmFree was one of our major national campaigns. Another was universal health care, for which AMSA had established the Jack Rutledge Fellowship, which allowed another med student to also take a year off to devote their full-time energy to this cause.

That year, the "JRF" (as we called him) was my good friend Kao-Ping Chua from Wash U. Kao was one year behind me in medical school, and I'd recruited him to join AMSA during his first week of orientation. We became close friends, and I was thrilled to work with him in D.C. Kao and I, along with other national and regional AMSA leaders, organized rallies where we invited elected officials to join us as we spoke about how the next generation of physicians was committed to ensuring that health care was a human right guaranteed to all, not just a privilege available only to some.

I will always remember the energy and the hope exemplified by the thousands of AMSA members as we marched across the Brooklyn Bridge in New York City to proclaim that we were fighting for a world of "everybody in, nobody out." We were not waiting for others to step up; we were the ones leading the charge.

The national presidents before me had pressed Congress to introduce legislation to limit working hours for residents. This effort was instrumental in getting hospitals to agree to a maximum eighty-hour-a-week rule, to protect resident work rights, and to safeguard patient safety. AMSA's legislative affairs director, Chris McCoy, and I built on this success and worked to introduce legislation on universal health care and student loan debt relief. We wrote a concept paper for loan forgiveness in exchange for service along with a new program that combined public health and community health training, which we called a "Public Health Medical College." Together with our allies and mentors, including Fitz Mullan, we championed efforts to improve diversity in the health-care workforce.

It was exciting to lead national-level policy making, and at the same time experience the grassroots energy of student activism on the local level. I traveled to several dozen chapters, where I met medical students who had gotten off the sidelines and were jumping into the fray. They were bucking convention and taking a stand, and each was making a difference in their own way. They reinforced the central message I took from my years at AMSA: that medical students and physicians shouldn't keep their heads down and mouths shut in the face of injustice. It was our obligation to be at the forefront of the fight for the patients we serve.

Perhaps most important, I saw for myself that change can and does happen. As a quote often attributed to Mahatma Gandhi goes, "First they ignore you, then they laugh at you, then they fight you, then you win."

THE MORE I BECAME INVOLVED in policy and advocacy, the more convinced I was that a career in the laboratory as a clinician-researcher was not the right fit for me. I still liked the pursuit of the science and was drawn to teaching, but more than anything I wanted to be on the front lines of the fight for better care for everyone. My colleagues in the lab loved that work more than anything. I didn't. I couldn't spend four or more years in the lab when I knew that I could be advocating to help the forty-five million people who were uninsured.

Leaving the MD/PhD track was going to be a challenge. For one thing, I had to tell Dr. Atkinson, whom I respected so much. He had personally secured grant funding for my PhD years and already invested two years in training me. I feared his disappointment and anger that I was reneging on my promise to join his lab.

Contrary to my expectations, not only did he understand my decision, he told me that he was far from surprised. He had seen my evolution and was waiting for me to come to this decision myself.

"I have every confidence that you will make a big difference in policy and advocacy," he told me. "This is what you were meant to do, and I'm glad to have been here for you when you figured it out."

Dr. Atkinson and I have stayed in touch over the years. In 2017, ten years after my graduation, I came back to Wash U as the medical school's commencement speaker. I saw Dr. Atkinson then and told him about how I've aspired to be a mentor like him, someone who—like Dr. Garcia and Dr. Paulson—always strove to help their students find their dreams and reach their potential. They all saw something in me when I didn't see it in myself. Though what I wanted to do was not always something that they had expertise in, they encouraged me every step of the way. Coming from the background I did, without well-connected family or other personal networks, it was these mentors who made all the difference in my life.

Leaving the MD/PhD track also meant that I would have to forgo my full scholarship. I had heard of students in other schools who were required to pay back the first two years. Wash U never asked me for this and, in fact, helped me identify a combination of need-based and merit scholarships that covered most of my remaining tuition.

In retrospect, it was incredible that the med school's administrators supported me as they did. The dean, William Peck, was well known in Missouri's Republican establishment and hardly shared my burgeoning political views. However, he took a keen interest in my desire for policy training and encouraged my efforts to pursue opportunities outside of the medical curriculum. Wash U's administration supported me when I took time off by ensuring that I received loan deferments and travel scholarships. One summer, when I didn't have health-care coverage, Dean Peck personally helped me secure health insurance. I could not have asked for a better place to receive my medical education.

My medical training was significant for another reason: it was during medical school that I finally faced my greatest shame.

I stutter. It's easy for me to write this now, but until I was in my midtwenties, I could not accept that fact, even as it dominated every aspect of my life.

In China, my stutter was so severe that I often couldn't get out any words at all. One of my most vivid memories from elementary school was a class where I had to give a talk on the Roman Empire. I could feel myself stuttering on the very word—Roman—so I stabbed myself with a pencil to get out of the class. That piece of pencil lead is still in my leg today.

As I learned English, I realized that there was a trick I could use: I knew which sounds would trip me up, so I avoided words that had those sounds. I never asked for a pencil, because *p* was the most difficult. I never ate sandwiches, because words that began with a solid *s* sound often tripped me up. I did everything I could not to introduce myself, because my name wasn't something I could substitute. I became so good at hiding that people around me rarely heard me stutter. But I lived in constant fear that I'd be found out.

I was able to make it through all of college and most of medical school by finding other ways to say what I didn't want to say. There were moments when I thought I'd be outed. *N* was another trigger, and I didn't know how I'd manage to introduce myself on my neurology rotation. (I became very creative, explaining that I was part of the "stroke team," for example.)

Another time, I was asked to answer a question in a large lecture for which the answer was a particular parasite, "schistosomiasis," a difficult word even for people who don't stutter. I couldn't get the word out, and the professor mimicked my block.

"It's 'schi-schi-schi-schistosomiasis.' Why don't you come back when you're not so nervous," he said. A few students laughed. I felt the sting of the slight, but mostly I was relieved that my secret was still safe.

It was not at all rational, but I had gotten away with my secret all these years. And still, my worries dominated every professional interaction. What if people found out I stuttered and no longer wanted me to be their doctor? After all my hard work, what if this was the reason I failed out of medical school? And what about my desire to be an advocate to speak for my patients—who wants someone to speak for them who can't speak themselves?

Things came to a head during the year I was AMSA president. With all the responsibilities to give speeches and represent AMSA at high-pressure meetings, I tried very hard to sound fluent at all times. The problem was that the harder I tried to hide my stuttering, the worse my speech became. There was one board meeting during which I felt myself blocking on words that involved almost half the alphabet. It soon became nearly impossible to say anything at all. Soon, I was canceling nearly all of my meetings. In my mind, I was letting everyone down. I thought about quitting my position. I couldn't bear to have anyone hear me like this, and I wanted to die.

For the first time, I sought the help of a speech therapist. And here I got lucky, twice. The first person I went to listened to me and told me that she wasn't the right person to help me. "I can help you a bit to get you started," she said, "but there is someone much better, an expert in speech disorders for adults. The stakes are so high for you. You need to see the best."

I've always remembered her words. They demonstrate humility and a recognition of one's own limitations, as well as generosity for a fellow professional. I was paying out of pocket for her services. On paper, she had the right credentials. She could easily have continued to accept my money and seen me as her client. By referring me instead, she showed that she had my best interest at heart.

It's because of her that I met my speech therapist, Vivian Sisskin. Through Vivian, I learned that I was a covert stutterer, able to hide my stuttering and thus not sound like a person who stutters. The ability to hide intensified the shame because it allowed me to hide under a veil of fluency, which brought on more pressure and self-doubt. The key to recovery? Acknowledging, first and foremost, that I was a person who stuttered.

I had seen Vivian for a few private sessions in her office at the University of Maryland, and she could see that changing my self-identity was not something I was ready to do yet. Instead of giving me an ultimatum, she invited me to come to a group that assembled at her house every weekend.

I remember sitting in my car in her driveway. I was debating whether I should go in when a middle-aged man knocked on my window.

"Are-are-are-are you going to Vivian's?" he asked.

I had heard people stutter before, but never seen anyone stutter so easily and comfortably. I followed him in. There, I met a dozen other people from all walks of life—a trial lawyer, a NASA astronaut, a stand-up comedian, a college student, a few retirees. There were people who openly stuttered, with repetitions and blocks. There were other covert stutterers who, like me, sounded fluent but were actually just good at replacing their words. We all had one thing in common: we stuttered, and we no longer wanted to live with fear and shame because of it.

Coming to terms with my stuttering was a difficult process that took years of intense work with Vivian. There were moments of unexpected revelation. When I told my mother over the phone, she was silent for a few moments. She then told me that Nai Nai had heard me stutter as a child and urged that I get help. My mother thought it was something I would grow out of, and after we came to America, she didn't hear me stutter.

"It's because I hid my stutter from you," I told her. "But how did Nai Nai know about stuttering and treatment for it?"

"Because your father stuttered, too," she said. That blew my mind. All these years, I had tried so hard to hide from my family something that they already knew. I couldn't help wondering how different things might have been if I had gotten treatment earlier. Could I have been spared all those years of misery and self-doubt?

As I went through my treatment, I became acutely aware of how little attention medical schools devoted to speech disorders and other disabilities. While nearly 20 percent of Americans have a disability, only one in four medical schools included disability education as part of its curriculum. Not surprisingly, studies show that people with disabilities experience many barriers to care, and two surgeons general's reports recommended additional health professional training in this area.

I began to speak out on this need. Over time, I started to talk about my own stuttering and the biases and misconceptions around speech disorders. I also began to mentor young people who stutter. One of my mentees and also a client of Vivian's was a college student who, like me, was terrified that he might have to abandon his dream of becoming a doctor because of his stutter. Today he is a practicing internist in Los Angeles.

Just as Vivian predicted, the key to recovery was acceptance of my identity as a person who stutters. I still struggle with fluency from time to time, and there are still moments when I wish I didn't have to cope with stuttering. But I also see that my lifelong source of shame is a core part of my identity. As a doctor, I encounter many people who feel that society has cast them aside: individuals who struggle with drug addiction, who are HIV positive, who are experiencing homelessness, who have mental illness. I may not know all their life circumstances, but I do know that I can help them leave shame at the door, show them that they belong, and treat every person with dignity and humanity.

4

Opening Pandora's Box

During my final year of medical school, in 2006, I decided on emergency medicine as my specialty. I loved the "predictably unpredictable" nature of the ER, and my personality was suited to its fast-paced, high-intensity environment.

I also loved that the ER was the one place where every patient had to be seen and no one would be turned away. These were the days before the Affordable Care Act, and I never wanted to be in a situation where I had to deny a patient lifesaving care because of their insurance status or inability to pay. The ER was the ultimate safety net. It was where I could treat the most vulnerable: those in critical condition who needed life-sustaining care, and those who otherwise had nowhere else to go for basic services.

Going into emergency medicine was also a strategic career decision: I knew I wanted to work in health policy, and the ER was where I would see the problems of our health-care system firsthand. Through my years of advocacy with AMSA, I had seen that it wasn't enough to provide care for my patients if what was making them sick wasn't just the disease but the limitations of the health-care system. I felt an obligation to advocate for policy changes that would help all patients to access quality, affordable care. The patient I saw in medical school, Eric, could have been alive and raising his children if he'd been able to afford his seizure medications. Tony and so many other people from my childhood could have had different trajectories if there were laws that protected their ability to obtain care when they were sick.

I also saw that so many people could have better lives if only they had a fundamental right to health care. In medical school, I took care of Eileen, a woman in her early forties, who came to the ER because of a fever. She had just started on dialysis, and although her fever was likely due to the seasonal flu, her nephrologist wanted to make sure she didn't have an infection in her new graft.

I asked Eileen how she was dealing with dialysis. It was, after all, a big change in lifestyle. She'd previously been working and was the primary caregiver for her grandchildren. Now she had to spend three afternoons a week in the dialysis clinic.

"Doc, I can't even tell you. I was so relieved the day my doctor told me my kidneys no longer worked," she said.

I thought I'd misheard. "Relieved?" I asked.

"Yes, relieved. Like, happy."

Eileen told me that she had long-standing high blood pressure and diabetes. Like Eric, she had "preexisting conditions" that made health insurance prohibitively expensive. Every month she'd scrimp together what she could to buy her blood pressure pills and insulin. Halfway through the month, she'd be cutting her pills in half and lowering her dose of insulin to make the supply last. Her doctor told her that her blood pressure and sugar levels were out of control, and although she knew what she needed to do to treat them, she had no means to do so.

"The day I started on dialysis was the day I qualified for Medicaid," she said. She could now afford her medications. In exchange, she'd be tethered to a machine three days a week. She had to sign up for disability and couldn't work anymore, and she could no longer care for her grandchildren as she did before. But at least she had health insurance.

There is something extraordinarily perverse about a health-care system that makes people thankful to be ill just so that they can receive medical care. This is the "sick care system" that dominates our medical system. To be sure, providing "sick care" is important. Patients coming to the ER need to receive immediate, state-of-the-art treatment. But as I provided this emergency care, I came to see how many patients ended up needing it because of a broken health-care system that could have kept them healthier in the first place. It was my job to provide the "sick care" now, while working toward long-term policy change to ensure that health care is available, affordable, and accessible for all.

I WAS ALSO BEGINNING TO recognize another related need: there were many factors that determined someone's health beyond the health care they received, issues outside the health-care system that had a profound impact on health and well-being.

That realization came to me through international health work. In addition to the year I took off from medical school to serve as AMSA national president, I had taken another year off to do community health work. Through AMSA I had met Anthony So, a physician who was also a professor of public policy at Duke University, who sparked my love for global health. Dr. So directed a global health fellows program that placed me at the World Health Organization in Geneva, where I worked on access to essential medicines. This led me to Rwanda, where I was on a Department of Defense fellowship to care for women infected with HIV/AIDS in the aftermath of the genocide a decade earlier.

Then, after my graduation from medical school in 2007, I had the opportunity to travel with and learn reporting from *New York Times* columnist Nicholas Kristof as part of his Win-a-Trip essay contest. Nick is an extraordinary reporter with a unique talent for finding the story that puts world events into perspective and jolts readers thousands of miles away out of their complacency and into action. I wanted to see his work up close and try to apply this skill in my own burgeoning advocacy.

Nick and I have another connection. He and his wife, Sheryl WuDunn, were reporters in China during the Tiananmen Square uprisings. My mother was such a fan of their work that she chose my American middle name, Sheryle, after Nick's wife. Growing up, I heard many stories of the foreign reporters who, along with brave Chinese revolutionaries, helped expose the Chinese government's human rights violations. My parents always emphasized to me how critical free speech is. For much of their lives, they and their families lived in constant fear that the government would police what they did, what they said, or even what they thought. Now we were in a country that guaranteed our right to think, speak, and write as we wish.

I was surprised and honored be selected as one of the two winners of the essay competition who would get to travel with Nick to Rwanda, Burundi, and the Democratic Republic of the Congo. In the Congo, I watched as Nick stopped various people on the road to ask where it was that massacres were happening. They'd point in a certain direction. "Dozens of people were just killed a couple of miles down there," they might say. Upon hearing this, the normal reaction would be to run in the opposite direction. But that was not Nick's instinct. He would go toward the horror and seek to understand it. That was how he tracked down stories no one else did and then shared them with the world.

In the small village of Malehe, Nick had asked villagers to point us to a family that was most affected by the civil war. They directed us to a hut, where we saw an elderly woman who was little more than skin and bones. She was so frail that she could barely stand up. But she was not the person who needed help the most.

That person was her daughter, a forty-one-year-old woman named Yohanita. We were directed behind the hut, where a person the size of a child lay on a bed of dried leaves. Yohanita barely weighed sixty pounds and was completely immobile. Her family farm had been pillaged by soldiers months ago. She hadn't eaten in weeks and was literally dying from starvation. She couldn't move, and when I turned her, I saw that she had deep and infected bedsores.

Yohanita was the first patient I treated as a newly minted doctor. She needed help far beyond what we could provide in the village. We brought her to a nearby hospital to receive care. She received fluids, antibiotics, and management of her deep bedsores.

Though she seemed to be doing well for a short time, we soon learned that the interventions were too little, too late. She died. The cause of death was malnutrition and infection, brought on directly by the civil war around her.

The circumstances surrounding Yohanita's death were tragic and dramatic, but they were in reality just a more extreme version of the plight that many patients faced back in the United States. Just weeks before I saw Yohanita, while I was finishing my final year of medical school, I had taken care of a patient in St. Louis who could barely breathe because her lungs were filled with fluid. She had kidney failure and was on dialysis but had missed all three of her dialysis appointments that week. Her son, who normally brought her to the clinic, had just been arrested, and she had no means to pay for a cab. As it was, she couldn't pay her bills, and her electricity had been shut off.

She was suffocating on her own bodily fluids and could have died, all because of issues that had nothing to do with her health but everything to do with her other life circumstances.

When I relayed her story to the attending physician, he cut me off. "It's not your job to open Pandora's box," he said. "Don't ask questions you don't want to know the answers to."

I had heard this sentiment expressed many times before. Each time, I was worried for my patient and disappointed for our profession. I knew all too well the choices that families are forced to make—between transportation and food, between medicines and rent. How could we deny that these trade-offs were literally making our patients ill? At the same time, I also understood the predicament that health professionals are in and the point the attending physician was making: Why ask about these social factors when there is nothing we can do about it anyway?

In the ER, I'd see a patient with heart disease. I could advise her on eating healthier and getting exercise, but then she'd tell me that the closest grocery store was two bus rides away and that she felt unsafe to walk outside. I'd help a child with asthma, only to have his mother bring him back a week later because their house had untreated mold. So many patients would come in for illnesses that were caused not only by the disease that they had but by social factors outside the traditional purview of medicine.

These "social determinants of health" play a major role, in fact, *the* major role, in determining a person's health and well-being. Studies have shown that as much as 90 percent of a person's life expectancy depends on these factors, and only 10 percent on medical care.

It was the field of public health that looked to assure the conditions in which people can be healthy. It was public health that focused on preventing diseases to keep people from needing health care in the first place. It was public health that urged policy makers, health professionals, and patients alike to regard education, housing, food, and transportation as health issues, too. It was public health that literally is about protecting and safeguarding the public's health.

I hadn't previously thought about this field, but I began to see that if I wanted to be the most effective advocate for my patients, I needed two key skill sets. I needed to gain formal training in health policy so I could help shape better health-care systems. And I needed to learn the discipline of public health to influence the social factors that determine health and overall well-being.

THERE ARE MANY EXCELLENT INSTITUTIONS to pursue formal training in health policy and public health. I had one particular place in mind: Oxford University.

The education available at Oxford was reason enough to study there. For me, there was a much more important reason. My goal was to win a Rhodes Scholarship and go to Oxford because I wanted the college experience I had never had. I wanted to make the friends that I had never made before and for once to have a "normal" life.

During medical school, I read Bill Clinton's autobiography, *My Life*. President Clinton wrote about his Oxford years as being instrumental to his intellectual growth and political awakening. Through the Rhodes Scholarship, he met people with connections that a young man from a working-class family in Arkansas otherwise couldn't have access to.

All of these aspects spoke to me. Medical school had taught me technical skills to become a doctor, but I wanted a broader education—and a wider network beyond medicine—that would prepare me for what I wanted to do. Most of all, I loved President Clinton's description of how Oxford was where he made lifelong friendships.

I craved these friendships more than anything else. Up until then, I had one, perhaps two, real friends. I knew and spent time with many people, but I never let them get close. Part of the reason was my deep shame about stuttering. Another was my insecurity about age. Toward the end of medical school, I had finally come to terms with stuttering and had reached an age (twenty-four) where my relative youth didn't matter as much. I thought that if I won a Rhodes Scholarship, I could start over. I could be honest with myself and those around me and start forming real friendships at last.

Every year, nearly a thousand applicants from the United States vied for thirty-two scholarship slots. I didn't think my chances were very good, but I did my best at writing an essay and compiling the requisite eight letters of recommendation. I made it to the final interview, which was a nerve-racking experience that started with a cocktail party with all the candidates and selectors. I thought I'd done reasonably well with this social event and the interviews the next day, but I was rejected.

I was furious at myself because I should have realized that there were unwritten rules of the road just as there had been for medical school admission. During the interview, I'd found out that elite universities had entire offices devoted to preparing students for Rhodes, Marshall, Fulbright, and other prestigious scholarships. All the other finalists seemed to have spoken with numerous Rhodes alumni, many of whom had written their letters of recommendation. I hadn't. In fact, I hadn't ever met any Rhodes Scholars until my interview.

Over the next several months, I thought hard about whether Rhodes was truly something I wanted to do. It was. That, then, was my mission, just as getting into medical school had been. So I asked all my contacts to see if they knew any Rhodes Scholars. Eventually, I found six scholars who shared with me their experiences and advice. I applied again, and this time, I was successful.

That second year, during the interview process, I got to know another finalist, Aaron Mertz, who also had Wash U connections. He had graduated from Wash U and was in a physics PhD program at Yale. Aaron and I became instant friends. We spent hours speaking the night of the social, and vowed that we'd remain close no matter the outcome. The next day, we were so thrilled that we were the two scholars chosen from our district. From that day in November until when we started over the summer, Aaron and I spoke on the phone every day.

Both of us looked to Rhodes to build our personal and professional relationships. There were many opportunities to do so, starting with the "Bon Voyage Weekend," when the Rhodes Scholars from the United States first met each other. It used to be that all thirty-two would sail across the Atlantic together and have additional time to bond during the trip. With England now just a six-hour flight away, the ocean crossing had been replaced by a series of formal and informal events the weekend before our departure. My year, we had off-the-record meetings with prominent alumni including Supreme Court Justice David Souter and U.S. senators Dick Lugar and Paul Sarbanes. In the evenings, we attended grand receptions hosted by the British ambassador to the United States and the American secretary of the Rhodes Trust.

Many times that weekend, I asked myself if this was real. Just seventeen years earlier, my parents and I had come to America bearing little more than our hopes and dreams. Now here I was, meeting people whom I'd read about, studied, and admired from afar.

My coursework was intellectually broadening as well, as I moved out of the structured world of medical instruction to delve into social, cultural, and political issues. I pursued two master's degrees that would provide broad exposure through interdisciplinary coursework, and I took classes in economics, history, and anthropology. I worked with superb professors like Avner Offer who encouraged and praised me for opening Pandora's box. With their guidance, I sought answers to the questions I had during medical training, through the lens of health policy and public health.

My two years at Oxford gave me the time and space for personal growth and the opportunity I'd sought to finally form deep friendships. My cowinner, who by that point had become my best friend, Aaron, was going through a similar personal transformation: just before he started at Oxford, he came out as being gay. Rhodes was also the first time he was living his true self. It was quite a journey to go through with him, being authentically and unapologetically who we are with each other and with the new people we were meeting.

I completed my coursework, but for the first time I didn't keep my head down in the books. I had already graduated from medical school and had deferred my residency; I wasn't worried about grades and "making it" to the next stage. My primary focus was getting to know people and having them get to know me.

So I filled the days with long meandering conversations with class-mates over leisurely teas at the Rose café, pints at the Turf Tavern, and late-night port in the Merton Middle Common Room. To meet new people, I joined the college rowing team, dabbled in chamber music, and went on day trips around England. My classmates were seeing parts of me that I had kept locked away for so long. They embraced me, as I did them. I was at peace in a way that I had never been before.

THE SUMMER BETWEEN MY FIRST and second year at Oxford was when I met the most important person in my life.

Many of my friends were in London for the summer, as was I. I had applied for and received an internship at Lehman Brothers so that I could better understand health-care financing, and I planned to spend the second half of the summer in South Africa, a country that had long fascinated me, to study its health-care system and to do a rotation in trauma medicine.

One Saturday morning, two days before I was to leave for Cape Town, I headed into Foyles bookstore on Charing Cross Road. I had been so busy hanging out with my Oxford friends that I was totally unprepared for my South African trip. I needed to buy a guidebook before I left.

I was deciding between Lonely Planet and Fodor's when I heard a voice behind me: "Excuse me, may I ask you—are you from China, by any chance?"

I didn't look up. I was annoyed. In England, as in the United States, strangers often assumed that I came from an Asian country and would say words in a random Asian language as a greeting. Usually, it was "*ni hao*" or "*konichiwa*."

I thought this man was about to do the same. "No, I'm American," I said, and went back to my books.

He kept on talking. "Are you headed to South Africa? I can help you, because I'm from there."

I turned around and finally looked at the man speaking to me. He was tall, a whole foot taller than I was, with dark brown hair and a kind smile. I suddenly became eager to learn more about South Africa.

We talked a bit at the book stacks, then went to the café in Foyles to continue our conversation. I learned that his name was Sebastian Walker, that he was born in Johannesburg and had trained as an aeronautical engineer at the University of the Witwatersrand there. After college, he emigrated to the United Kingdom and was working as a real estate project manager for Reuters. One of his upcoming projects was in China. That's why he was also looking for travel books.

Coincidentally, the Reuters building was right across from Lehman's; we figured out that our offices were on the same floor and faced each other. Yet if we hadn't met that day in Foyles, we probably would never have met at all. We had no friends in common. He was an avid cricket player and followed rugby closely; these were two sports I knew nothing about. I knew that my life was back in the United States; he'd never been to America nor did he have any desire to visit, much less to live there.

Still, there was something that kept us talking and talking. We canceled all our plans that day and continued our conversation over dinner. It was the best "date" I'd ever had. We saw each other again the next day, and then early the following morning I left for South Africa.

Sebastian and I would text or e-mail each other nearly every day while I was in his home country. When I came back to the U.K., we became inseparable. After I learned that I would be doing my emergency medicine residency at Brigham & Women's Hospital and Massachusetts General Hospital in Boston, he came with me to find a place to live there. I returned to South Africa to meet his mother, Veronica, and his brother's family, in Johannesburg. Sebastian came to Los Angeles to meet my parents and my sister. There were a lot of logistical challenges to overcome, but there was no question in either of our minds that we would continue our relationship.

When I graduated from Oxford and started my residency, we began our transatlantic romance. Sebastian shouldered the lion's share of travel. Every month, he would spend a week or so in Boston, while still working London hours. That, combined with my punishing residency hours, made for two very tired people.

In my second year of residency, Sebastian showed up in Boston unexpectedly. I was coming home from an ER shift nearly three hours after it was due to end. It was almost midnight. I was exhausted. I still had notes to finish, and my next shift would start just eight hours later.

When I entered my apartment building, I found Sebastian sitting on the stairs.

"What are you doing here? I need to finish my charting and get some sleep." This is what Sebastian remembers me saying. (I thought I was more gracious and simply expressed my surprise that he was there.)

He took my hand. "Take a walk with me," he said.

Sebastian recalls that I resisted and said that it was too cold and too late. I don't remember that part, but I do remember the late-night walk to the Boston Common, where he proposed.

We got married in South Africa, at a vineyard outside Cape Town, the following year. Aaron was my "man of honor." Angela and Sebastian's brother, Alastair, were part of the wedding party, along with Kao from AMSA and another close friend from Oxford, Lyric Chen.

After three years of long-distance, Sebastian moved to Boston for good. It was the first of many moves he'd make for us to be together.

The Rhodes Scholarship was life-changing for many reasons. It was where I met my closest friends and felt like I finally belonged for who I really was. And, of course, without the Rhodes, I would have never met Sebastian. I will be eternally thankful to have found someone so thoughtful, kind, and generous who shares my values on family and who has always been 100 percent supportive of my career ambitions. As many have said, the person you end up with, with whom you build a family and a life, is the most important decision that you will ever make.

It certainly was for me. And it couldn't have happened without a chance meeting one Saturday morning in a bookstore.

5

When Doctors Don't Listen

Throughout my childhood and adolescence, I had what can euphemistically be called a challenging relationship with my mother. I looked up to her and was always seeking her approval, which she never gave. If I received a grade of 99 on a test, she'd ask what I got wrong and why I was careless. If I got 100, then the test must have been too easy. I loved music and played the piano and the violin. If I entered a competition and didn't win, she'd say others must have done better. On the rare occasions I did triumph, she'd comment that music was a waste of time and a distraction from studying.

I don't think I ever heard her say that I did something well, and I'm certain she never told me that she was proud of me. Unlike Nai Nai and Ye Ye, she was not physically affectionate. There are pictures of her holding me when I was a baby, but I can't recall if she ever held my hand or gave me a hug.

My mother showed her love in other ways, which I did not understand or appreciate at the time. When we first came to America, she pushed me hard academically because she knew that I needed to learn English and had to catch up fast. Every night she'd drill me on vocabulary words. I was often asleep when she got home after work, so she'd wake me up. I was groggy, but she must have been many times more tired. If I complained, she'd remind me of the sacrifices she and my father were making.

"We do this for you," she'd say. "We gave up everything and now you must do your part."

It was true that she and my father worked exceptionally hard. They were both so frugal with both time and money that they never did anything that was considered a "waste." Neither ever bought anything new. Clothes were hand-me-downs from their coworkers or purchased from yard sales. Furniture was scrounged from dumpsters. We never ate in restaurants, and even fast food was a luxury we couldn't afford. There was no such thing as "free time": if there was time in the day, that meant they could take on another side job.

My mother, in particular, thought of her children as her reason for being. I was her life, and after Angela was born, we were her life. She just would never tell us so with words. Being hard on us was her way of showing love. After all, this was how she was raised, and the world in which she lived was pretty hard on her.

Even though I could intellectually understand why my mother acted as she did, I was constantly resentful. I would lash out at her and tell her she was a terrible mother who didn't care about her children. When Angela was sent away to China as an infant, I'd talk about her, knowing that it would hurt my mother when I did. After Angela returned, I'd say to my mother that I'd never do this myself, that one day I wanted to be the warm and loving mother for my children that I wish I'd had. I vowed to never be anything like my mother.

It would take many years for me to see how much my cruel words must have hurt her, and to recognize how many of my mother's character traits are deeply ingrained in me. She exemplified persistence and resiliency. At a time when fewer than one in a thousand Chinese students tested into college, she studied until she became one of the few who did. Then, when it was just as unlikely to get into an American university, she figured it out. In the United States, when one job after another fell through, she kept going. She never gave up, because failure was not a result she'd ever accept.

Yet whenever good things happened because of her hard work, she would never take credit. It was always because "we are so lucky," as she'd say. She would remind me of the many ways luck was on our side. If our asylum status hadn't come through when it did, who knows where we would be. Maybe we would be living in Canada. Or maybe we would have continued to live in the United States, and I would be among the half million Dreamers whose legal status continues to be in jeopardy.

GROWING UP, I WAS TOO caught up in the everyday conflicts and too stubborn to see that what I sought from my mother was her love and approval. By the time I left for medical school, my mother and I were not on speaking terms. I wouldn't see her for nearly my entire first year in St. Louis, until I came back to visit my sister for her eighth birthday. I took Angela to the zoo, and when we came back home my father convinced my mother and me that we should all have dinner together. We went out to a Chinese restaurant in San Gabriel. Before the food came, we got into a fight, and my mother and I both left the table in tears.

We wouldn't talk again for months. I left an occasional voice mail to let her and my father know that I was doing fine.

Then one day, my mother called me. This was something she had never done before. I didn't even know she had my number.

"Duo Duo, something is wrong," she said.

I assumed that she meant with my father, whose stomach ulcer was a continuing source of problems. "Is Father in the hospital?" I asked.

"No, he's fine. The trouble is with me."

She told me that she was feeling run-down and out of breath. By noon, she was so tired that she could barely make it through her afternoon classes. She was getting winded walking from her classroom to the car.

"Have you been to see a doctor?" I asked.

"Yes, to the primary care doctor," she said. "He said it was a virus. I'm around all these kids who are sick all the time."

"If it's a virus, it should go away. How long has this been going on for?"

"A while."

"What's a while? A few weeks? A few months?"

She sighed. "Probably six months."

Which meant that she had been ill when I last saw her.

"Why didn't you tell me when I was in L.A.?"

"What would you have done? You're only a medical student."

"I could have helped you and gone to the doctor with you."

"Well, I'm telling you now."

She'd been back to her doctor, who ordered some tests. She didn't know which tests they were, but she said that she had some blood drawn. I assumed they were basic tests looking for anemia, hypothyroidism, and kidney problems. "He thinks that I have depression and gave me some medications for that. But I know I'm not depressed. There's something wrong."

My worries were growing by the minute. This was the first time I had ever known my mother to voice concern about anything related to herself. I had seen her work three jobs and go to school full-time, sleeping no more than four hours each night. I had seen her return to work right after a C-section and go through some terrible abuses from her bosses. Not once did I ever hear her voice any complaints. Not once did I ever hear her ask for help.

Something had to be really wrong. I didn't know what it was, but I knew her problem wasn't a cold or depression.

I flew back to L.A. the following week and made an appointment for her to have a second opinion. This doctor's office had asked us to send over her medical records, and we did.

My mother and I were sitting in the waiting room when she made a request that I will forever regret agreeing to. She asked me not to say anything—not to speak up.

"Don't make the doctor angry," she said. "I just want to see what he thinks, not to have an argument."

I started explaining that it was a patient's right to ask questions. I had learned this in medical school; this was what doctors expected.

She was insistent. "Don't make trouble for me. This is my health. Let me do the talking. You just listen."

So I did. I listened as the doctor asked questions and then rendered his opinion. He thought my mother's problems had to do with her mind. He saw that she was on antidepressants, but she didn't tell him that she wasn't taking them. Since the drugs didn't seem to be working, he prescribed another medication: Valium.

"Your mother is just anxious," he said to me as we left. "She will be fine."

She was not fine. The next time she sought medical care was after she started coughing up blood. This time, she was hospitalized and had a whole battery of tests done. One test led to another, and soon she was having a biopsy and then surgery.

Then came the diagnosis: she had breast cancer that was widely metastatic, to her lungs, her brain, and her bones. It was a rare form of cancer that spread quickly and was hard to treat.

My mother was forty-seven years old. She was given six months to live.

THERE IS A CHINESE PROVERB that roughly translates to: If you fall down, stand up and fight on. This could have been my mother's motto. Her life was about *chi ku*, which she had done so many times before. She had beaten the odds many times over. There was no question that she was going to fight this cancer head-on.

The first question she had was where she could find the most aggressive treatment. That's what she wanted. Surgery, chemotherapy, radiation, experimental immune therapy—whatever there was, she was going to take it on. Cancer wouldn't keep her down. Failure was not an option with anything else, and this was no different.

"Your sister is only eight," she said. "I'm not going to die before she's grown up."

My mother lost her beautiful thick hair. The fullness in her cheeks disappeared. She had painful ulcers down her throat. Her blood counts became so low that she was in the intensive care unit for weeks fighting infection after infection.

I came back to L.A. so I could accompany her to the treatments. Wash U was more than accommodating, allowing me to take exams remotely and pursue independent study. What I missed from classroom instruction, I was learning through observing my mother's care.

Every day, I was struck by the disconnect between what patients and families needed and what doctors and nurses were doing. The doctors who had misdiagnosed my mother were not trying to practice poor medicine, but their dismissal of her symptoms resulted in a one-year delay in her ultimate diagnosis. My mother was so hesitant to speak up herself, and I wondered what would have happened if she—and I—had been more insistent that something was wrong.

There were numerous other examples of this disconnect and how it affected her care. Once, I had just flown in from St. Louis when my father told me that my mother was in the ER. When I arrived there, I found her lying on a gurney in the hallway. She was wearing a flimsy gown and curled in a ball, shivering. She was being admitted for dehydration and had an IV pumping cold fluids into her. She'd asked for a blanket hours before, but nobody had followed through to give it to her. The staff were almost certainly busy and overwhelmed with pressing requests. But one simple act could have made a big difference in her care.

I was beginning to understand why medical care seemed devoid of the humanity that patients and their loved ones needed in their time of extraordinary vulnerability. My mother and I would talk about this, a lot. It was one of the few topics we could discuss without arguing.

Prior to her treatments, we'd never spent this amount of time together, just the two of us. It wasn't easy. Before every appointment, we'd fight over how much she should say to her oncologist. She still had the mentality that the doctor-patient relationship was like a parent-child relationship. The doctor had the final word, and she was being insubordinate if she spoke up at all.

"I don't want the doctor to be so mad he will fire me," she said.

"He won't fire you. He can't."

"He could treat me badly and not give me the best medicine."

"Then he's committing malpractice. That's not how it works in America."

"How would you know? You're not a real doctor yet."

We'd go back and forth. At some point, I realized that my efforts at convincing her were futile. I tried a different route and spoke to the nurse practitioner, Pam, a kind woman who took a liking to my mother. Pam reassured my mother that the oncologist wanted her to ask questions. We would come up with the questions together, and my mother began to take solace in my asking on her behalf.

"He can become angry at you, not me," she said.

I would later understand how many other patients harbored a similar fear. Part of it was cultural—the traditional Chinese doctor-patient relationship was as she described. Another was generational. I met plenty of older patients who believed that to ask questions meant that they were doubting the doctor. It wasn't always easy to convince patients that good medical care requires a partnership and that not speaking up can result in misdiagnoses and worse outcomes.

My mother and I didn't talk much, other than about her health. There was too much baggage, and virtually every topic was laden with land mines that could explode at any moment. When she discovered that I had quit my PhD, she was very upset that I'd given up my scholarship. She couldn't fathom that I wanted to do policy work when medicine was such a good career. She didn't approve of the boyfriend I was dating at the time, or really the fact that I was dating at all and not focused entirely on my studies. There were problems with my hair (too long), my weight (too high), and my appearance (name the flavor of the day).

I didn't want to upset her, so I did my best to bite my tongue and not respond when she went on a tirade. Soon, we found comfort in being together in silence. As she received infusions, she'd read mystery novels and I'd study my medical texts. There were many times when I thought about asking her how she was coping. When she got very ill, I came close to apologizing to her for the awful things I'd said to her. I never did, and she never tried to make amends, either. In our silence, there was an understanding that we sought—and received—from each other.

Six months after her diagnosis, she was weak but very much alive. Her oncologist said she was beating the odds, as she always did. After a few more rounds of treatment, he told her that she was in remission.

She started to eat and to put on weight. In a year and a half, she was back teaching full-time at her school.

When she received the news that she was in remission, the four of us went out to celebrate. For years, she'd spoken about wanting a "new" car. All the cars we'd driven before had been found in junkyards and brought back to life by my father. My mother and I both experienced many breakdowns, and she wanted the luxury of choosing a car herself, one that she could test-drive. It didn't matter that what we could afford would still be a used car; it came from a real store and would have that new car smell.

We went to a car dealership and she tried out a couple of Toyotas and Hondas. The Honda Civic was her favorite. When she finished the lease paperwork, we drove the car home, cooked dinner, and rented a movie to watch together.

At some point that evening, my mother turned to me and smiled. "Now everything can go back to how it was," she said.

OUR RELIEF WAS SHORT-LIVED. A follow-up scan found that her cancer was back. She got treatment and at some point was told that she was in remission again. Then the cycle would repeat itself. For seven years, my mother would go through multiple more rounds of treatment, followed by cautious optimism that her cancer was back under control.

I was in my second year of emergency medicine residency in Boston when my father called me one day.

"I think you should come home," he said. "She has a different look in her eyes."

"What do you mean?"

"She doesn't look at me anymore. Sometimes, I don't think she sees anyone."

I flew back immediately, after finding another resident with whom to switch my next ER shift. When I got home, my mother seemed to be her usual self. She was undergoing yet another round of chemo and I could see that the treatment was taking its toll on her. Her fingernails were black and she was visibly in pain when she tried to eat. But her eyes were as bright as they had always been.

One of her favorite places to visit was the Los Angeles County Arboretum, a short drive from the house. It was during the week and Angela was in school. I drove to the arboretum and we started walking.

She wanted to take a break once we got to the waterfall. We sat on a bench, and she stared at the water cascading and crashing onto the rocks. I turned toward her and saw what my father meant. She was looking straight ahead but it was as if she wasn't seeing anything at all.

Suddenly, she started talking. She began telling me about her life in China and how much she hadn't wanted to leave. It was what she had to do for our family, but it was a regret she would always have—to leave her life there behind. She told me that she knew I loved Nai Nai and Ye Ye and that she was sorry to take me away from them. They'd both died by then—Ye Ye first, and then Nai Nai a few months later. They both loved me so much, she wanted me to know.

She told me about her relationship with my father and many things I had not known about their turbulent times. She was certain he would quickly move on to find someone when she was gone. He was going to be fine without her.

"You will be fine, too. You're already a doctor. I'm glad I got to meet Sebastian. Now get married and start your family," she said. "What I need you to do is to promise me that you will always look after Angela."

"Of course," I said. "You know I will always do that."

She told me that she'd taken out a life insurance policy that would provide for Angela's college education. She wanted me to make sure that Angela was cared for financially until she was able to find a job herself.

My mother had one more request. She had gone to a lawyer and made a will. The will included a "do not resuscitate" order. In the event she became critically ill, she did not want extraordinary measures like CPR or being put on a ventilator. She had designated me as her health-care proxy to make sure her wishes were respected.

She was still staring straight ahead, the same blank look in her eyes, when she told me that she had suffered enough. She was done fighting. This was not failure; it was acceptance. She would continue her treatments if they could extend her life, but if she ever got to the point that she was dying, she wanted to die in peace.

I was crying by then. She put her hands over mine and told me to stop. "Don't be sad for me," she said. "The best thing you can do for me is to live your life. You and Angela have been my life, and now you live your lives for me. Everything I did, I did it for you."

Over the next couple of months, we had many more painful conversations. Initially, I couldn't accept that she was giving up. She was still young; her doctors were hopeful; and there were still some therapies she hadn't tried. But the more we talked, the more I came to see that she had thought through everything. It was her choice to die as comfortably as possible and at home. She signed paperwork to this effect and entered home hospice care. She told me that she had prepared everything, so that all I had to do was execute her wishes.

Looking back, these were the conversations where I learned the most about my mother. She was finally letting me see her, and I was finally beginning to understand her.

I was finishing a rotation in the Brigham & Women's ER and due to return home in a week when I received a call from my father. "She's in the hospital," he said. I was aware that she was being treated for pneumonia at home, with IV antibiotics. That afternoon, she took a turn for the worse. Her coughing was so bad that she choked and turned blue. My father panicked and overrode the hospice order by driving her to the hospital.

By the time I arrived, her pneumonia had turned into a full-blown infection that had spread throughout her body. Her blood pressure was low. She was barely breathing on her own. She had lost consciousness.

The ICU doctors were at her bedside and getting ready to put her on a ventilator. Angela was crying and pleading with them.

"Please, she doesn't want this," she said. "She signed paperwork."

"My sister is right," I said. "She's on hospice. She wouldn't want this."

"You brought her to the hospital," one of the doctors said. "You're her daughters. Do you want to let your mother die?"

"We can get her through this and she can live weeks, maybe months," someone else said. "You are her health-care proxy. You can change the order."

I was watching my mother's blood pressure hover in the 80s and her oxygen saturation dip below that. The monitors were flashing and sounding their alarms. Half a dozen people in scrubs and masks were waiting for my call. My sister was holding my mother's hand. She and my father were both sobbing.

My mother had been so clear with her wishes. I knew that honoring them was the right thing to do. Yet, it was also the hardest decision I'd ever made, to ask everyone to stop their efforts and let my mother die.

The doctors signed orders to give her medications that would keep her comfortable. My father, my sister, and I stayed at her bedside all night. On the morning of July 26, 2010, my mother, Sandy Ying Zhang, took her last breath and died.

ONE OF MY HEROES, CONGRESSMAN Elijah Cummings, liked to talk about how one's pain is what forms one's passion, and then that passion becomes one's purpose. For all that I had wanted to do to shape national health policy and work in public health, there was a much more urgent calling following my mother's death. I had no greater drive than to turn the deeply painful experience of her illness into something that would help patients and families in their time of greatest need.

Not long after my mother died, one of the attending physicians at Brigham & Women's Hospital, Josh Kosowsky, approached me about writing a book with him about preventing misdiagnoses. His thesis was that medicine has become so focused on high-tech advances that doctors have forgotten the lost art of listening to the patient. I had experienced this acutely with my mother and also saw it in my own clinical practice. It was astounding that 80 percent of all diagnoses can be made based on a patient's history, yet studies showed that doctors interrupted patients within eight to twelve seconds after they began speaking.

Josh was a master clinician and a brilliant diagnostician. His insights on how doctors can make better diagnoses would be a needed addition to better train health professionals. I thought that we should make the audience for the book even broader: I wanted to share the lessons that I had learned with my mother and target the book to patients as well. While it is the duty of the doctor to listen better and for the health-care system to more ably support the doctor-patient relationship, there are concrete steps that patients can take to advocate for the best care possible.

For two years, I conducted research and interviewed health professionals and patient advocates. Josh and I went around the country to understand best practices. In 2013, we published *When Doctors Don't Listen: How to Avoid Misdiagnoses and Unnecessary Tests*. Part of it was a guidebook for clinicians to improve their diagnostic skills. Another part was a guidebook on why and how patients need to be equal partners in their care.

In the meantime, I began working with hospitals on improving their systems of practice. A critical component was involving patient and family representatives in the feedback process. This was common sense but not the norm. I'd often begin seminars with hospital leaders about patient-centered care by asking them who was in the room. How many people were there as administrators? How many were doctors, nurses, and other practicing health professionals? And then: How many were there in their primary capacity as a patient or the family member of a patient? Nearly all of the time, no one would raise a hand. That made my point: How could there be a conversation about including patients in decision-making if patients were not at the table?

I talked about the challenges my mother and I encountered, from her initial misdiagnosis to the problems following her end-of-life wishes. I also shared experiences from those hospitals that had begun including patient input. One hospital started engaging patients as part of its advisory committee and found, to the staff's surprise, that some of the cases they were most proud of also had the worst ratings from patients. One case involved a middle-aged man who was diagnosed in the ER with a heart attack. The "door to balloon time"—the time it took from entering the hospital to clearing the coronary artery blockage—was twenty-two minutes, far below the national average of forty-two minutes. The patient recovered without incident, and the hospital considered the case a resounding success.

The patient, though, saw his care very differently. He recalled having his shirt and pants cut off without explanation. His wife wasn't allowed to accompany him into the ER, and she waited for hours before someone told her that he was in the ICU. They both reported being in the dark about what had happened; it wasn't until he was being discharged, two days later, that they understood he'd had a heart attack.

There was no medical mismanagement. To the contrary, every measure of sound medical care was met: prompt diagnosis, speedy and effective treatment, and an uneventful, full recovery. There was no doubt that every doctor and nurse involved had good intentions and worked hard to respond to the medical emergency. But in their rush to open the blocked heart vessel they neglected the person they were caring for.

This patient's wife ended up serving on the hospital's advisory board. She told me that she had a whole new perspective on medical care and could see that the doctors and nurses were trying so hard to do the right thing. She was eager to help them do even better. The hospital incorporated new processes into their protocols, including changing their policy to allow one person to accompany the patient into the resuscitation and assigning a team member to explain to the patient and family member what was occurring each step of the way. As I had experienced with my mother, these seemingly simple measures can make a world of difference in someone's perception of their care.

The movement toward shared decision-making and patient-centered care was taking off across the country. With my dual perspective as a provider and family-member advocate, I wanted to be part of that movement. Working in public health and policy was still a goal, but for the moment it would have to be put on hold.

FOR THE TIME BEING, MY waking hours were entirely devoted to delivering and improving patient care. Most days were business as usual in the ER. Some were moments of extraordinary crisis.

At 2:50 p.m. on Monday, April 15, 2013, the emergency department at Massachusetts General Hospital was filled to capacity. In the area of the ER where I was working, my patients were critically ill, with strokes, heart attacks, and overwhelming infections. Even the hallways were packed with patients receiving emergency treatment.

A call over the loudspeakers announced that there had been two explosions at the finish line of the Boston Marathon, a mile and a half away. Many people were injured. That's all we knew.

Doctors, nurses, and techs started clearing the trauma bays. We rushed to send as many patients to other areas of the hospital as we could.

Then there was a second call. These were bombings. There were fatalities and dozens, maybe hundreds, of injured people. How many were coming to Mass General? Nobody knew.

Three minutes later, the doors flew open. Stretchers rolled in, one after the other. Some victims had no pulse and weren't breathing. Others had had their legs blown to shreds. All were covered with blood and soot. The ER was soon filled with the smell of burnt flesh, and each stretcher left behind a fresh trail of blood.

My first patient was unconscious and bleeding profusely. I knew what to do. Within minutes, he was on a respirator to help him breathe and had two tourniquets to stop bleeding.

My second patient, a young woman my age, was screaming and crying. One of her feet was gone and she had severe burns. She was wailing for her family. Where was her husband? Where were her children? For her, I had no answers.

Screams mixed with ambulance sirens. The loudspeaker sounded again and again, announcing that more patients were on their way.

A cell phone rang. A nurse, a surgeon, and I all reached for our pockets, but it wasn't ours. The phone was in a pile of clothes in the corner, in the tan slacks of a patient who had gone to the operating room to complete his amputations. I picked it up and saw the messages that had come through. His loved ones were asking: Where are you? They also told him: I love you.

The Mass General ER would see thirty-nine bombing victims

during those chaotic first hours. That day is inscribed in me. This was the essence of the work for which I had trained: triaging situations, resuscitating patients, and responding to crises. I was on the front lines, where I belonged, and fulfilling my desire to serve those most in need.

At the same time, though, my clinical work opened my eyes to other routes to improving medical care. There were many well-meaning people trying to do the right thing for their patients, but people like my mother were sometimes not getting the care that they deserved. That type of health system reform—at the level of the individual patient and provider—was what I needed to work on next.

AFTER MY RESIDENCY IN BOSTON was over, I moved to Washington, D.C., to join my mentor, Fitzhugh Mullan, and to start a center focused on patient-centered care in the department of emergency medicine at George Washington University. Building on the research that went into *When Doctors Don't Listen*, I assisted patient groups on effective advocacy tools and advised hospitals on incorporating patient- and family-centered care. As an attending physician in the ER, I also directly translated what I was seeing into practice, and taught medical students and doctors in patient-centered care practices.

My work included interviews and surveys of patients, providers, and administrators in forty-eight cities. I found that when it comes to health care, people want the same things. It doesn't matter if they are poor or wealthy, if they are Democrats or Republicans, or if they come from small towns or large cities. People want high-quality affordable health care. They want doctors they can trust, and they crave connection and caring. They don't expect perfection, but they do expect honesty. They know that the current health-care system is unsustainable at best and irreparably broken at worst, and while they recognize the importance of long-term change, they are glad to know that there are things they can do now to help their loved ones.

I met some remarkable patient advocates along the way. Like me, they all became involved in this work because of a painful personal experience. I learned from Julia Hallisay, who founded the Empowered

Patient Coalition after her daughter, Katherine Eileen, suffered medical errors and miscommunication in the course of her fight with cancer. Patty Skolnik, whose son Michael died after an unnecessary brain surgery, started Citizens for Patient Safety to call attention to the importance of informed decision-making. Regina Holliday honored her husband, Fred's, final wishes to use her talent in art to advocate for patients. Her "Walking Gallery," featuring patient stories painted onto suits and jackets, could be found at many medical conferences.

All of these individuals had channeled the most painful moments of their lives into their calling, their pain into the passion that became their purpose. Those who have suffered grave harm or have lost loved ones know that their work now won't undo the damage or mitigate the loss. Their drive to do the work is to prevent others from going through the same tragedy. Knowing that the world as it is is broken, they cannot live without doing everything they can to work for the world as it should be. For them, as it was for me, their journey to better care for all was also their personal journey of healing.

WHENEVER I AM BACK IN L.A., I visit the arboretum. I sit at the waterfall where my mother and I had our fateful conversation. I stare at the cascading streams and I hear her voice as clearly as I did so many years ago.

Sometimes, my father or Angela would go with me. My father retired soon after my mother's death. As my mother predicted, he quickly remarried. He met a kind Chinese woman named Livia and moved to live with her in Vancouver.

Angela went to her college of choice, the University of Southern California, and then joined the Peace Corps. After serving in the Republic of Georgia and then working in China, she's now living in Seattle and working in the tech industry. She's beautiful, brilliant, and has a heart of gold. I am so proud of the incredible person she has turned out to be.

Angela thinks about our mother every day. I do, too. The pain of her passing has been dulled with time, but it comes back with every milestone that she is not there for. How proud she would have been at Angela's graduation. How happy she would have been when Sebastian and I got married. How much she would have wanted to be at the birth of her grandchildren and how much she would have adored them.

A few years ago, I was cleaning our old house when I found a large box with my name on it. Inside were clippings of every news story I had ever appeared in, dating back to my college years. There were college newsletters that featured awards that she said at the time were worth nothing. There was my graduation program, which she must have hunted down from somewhere, and some photos from the ceremony I'd never seen.

There were also handwritten letters from her to me, letters that were never sent. One of them, dated the day of my college graduation, read, "Duo Duo, today is the day my dreams have come true."

I wish I had known this before, when I could have told my mother that she is the reason I am able to live our wildest dreams—hers and mine both.

PART TWO

Leading

6

Doctor for the City

It was an unseasonably warm November day, the day after the 2014 midterm elections. I was on the second floor of Baltimore's city hall, sitting alone inside the mayor's executive conference room. This was where the mayor brought together her cabinet: the heads of police, fire, housing, public works, health, education, and other departments that together ran the city. I recognized the room from the evening news; it was also where she and other city officials often held press conferences.

At any moment, Mayor Stephanie Rawlings-Blake was going to walk in. I was about to interview to become the Baltimore City health commissioner.

My patient advocacy work at George Washington University had been personally fulfilling. After my mother's death, it was what I needed to do for myself and for her. The movement for patient- and family-centered care was growing all around the country, and I was proud to have been part of building it for several years.

Now I was ready to come back to the world of health policy and public health.

Specifically, I wanted to work in local public health. Although it was through AMSA and national-level advocacy that my passion for health policy first started, my true home was on the front lines, working in the community, because of the immediacy of the impact on people's lives. I liked the idea of working in city government because it was hands-on, providing a direct service to residents. I also liked that I'd be engaged with policy formulation and implementation, but didn't need to be overtly political. Filling potholes and cleaning trash isn't about ideology and party politics, and neither is serving as the city's health safety net.

In many ways, I thought of local government as I thought of the ER: we had to care for everyone and no one would be turned away. But unlike the ER, where I couldn't open Pandora's box because there was nothing I could do about transportation, housing, or food access, local government could address these issues, and that would have a direct impact on my patients' medical conditions. Not only could I open Pandora's box, it was my job to do so and figure out how to address the ills that we uncovered.

I'd first gotten to know Baltimore when I was interviewing for residency during my second year at Oxford. There were two excellent emergency medicine programs in the city, at the University of Maryland and at Johns Hopkins, and I'd come back from England to interview at both. I stayed with a medical school colleague who'd grown up in Baltimore. He and his wife lived in Fell's Point, a bustling neighborhood just east of downtown, on a quaint cobblestoned street facing the harbor.

My colleague gave me a tour of the city. We drove through the high-rises of downtown to the tony neighborhoods of North Baltimore. In between were entire blocks of boarded-up houses and blight. As we approached the world-famous Shock Trauma Hospital in West Baltimore, he remarked that there was no shortage of training opportunities in emergency care: this was a city where there were shootings every day and where far too many people suffered from untreated chronic illnesses.

In many ways, Baltimore reminded me of St. Louis. Both cities faced major challenges as a result of declining populations. In 1950, Baltimore was America's sixth-most-populous city, with nearly a million residents. In the last few decades, after the closure of several large manufacturing businesses, the population has been in sharp decline,

with middle-class families moving to Baltimore County and other surrounding suburban areas. This decimated the city's tax base and left a
growing number of structural problems including vacant properties,
underperforming schools, and rising unemployment. By 2008, when
I was visiting Baltimore, the city had approximately 650,000 residents;
by 2014, when I interviewed for the health commissioner's position,
the population had fallen to 620,000.

Like St. Louis, Baltimore is a majority-minority city, with 62 percent
of its population African American. In both cities you can find neighborhoods a few miles apart that have a difference in life expectancy of
twenty years. These present-day disparities are inextricably linked to
a history of discriminatory policies in housing and criminal justice that
mired generations in cycles of poverty and poor health.

I'd been drawn to St. Louis because its neighborhoods reminded me
of the areas in L.A. where I grew up. When my colleague showed me
around Baltimore, I felt the same familiarity. Eighty-four percent of
the children attending Baltimore's public schools qualified for free or
reduced-fee lunches. Many of them would go hungry if not for their
school meal, just as had been the case for me and my classmates. On
any given day, a few hundred school-age kids were homeless or otherwise without stable housing, just as I had been at different times in my
childhood.

My colleague told me about the patients he'd seen who were ill not
because of any specific disease but because of the conditions in their
lives. I thought about all the children who were in vulnerable circumstances by virtue of their birth, about all the parents who wanted more
than anything to give their kids a better life than they had. My parents
had worked very hard and succeeded (eventually) in getting stable jobs.
They were able to move us to neighborhoods with better schools and
safer housing, but there were so many times when we were walking on
a tightrope and just as easily could have fallen off.

As my mother frequently reminded me, we were the lucky ones. We
came so close to losing our immigration status. It wasn't until I was a
medical student that I was finally able to apply for citizenship in the
United States, the country I had long considered my own. My family

and I were once without a home and doing anything we could to make ends meet. I remembered how it felt to beg for money in front of a supermarket. Every time I saw young people hanging out on street corners, selling drugs or their own bodies, I thought that this could have been me under not so different circumstances. Our family was no different from the families around us in L.A., or the families I had gotten to know in St. Louis and was now seeing in Baltimore. I was no different from so many other kids. Coming from the background I did, I just could not accept that geography has to be destiny. I felt that Baltimore could be the place to fulfill my obligation to serve the communities most in need.

But it would take me several years to find my way back to Baltimore. The residency program in Boston was a better fit for me—with the clinical and research experiences I'd sought at the time—and then I had the opportunity to work with Fitz at George Washington University, a long-standing wish. Still, I felt a pull. Through my patient advocacy work in D.C., I met incredible community organizers from Baltimore who were working to right the legacy of Henrietta Lacks, a patient at Johns Hopkins Hospital whose cervical cancer cells were used for research without her or her family's permission.

"We don't want doctors and researchers coming in and doing things *to* us, rather than *for* us," these activists said, mirroring the mantra of our patient advocacy work of "nothing about us, without us."

I saw the energy and the dynamism of Baltimore's community leaders and marveled at how much they were able to do with very few resources. One was the Reverend Debra Hickman, who founded an organization called Sisters Together and Reaching (STAR) to assist women infected with HIV/AIDS. When STAR first began, in 1991, she faced enormous stigma and an indifference "that was sometimes even worse than the stigma," as she put it. She provided medical treatment and access to antiretroviral medications, but then saw that the women needed more support—housing, jobs, and mental health assistance.

In our first of many meetings, I told her about my experience working in Rwanda, providing antiretroviral drugs to women infected with

HIV. While these women welcomed the medical treatment, they identified other urgent needs. They were hungry and didn't have food to feed their families. They were living in extreme poverty without a path to employment and stable incomes. Many had suffered the horrific trauma of watching their husbands and children murdered in front of them, yet mental health help was stigmatized and inaccessible. Providing antiretroviral medicine was one component that was essential to their health, but it alone would not make a difference unless we also tended to these other factors in their lives.

Reverend Hickman nodded as I shared this story with her. "What they need, what we all need, is love, compassion, and hope," she said. This was what she and her staff delivered, every day. More than forty thousand women, children, and families have benefited from her service; some of them have since become part of her team as staff and volunteers.

What an opportunity it would be to work with amazing people like her! Yet when a colleague mentioned to me that the role of Baltimore City health commissioner was open, my first reaction was to think about all the qualifications I should have had but didn't. I'd later learn that my response was typical of many women, whose first reaction about applying for a higher-level role is often "I can't, because I only have eight out of the ten qualifications." Many of my female employees and mentees would respond this way. I'd point out to them what their male counterparts with far less experience would say: "I'm a shoo-in, because I have three of the ten qualifications!"

Various studies have shown that women have to be asked an average of three to five times to take on a leadership role. There's something about our upbringing and societal expectations that got us to this point, and all of us in positions of authority must be the ones to ask women— and people of color, immigrants, and other traditionally marginalized groups—to step up.

I was fortunate to have my colleague encourage me, then for my husband to give his unequivocal support despite the change it would mean for his life. Sebastian had moved to Boston and then to Washington for me. We were settled with a house and he had a job he liked as a consultant to IBM. He'd found a group of friends and had started a D.C.-based cricket team. Even though it would require another move for our family, applying for this job was a no-brainer, he told me.

"This is what you've been talking about ever since we met!" he said. "Everything about this job is what you've been preparing for all your life." I could finally put to use my training and experience in policy, advocacy, and public health, to make a difference in a city with huge unmet needs. I had to go for it.

As I WENT THROUGH THE application process, I got to know more about the health department and the city. Founded over two hundred years ago, the Baltimore City Health Department was the oldest health department in continuous operation in America. Despite its long history, the health department was known for innovative practices under bold—and youthful—leadership. Two of my predecessors, Peter Beilenson and Josh Sharfstein, had been in their thirties when they were appointed, which made me even more encouraged that I could do the job. Peter and Josh launched numerous initiatives that defined progressive public health leadership and approached controversial issues head-on. Baltimore was one of the first jurisdictions to begin needle exchange in the early 1990s, with the result that the percentage of residents with HIV from intravenous drug use dropped from 63 percent to 7 percent. School-based health clinics provided health-care services, and ongoing efforts for comprehensive sex education reduced teen birth rates by 61 percent.

The health commissioner in Baltimore had the potential for significant influence by virtue of the position's unique structure and funding. The mayor of Baltimore held more formal powers than just about any other big-city mayor in America, because she set the entire city budget. The Baltimore City Council had the power only to subtract from the mayor's budget; it could not add funding or shift money around. Agency heads worked with the city council, but their sole reporting was to the mayor. In addition, while most other local health directors in Maryland reported to both the state health secretary and to their local elected official, the head of the Baltimore City Health Department answered only to the mayor.

Another unique element of this health department was the source of its funding. Of the $130 million annual budget, less than 20 percent came from the city. Federal and state grants constituted the majority, with private foundation contributions making up the rest. Because the agency was not solely dependent on the cash-strapped city, new projects didn't have to wait until the next fiscal year, and urgent health priorities could avoid competing for funds with other city needs like policing and education. As long as the money could be raised, and as long the mayor was in support, the health commissioner had the latitude to spearhead new health programs. My predecessors did this, empowering the health department to have rapid, on-the-ground impact, with the trifecta of service delivery, public education, and policy change.

As the search committee went through its rounds of interviews, I spent time with Peter and Josh, with former and current staff, and with elected officials and community leaders. Two of the most helpful people I met were veterans of the health department, Olivia Farrow and Dawn O'Neill. Olivia was a previous deputy and acting commissioner who had served the city in a number of roles for thirty years. She had started her career conducting inspections for the health department, then went to law school at night before becoming the city's first prosecutor for lead paint violation cases. At the time I met her, she was the head of the city's human services agency. Dawn had been Peter's chief of staff and then followed him in his next several roles, including managing his run for Congress, serving as his deputy at another health department, and then becoming COO for a health insurance co-op that he cofounded.

Olivia and Dawn knew government—and Baltimore—inside and out. They gave me insights into the programs that were successful and those that weren't and why. They helped me to understand the broad scope of the day-to-day work, which included areas in which I had little experience, such as animal control, restaurant inspections, and senior center operations. Because they'd also worked in other parts of government and were familiar with the private sector partners in the region, they would complement the many staff who'd worked their entire career in the health department. I knew that if I were to become commissioner, I would want to recruit them to work with me.

To get to know the city better, I started attending neighborhood forums. One of the first was a community meeting with a group of young people, ages eight to fifteen. I'd predicted that the topics would evolve around sexually transmitted infections (STI), smoking, and condoms—after all, the nickname of the health department among teens was the agency of "Bugs, Drugs and Sex."

What the young people told me shocked and saddened me. They wanted to talk about the biggest problem they experienced: addiction and mental health. They didn't say those words, but there was no mistaking their meaning. A young boy, just nine years old, told me about how he had resuscitated his mother, who had passed out from intoxication, by pouring ice water over her face. A teenage girl recounted how she and her younger siblings were repeatedly beaten by their mother's boyfriend, who was high; their mother, too, was on drugs. Other kids talked about the trauma they faced: the trauma of watching their fathers and brothers shot and killed, the trauma of starving for dinner night after night, the trauma of being the only person in the household who got up in the morning because everyone else was addicted to heroin.

One of the people leading the meeting asked these kids, some of whom were just in the third grade, how many knew someone close to them who was affected by drugs. Every single child raised his or her hand.

I had known that the overdose rate in Baltimore was escalating and that addiction was a major problem in the city, but I didn't expect to see how it affected virtually every aspect of life there.

I was also beginning to see what members of the community wanted the health department to do for them. When I visited a senior center to ask what more the health department should be doing, an older African American woman took my hand and said, "Sweetie, you seem nice. I like what you're saying. I just hope you'll do some of what you say, and that you'll tell us about it when we see you again in four years."

These residents were expressing that they were used to seeing local officials visiting them for their own needs, to get votes, every four years.

But they wanted us to come not just when we needed something from them. They wanted us to listen to what they needed and to deliver on our promises.

What they wanted wasn't simply a presentation of the problems. The health department produced a lot of data, and the staff were proud to present these data at community meetings. I attended such a meeting, where an epidemiologist presented a series of slick slides showing health metrics for various neighborhoods in Baltimore: average life expectancy, infant mortality rate, hospitalization rate for addiction, cardiovascular disease incidence, and so forth.

When she finished the presentation, the organizer thanked her. "I just have one question for you," she said. "How come this is just the same map you're showing over and over again? Every page has different colors and different codes, but it's basically the same map."

The epidemiologist flipped back through the slides. Everyone saw what the organizer did, that the same areas of the city with the lowest life expectancy also had the highest infant mortality rate, the highest rates of addiction and overdose, the greatest incidence of cardiovascular disease and deaths from gun homicide. These were also the areas with the highest rate of incarceration, the lowest rate of educational attainment, and the greatest poverty. The health map of Baltimore was a map of inequalities and disparities, one map that showed the impact of social determinants of health.

The city's residents might not have known the exact statistics, but they were certainly aware of these inequities. They were also tired of hearing about them without a subsequent conversation about what was to be done.

Getting good data was necessary but nowhere near sufficient. I was beginning to formulate a vision for health in Baltimore that was based directly on what the residents experienced and expressed. I could see that they were sick of simply looking at map after map of disparities and being presented with the problems they live with every day. We needed to understand what they were saying and then quickly pivot to what we could do. With all the issues that we faced, we had to start somewhere—and it would be through ongoing engagement with citizens that we'd determine priorities and measure impact. It was a daunting task, with the odds against us, but if we were able to move the needle in Baltimore, we could change the trajectory for so many in our city and set a powerful example for the rest of the country.

THE SEARCH PROCESS TOOK MORE than four months. By the time I met the mayor in the executive conference room that November, I had made it through vettings with a search firm and was one of the final candidates recommended by a committee composed of prominent civic leaders.

I had learned a lot about Mayor Rawlings-Blake. She came from a political family and was first elected to the city council when she was twenty-five, the youngest person ever elected in Baltimore's history. She had served on the council for nearly twenty years before being elevated from council president to mayor upon the resignation of her predecessor, and then won her own term as mayor. At the time I met her, she had a growing profile nationally and would go on to serve as the president of the U.S. Conference of Mayors and the secretary of the Democratic National Committee. She had a reputation for choosing strong agency heads, and I trusted that she would see a bold vision for health as reflecting her own leadership style and ambition for the city.

Her goal for the city was clearly defined: she wanted to reverse the population decline and attract ten thousand families to Baltimore. To retain families and attract new ones, she needed to ensure that the city had good schools, improved safety, and ample job opportunities. As the daughter of a pediatrician, she spoke often about how integral health was to all of these goals.

In my interview, I described to Mayor Rawlings-Blake what I had learned about the city and its health challenges. I told her that everything in my life had prepared me for this role. I wasn't from Baltimore, but I grew up in neighborhoods not unlike the ones that I'd be serving. I didn't come from government, but it was my experiences in the ER and advocating for patients that made me see why the work of the city health department was so needed—and what more could be done.

Over the next hour, we spoke about our leadership philosophies and how we approached challenging problems. We were both of the mind-set that better is good—perfect is not on the menu. We both understood that governing requires finding common ground. Making progress in local government requires putting aside ideological differences to focus on points of agreement. She was well regarded in the business commu-nity for promoting economic development and encouraging public-private partnerships. While she and I were prepared to compromise on issues necessary to move policies forward, we were proud of our deeply held personal values such as faith, integrity, and loyalty.

Mayor Rawlings-Blake appreciated my background in the ER, say-ing that she knew I wouldn't just sit around and study problems: I had a history of getting things done and I'd bring that to the job.

I had previously met a former mayor of Baltimore, Kurt Schmoke, through the Rhodes Scholars network. He told me that he learned that the word "mayor" was not just a noun—it was a verb as well. "To mayor" meant to show up and be present for the people. I said to Mayor Rawlings-Blake that this was my belief in being health commissioner, too. I needed to be in the community as much as I could. I wanted to start with a one-hundred-day listening tour to identify the key areas of work.

"What do you need from me for you to succeed?" she asked me.

This was my opportunity to ask for the moon. The people I met with had advised that I try to get a guarantee of resources. Agency budgets would be reviewed a couple of months into my tenure, and this was the best chance I'd have to secure the next year's funding. I also received the advice that I should ask for her support on a few key policies to intro-duce in the city council or the state legislature; that way, I could see just how committed she was to public health, and if I got the job, this would secure my "early wins."

I took a different direction. "Madam Mayor, you've often said that the most important resources in the city are its people. I strongly believe this as well. My vision is to build and to run the best health department in the country. I know you'd want to me hit the ground running. To do that, I need to be able to recruit and retain the best people. And I need to have your support."

Mayor Rawlings-Blake nodded. She knew exactly what I was getting at. "Look, I'm not the mayor who's going to make you hire my cousin and uncle and everyone on my street," she replied. "I want you to hire the best people who can get the job done. Period."

There was one more step I needed to take, and it was a delicate matter. "I understand that there are a lot of great people at the health department," I said. "Some should be promoted. Others may not be doing good work and need to be moved out."

"It's your department. It's your decision," she said, with a smile. "And if you're worried about any of those council people getting on your case, leave it to me. I'll have your back."

It would take me years to realize how her unconditional support set me up for success, and how blessed I was to work for someone who had this philosophy. City governments across the country have long been regarded as a bastion of nepotism and personal favors, where donors who got the mayor and council members elected would be rewarded with cushy jobs. My predecessors had told me horror stories of incompetent employees who held high-level positions and had no accountability to them, because they were "protected" by some elected official.

There was the story of an interim leader who felt so protected by the council that he refused to vacate the commissioner's office when a new commissioner was selected by the mayor! It wasn't until the interim commissioner died that the new commissioner was able to move into his own office. Other agency heads told me about the "dance of the lemons": how they had to move protected individuals around so that they could do the least harm while still keeping in the elected officials' good graces.

I never had to contend with this under Mayor Rawlings-Blake. She stuck to her word. Never once did she apply pressure on me to hire someone who wasn't qualified for the work. Complaints from other elected officials who were frustrated that I wasn't playing their game were met with a shrug.

As a result, during the weeks between the mayor offering me the job and the day I officially started, I was able to assess my new agency and the capabilities and needs of the existing team. On day one, I had enough sense of the lay of the land that I reorganized the agency, with Olivia and Dawn agreeing to return to the health department as my deputies.

They would stay with me for three years, before Olivia retired from government service and Dawn left to become vice president for population health for a regional hospital. For those three years, they provided the stability I needed as I instituted major programmatic and organizational changes. Within twelve months I would have an entirely new senior team to lead the major streams of work in finance, administration, policy, communications, and program delivery. Some people were stars within the department who were promoted; others came from outside the city.

Kristin Rzeczkowski was one of my early external hires. She had previously worked in the U.S. Senate and was part of the Obama administration in the Office of Management and Budget. She'd quickly prove herself to be indispensable, and I soon promoted her to be my chief of staff. Another early hire was Joneigh Khaldun, my first chief medical officer. Joneigh would help me build key relationships with local hospitals, before leaving to head up the Detroit health department and then become the top medical official in the state of Michigan.

On my book tour for *When Doctors Don't Listen* in 2013, I had met a Malaysian American immigrant named Shirli Tay, who had introduced herself as a paralegal who wanted to pursue a career in medicine. She started working with me at George Washington University while pursuing her premedical studies. When I was offered the Baltimore job, I asked her to postpone her medical school plans and come to work with me as my executive assistant. It is impossible to overstate how important it was to have someone in that role who was supremely competent and unfailingly loyal. One of my proudest moments was when Shirli got accepted to medical school at my alma mater, Washington University, and I accompanied her to visit St. Louis. I knew from the moment I met her that she would be a caring and compassionate doctor, and I felt so proud to have played a role in her career growth as she did in mine.

My early hires were not without controversy. Those with deep city experience inevitably had detractors with lists of grudges from past conflicts. Those who were new were met with grumbling that they did not understand the city. My rapid changes to instill accountability were also met with internal resistance. But Mayor Rawlings-Blake never wavered. She saw that my team and I were delivering on our shared vision for the city.

Our growing, dynamic team drew other top-notch candidates who were willing to take significant pay cuts and relocate to Baltimore. I had received the advice early on that I could never spend enough time on recruitment, and I made sure that I personally interviewed every member of the senior team and their direct reports.

My most interesting recruiting experience was when someone called me after her interview to say that she believed she was not the best candidate for the job—but her husband was! I had liked her so much that I invited her husband, Gabriel Auteri, to come the next day, and then I hired him on the spot. Gabe started out as my special assistant, then would hold a number of senior roles during my tenure.

There were members of my team who came from other parts of city government. The mayor's speechwriter, a young man named Sean Naron, had caught my attention as a rising star. When I had the opportunity, I hired him to be the department's public information officer. He'd be instrumental in elevating our work in Baltimore and around the country.

My team and I also prioritized developing the pipeline of public health leaders. I partnered with a local organization called Baltimore Corps that brought in recent university graduates for one-year placements with agencies, nonprofits, and businesses. Some of my best team members started out as Baltimore Corps fellows. Together, we recruited Rhodes, Marshall, and Fulbright Scholars, and top-notch young professionals from around the world to Baltimore's city government.

WITH MY TEAM IN PLACE, I began my one-hundred-day listening tour to understand community concerns and to establish, with the community, our joint priorities.

I heard three recurrent themes. The first was the most dominant by far: there needed to be immediate attention to addiction and mental health.

The second was children's health. The health department ran numerous programs that directly affected health outcomes for kids and youth, including overseeing school health in every public school in Baltimore. This was a major area of opportunity, and also one that the mayor, through her pediatrician mother, was personally invested in.

The third area became a catchall—care for the most vulnerable—but it was one that I also heard with resounding clarity through the community meetings. People understood the need not just to improve health outcomes but also to focus on reducing disparities. They wanted us to provide services particularly for those who need it the most.

And instinctively, they knew the importance of going beyond health care when thinking about public health. Hardly anyone talked about the care they had received in hospitals as a priority focus: they wanted the health department to focus on the other aspects of their lives that determined their health. They knew that for them, for our city, that the currency of inequality equals years of life.

Now that I had my dream job, I needed to do the work to prove to the residents of Baltimore that public health—with an approach based on science and community-level advocacy and rooted in the principles of social justice—could level the playing field of inequality.

7

Saving Lives Today

In 2014, when I was first announced as the new "doctor for the city," there were 303 deaths from overdose, a 23 percent increase from the previous year. An estimated 60,000 Baltimoreans had substance use disorders. In a city with 620,000 total residents, that meant virtually every family was affected by addiction in some way.

The numbers from Baltimore reflected growing national trends. Overdose deaths were climbing around the country, taking the lives of more than 130 people every day. At the same time, there was a dearth of treatment availability: a U.S. surgeon general's report found that only one in ten people with addiction were receiving the treatment they needed. This was consistent with data from Baltimore, where about 50,000 residents needed treatment but did not receive it.

On my listening tour, I heard again and again about how addiction tied into every other issue in the city, from unemployment to crime to intergenerational poverty. Just as I heard from young people about how addiction affected every aspect of their lives, I heard the same from older adults, too. My agency was responsible for the oversight of senior centers, and not a day passed that I didn't hear from grandparents and great-grandparents about how they were the caregivers of young children because of lives and livelihoods lost to addiction. I met a seventy-two-year-old man who told me that he couldn't access addiction treatment himself and felt resigned to waste away the rest of his life. I met two women in their eighties who were scared for their lives because drug dealers used their senior living facilities as safe havens for drug sales.

Over and over again, I heard about the pervasive stigma around addiction. Despite what we in medicine know to be true—that addiction is a disease for which treatment exists and recovery is possible—addiction is regarded differently from other diseases. After all, for what other disease would we ever find it acceptable that only one in ten afflicted patients can receive treatment? What public outcry would there be if only one in ten patients with cancer could receive chemotherapy, or one in ten people with kidney failure could access dialysis?

A mother who lost her son to overdose told me that her tragedy was made worse by the shame imposed on her. "Everyone was so sympathetic until they found out how he died. Then they avoided me like the plague," she said. "Some people told me to my face that he did it to himself. If he died from a car accident, my neighbors would bring casseroles. Addiction is seen as a personal failing, when it should be a casserole disease."

During my residency training, I had a patient whom I'll call Jessica. She was in her late twenties and a "frequent flier," someone who came in so often to the ER that all the doctors, nurses, and technicians knew her. We'd remember the last time she received a CT scan and that her white blood cell count was always a little high. And we'd know what she wanted every single time she came in: treatment for her opioid addiction.

I knew Jessica's story, that she had been a competitive swimmer in college who had back surgery and became addicted to painkillers. When her doctor stopped prescribing them, she went to other doctors to seek more. Eventually she switched to heroin because it was cheaper and more readily available.

By the time I got to know her, she had dropped out of school and had no job. Her fiancé broke up with her and her parents kicked her out of their house. She had hit "rock bottom," in her words, and she came in night after night, desperate to get her life back on track.

Jessica knew she needed help for her addiction. We knew she needed help. Yet every time she came in, we'd have to tell her that our hospital had no treatment for her. We didn't have an addiction treatment ward where we could admit her. We could try to find her treatment at an outpatient clinic, but she would probably have to wait weeks or months for a spot to open. During that time, she'd go through withdrawal, relapse, and regret that would send her back to the ER.

Every time she came and left, I'd think about how differently she'd be treated if she had arrived with chest pain. If she were having a heart attack, no one would discharge her and ask her to come back in three weeks. Her situation was just as dire, but the medical system was not set up to handle her disease as it handles every other.

There were a couple of times that I remember Jessica being so desperate for care that she'd lie and say that she was suicidal. She knew that if she said this, it would buy her several more hours of evaluation—she'd have to be seen by the psychiatrist, and there was often an overnight wait for the consultation. It could also expedite her placement in a drug treatment program if she had an urgent psychiatric issue. But what a dire reflection on our system, when patients know they need to lie to get the care that they—and their doctors—know they need.

One day, Jessica came in with her usual request. A social worker saw her and got her a clinic appointment in two weeks' time. She was discharged, only to return in several hours on my same shift. The nurses told me that she had been rolled out of a car in front of the ER, presumably by "friends" who did not wish to get into trouble themselves. She was immediately put onto a stretcher and brought to the trauma bay.

When I saw her, she was unresponsive. Her skin was the same color as the sheet she was lying on, and her lips were blue. Her heart wasn't beating. We began CPR. The nurse gave her naloxone, the opioid antidote. My intern slipped a breathing tube down her throat. We kept on administering medications, giving chest compressions, and breathing for her.

But she had been unresponsive for too long. Half an hour later I pronounced Jessica dead.

This was someone who had walked out of our ER just a few hours before, who now was dead from a treatable illness. When I reviewed Jessica's chart, I found that in the year before her death, she had been to our ER more than a hundred times—an average of twice each week. She had begged us for treatment every time, and we had failed her.

IN THE ER, I HAD felt powerless to work on ways to increase access to addiction treatment. As Baltimore's health commissioner, this was an area where I could have an impact. There was a major problem, though: as much as people recognized the pervasiveness of addiction in Baltimore, they did not wish to have treatment facilities located near them.

The "not in my backyard" (NIMBY) contingent was loud and out in force during my listening tour. Homeowners who lived near methadone clinics talked about the patients who loitered on their doorsteps. Small business owners said that these patients were driving away their clientele. Everyone seemed to have stories of crimes they attributed directly to the clinics themselves, from car theft to shootings occurring nearby.

When asked where these clinics should be located, everyone had the same answer: somewhere else. Anywhere else, just not near us. They proposed abandoned buildings in industrial sites, far from where people live and work. This theme was so prevalent that a staff member at a treatment center joked that NIMBY in Baltimore should be renamed BANANA: "don't build anything near anything that's near anything."

But as I listened to their concerns, I began to see where these community members were coming from. In order to retain and attract new residents, the city had to have neighborhoods that were safe, attractive to families, and friendly for businesses. I knew that if people did not feel safe in their homes and if businesses were suffering, those who had the means would move. I could understand why community members would show up at town halls wishing to get rid of what they saw as a nuisance. On the surface, if there were in fact unused buildings in less populated areas, why not send patients there instead?

Except it wasn't random people who needed help for their addiction: those who needed help were neighbors and fellow residents in those same communities. Patients receiving methadone need to go every day to get this treatment, and many patients need to be on methadone for years, some for a lifetime. This is in addition to other treatments that they may require, including psychosocial counseling and treatment for other physical and mental conditions. It is difficult enough for patients with addiction to maintain a job, care for their families, and receive daily treatment. To require someone to take multiple buses or pay for rideshares to industrial sites far away from home is more than impractical: it presents yet another barrier to treatment that is already difficult to access.

It's also true that numerous studies have shown that evidence-based addiction treatment actually saves the community money and reduces the crime rate. A study done in Baltimore found that neighborhoods near methadone clinics were no more associated with crime than convenience stores. (By contrast, the radius around liquor stores had a 30 to 40 percent higher incidence of crime.)

But no matter how many statistics I cited or how many scientific experts I brought to speak at these community meetings, the NIMBY/BANANA mentality persisted. People may have recognized the dire need for addiction treatment in the abstract, but it was a nonstarter to suggest opening treatment centers anywhere around them.

One area of common ground was that most people agreed that hospitals needed to do more to treat addiction in their own facilities. If addiction is a disease, as indeed it is, then why wouldn't hospitals and doctors' offices treat it as they would treat any other disease? Couldn't one solution be to increase treatment in existing medical facilities?

This was a notion that I agreed with wholeheartedly. How different Jessica's life would have been if we had been able to admit her directly to the hospital to receive treatment! Another medication used for long-term addiction treatment is buprenorphine, also called Suboxone. Unlike methadone, which needs to be administered every day by a specialized facility, buprenorphine can be prescribed by a person's primary care doctor. It can even be administered in an ER for patients who need a bridge to longer-term treatment. The federal law was such that doctors must have special training to prescribe buprenorphine and there was a limit to how many patients a single doctor can treat, but surely increasing the treatment of addiction through existing medical systems would help alleviate the treatment shortage.

One could argue that medical professionals need to provide addiction treatment for another reason: doctors themselves have been complicit in the epidemic in the first place. When I began medical school in 2001, the concept of "pain as the fifth vital sign" was already in full force. In my training, I understood that my job was not only to figure out what the patients were suffering from but also to immediately take away their pain. Patient satisfaction was tied to pain management, further emphasizing that getting rid of pain was a goal unto itself—not merely addressing the cause of the pain. Drug sales representatives were everywhere peddling the miracles of narcotic painkillers, which we physicians dispensed because it was the standard of care.

I think back now to all the patients for whom I prescribed opioids for back pain and dental pain, without realizing the long-term potential for addiction. While pharmaceutical companies take the lion's share of blame for (as we know now) deliberately misleading doctors and using unethical sales tactics, the crisis would not have gotten to where it is without the central role played by the medical profession.

Now, the medical system had an opportunity to right this wrong by providing treatment to the very patients they led down the path of addiction in the first place. Yet even as they were well aware of the need, hospitals and physicians were reluctant to take the lead in increasing addiction treatment.

I tasked Joneigh Khaldun, a fellow emergency physician, to talk to local hospital administrators and leading physicians. She came back with disappointing findings. Many of these leaders held misperceptions of addiction. Some talked about the benefits of "detox" treatment and offered it at their hospitals, even though rapid detox was a scientifically discredited therapy that was associated with higher rates of overdose. Some spoke about how methadone and buprenorphine treatment was like "replacing one addiction with another"—despite every major medical society endorsing medication-assisted treatment as part of the gold standard for addiction treatment. (Every time someone would say this, I'd counter with whether we'd ever say that insulin for diabetes is "replacing one addiction with another." Obviously not. Insulin was treating a medical condition, just as methadone and buprenorphine were.)

Everyone Joneigh spoke with wanted more treatment available; after all, they were seeing the influx of ER patients requesting treatment, just as she and I had seen in our practices. But nobody was willing to step up and commit to providing more treatment themselves. A variety of reasons were cited, from lack of protocols to a dearth of trained specialists. One administrator was bold enough to say what the others did not: that they didn't want to become the place in the city where people with addiction would know they could go. The implication was that they didn't want "certain patients" to come to their hospital. Surely, this would have been different if the illness were anything else; hospitals don't shy away from being known as the center of excellence for cardiac care and cancer treatment.

The medical system, too, suffered from NIMBYism. They, too, were throwing up their hands. Yes, addiction was a problem. Yes, more patients were dying from overdose than before. Yes, there needed to be urgent action. But someone else needed to step up first.

MY TEAM AND I SPOKE at length about how we would approach the many layers of this problem. It was clear that what the city needed, desperately, was more treatment, on-demand, at the time that patients need it. But it was also clear that there was no quick path to getting there. The major constituencies actively opposed it, the political will was not there, and if we couldn't get hospitals and doctors on board, there was no one to deliver the increased treatment.

What we needed to do was to ramp up the pressure. We needed to select one action item that could be done rapidly, that would have maximal impact and draw maximal attention. And we had to take swift action ourselves. If others were not going to step up, the health department needed to step up first to do what we can do now.

That's how I chose to begin our addiction work by focusing on one component: increasing access to the opioid antidote naloxone (also called Narcan). Working in the ER, I knew naloxone well and had administered it to hundreds of patients. Naloxone is safe, with virtually no side effects for someone who is not on opioids. It works nearly instantaneously: someone who is overdosing can be walking and talking within thirty seconds of receiving it. I'd trained dozens of medical students to use it, and I knew that lay people could learn to administer it, too. Naloxone comes in two forms, a nasal spray and an auto-injector (like an EpiPen). Both can be taught within a few minutes.

Naloxone is a complete antidote to opioid overdose. If there were a deadly disease claiming three hundred lives yearly in our city and there were a complete antidote available, there would be no question that the therapy should be available to everyone. That was an easy case to make. We could also make the case that if someone is dying in front of us now, we have to save that person's life right now. If someone is having a heart attack, we do need to pay attention to their long-term cardiovascular health and to treat their underlying medical conditions like diabetes and hypertension. But first we have to resuscitate, or there is no purpose in talking about long-term treatment.

Politically, there were other reasons for starting with naloxone access. While there was initial opposition from some people who said that naloxone made it easier for people to use drugs, this was easily countered by the stories of community members who are alive because of naloxone. A mantra in public health is to meet people where they are, and I thought that naloxone was the least controversial and most expeditious way to get people to reconsider their notions of addiction and to start seeing it as a public health issue that we all had to be a part of solving—instead of a crime, a moral failing, or a community nuisance that's someone else's problem.

Increasing naloxone access was also something I could do, or so I thought. The city health department ran the only needle exchange program in the state. Our mobile van went to a couple of dozen sites every week, and outreach workers distributed clean needles and syringes and counseled on a variety of health topics. They were also teaching about naloxone. However, even though their clients were asking for the medication, the health department was not able to provide it.

These were people who were actively using drugs and therefore at the highest risk of overdose. They were also around others who used drugs and were in a position to revive their friends. If they wanted naloxone, why were they not able to get it?

The needle exchange staff shared my frustration. "Here's the problem," one employee said to me. "We can provide the training, but we can't distribute the medication. So the client, after he gets the training from us, has to go to his doctor and ask for naloxone. His doctor may or may not feel comfortable prescribing it. If he does get the prescription, he still has to go to the pharmacy to get it filled. The pharmacy might not have it, and he may not have insurance."

I was counting the steps involved. "Wow, that's a lot of hoops to go through," I said.

"Exactly. At the end of the day, the chance of our client actually getting naloxone is really low. Then there's the problem that if someone is overdosing themselves, they can't save their own life. We also have to figure out a way to get people naloxone so that they can use it for a family member or loved one, or if they just encounter someone on the street who is OD'ing."

Another outreach worker explained that he and his colleagues had tried to reduce the number of steps by having a physician physically present on the needle exchange van. If we could pay for the physician and get the city to pay for naloxone, then the client could get the training, get the prescription, and be given the medication, all at the same place and the same time.

"But it's expensive," he went on. "And it's unnecessary. We don't need a doc to just sit around and write prescriptions, when we are the ones who know how to do trainings."

Indeed, when I went out in the van the next day, I was impressed by the acumen of these outreach workers. Some of them were in recovery themselves. All of them knew exactly how to identify the symptoms of overdose, and they were expert in administering naloxone and teaching others to do so. They didn't need a doctor there—but they did need a way to get naloxone directly into the hands of their clients.

There was a solution to this, a legislative one. A few other states had recently passed legislation to allow for a senior health official to issue a standing order, which was essentially a blanket prescription for naloxone. A standing order in Baltimore would mean that the outreach workers could conduct a short training course (we called this a "training") and then be allowed to dispense naloxone under the order of the health official. This blanket prescription would take the place of individual prescriptions.

If we could get this legislation passed in Maryland, it would allow us to get naloxone directly into the hands of our high-risk clients and potentially save the lives of fellow Baltimoreans. We had to act quickly, though, because the 2015 legislative session was in full swing. The Maryland General Assembly is a part-time body whose annual session starts in January and ends in April, and we had a matter of weeks to identify sponsors, secure committee hearings, build public support, and get the bill passed through committee and through both chambers.

Thankfully, there were already several groups of advocates who supported this idea and were already working with legislators on similar bills. My legislative team worked with them to consolidate the bills and put our efforts toward one omnibus legislation. I had wanted a straightforward bill that would allow me to issue the standing order and make naloxone available everywhere in the city. But even though naloxone is one of the safest medications available, there were still concerns about this type of widespread distribution. The state health department pushed for an hour-long mandatory training requirement, and there were various versions of the bill that included additional restrictions including limiting who could write the standing order.

Eventually, a compromise bill passed that had the governor's support: I could issue a standing order to city residents, and as long as someone had proof that they had received the necessary training, they could be given naloxone. That would allow outreach workers on the needle exchange vans to give out naloxone directly, and anyone who received training could go to a pharmacy and receive naloxone through my blanket prescription. In addition, instead of the law taking effect on October 1, as the session's other bills did, it was marked as an emergency provision, allowing it to go into effect on June 1.

ON JUNE 1, 2015, I held a press conference with the advocates, health leaders, and elected officials who together had gotten this important bill passed. I stood with them as I declared addiction to be a public health emergency in Baltimore and officially signed the city's blanket prescription for naloxone. It was a proud moment: this was why I had come to local public health, to make an immediate impact on critical issues facing people in my city.

My team had done a lot of work in the interim. There were many logistics to figure out—starting with, how does one write a prescription for 620,000 people? The solution was to print hundreds of prescription pads with the dosage information for naloxone and my signature. It was another proud moment when those pads were delivered, but still a bit nerve-racking to sign a prescription for more than half a million people.

My team and I knew that a sound policy alone was not enough: we also had to get the services directly to people. We reached out to hundreds of community groups, health centers, and small businesses to see who would be interested in training people to administer naloxone and help us to distribute the medication. On day one, our needle exchange vans were ready to go, and we made sure that we had enlisted a few dozen partner organizations that had gone through "train-the-trainer" workshops. On June 1, trainings began in churches, libraries, recreation centers, public housing buildings, bus shelters, bars, and restaurants— wherever it was that people were.

I conducted some training sessions myself. We always began by asking attendees how many people had witnessed an overdose, and for the "on the street" sessions, it was always a high percentage; sometimes the entire group would raise their hands. People would volunteer their experiences and talk about how they put ice packs in someone's groin or poured water on a person's face. These individuals had come because they were around people who used drugs and wanted to be in a position to revive them using the proper procedures. Some were initially skeptical that they could provide medical treatment, but when we showed them how simple naloxone was to use, their faces lit up.

Mayor Rawlings-Blake was game to extending the training sessions to those officials over whom she had direct supervision. I trained the entire cabinet and requested that the Baltimore City Council permit us to train its members, too. Our goal was to reach every city employee, and thanks to the participation of my fellow cabinet members, the health department team began attending staff meetings with sanitation workers, teachers, and parks employees.

One of the most important—and most challenging—constituencies was the police department. The police commissioner, Anthony Batts, was a proponent of naloxone. It was a difficult time locally and nationally for police and community relations, and Commissioner Batts understood the optics—and necessity—of officers being trained to save lives. But not all the police officers saw it that way. When I went to a training session and talked about administering naloxone, the group of officers looked as if I was asking them to dissect a rat and then eat it.

"I can't touch these people," one officer said to me. Another threw down his naloxone kit and said he just wasn't going to do it.

This turned out to be a lesson in another key principle of public health: one must always find the most credible messengers. As a doctor, I wasn't relating to the frontline officers in the way that they needed. Our outreach workers were the most credible messengers in the community, but they did not hold sway with the police, either. And so we sought out allies within the police department, officers who had personal experience with addiction, whom we trained to be the trainers. One of them had a brother who suffered from addiction, and I watched a complete change in the officers' demeanor when he talked about how his brother was saved thanks to someone nearby who carried naloxone.

Within a month, Baltimore police officers had used naloxone to save four people. By the end of the year, Commissioner Batts relayed to me that officers were competing with each other to see how many "saves" they each had.

A year later, I attended another police training session and asked the officers what they would look for if they were called to the scene for an overdose. In the past, I would have received answers about "looking for drug paraphernalia and other evidence."

This time, officers answered that their job was "to find out what drugs the person might have taken, call an ambulance, and administer naloxone," because their duty is to save a life. Credible messengers matter. And culture change can happen quickly, even in a traditional culture with entrenched norms and a suspicion of outsiders.

IN THE MEANTIME, MY TEAM was hard at work identifying additional barriers to naloxone access. One major barrier was that many pharmacies were not aware of my standing order. We had limited city funds to purchase naloxone, and we distributed these kits to those who were most at risk—for example, the clients of our needle exchange vans. Everyone else had to go to the pharmacy to get their prescription filled. We began sending flyers to pharmacists and pharmacy techs with information about the standing order. Eventually, I would hire an overdose prevention director, José Rodriguez, who would visit every pharmacy in the city, in person—over a hundred pharmacies total.

Another barrier was insurance. Even though there was already a deal in place that patients on Medicaid would receive naloxone for $1, or if they couldn't pay, could receive it free of charge, patients and pharmacists were not aware of this. Sometimes, Medicaid erroneously rejected the reimbursement. We set up a twenty-four-hour phone hotline for anyone with issues filling a naloxone prescription, and helped to troubleshoot whenever there was a problem with the standing order.

Private insurance companies had varying levels of co-pay, and since there were different formulations of naloxone, we reached out to individual insurance companies to ensure that they put forth the cheapest rate. We also worked with hospitals so that patients who came into the ER for addiction could receive naloxone when they got discharged.

Every time there was a new partnership, whether it was with a new community organization or local business that provided training, or an insurance group, or a hospital or pharmacy that now worked with us, we thanked the organization publicly. We held press conferences, invited the media to interview the new trainers, and celebrated the people who performed the "saves." The positive publicity encouraged more organizations to work with us and provided educational opportunities about addiction. Not only did people learn about naloxone, they also received the message that I wanted to impart: that addiction is a disease and that what we needed was increased treatment for it.

In the meantime, my team also developed an online naloxone training that we believed was the first of its kind in the country. This broke down another major barrier—the need for in-person trainers. Now anyone could watch a video and take a short quiz; within ten minutes, they could download a certificate that they could display on their smartphone or print out to receive naloxone from a pharmacy.

All of these efforts drew national attention to our work, which attracted increased grant-funding opportunities. The manufacturers of the auto-injector version of naloxone donated ten thousand units to the city, which we were able to distribute rapidly via our community partners. We received much-needed funding from foundations and the federal government to roll out additional initiatives, like a citywide public messaging campaign called "Don't Die" that plastered naloxone and addiction awareness information everywhere in the city. For a few months, nearly every city bus had our messaging on the side of it: *You can save a life with naloxone. Addiction is a disease. Treatment exists.*

WITHIN TWO YEARS OF ISSUING my naloxone standing order, nearly two thousand "saves" had been documented; within three years, the number was up to three thousand. This was likely a significant underestimate, as not everyone who used naloxone called in to report it.

Every year, International Overdose Awareness Day is on the last day of August. Our health department held events to commemorate the lives lost due to overdose, calling attention to what more needs to be done and what each of us can do now.

One particularly memorable year, my team invited all those who had been revived by naloxone and their family members. Also in attendance were paramedics, police officers, and the leaders of community organizations and businesses who had taken part in naloxone trainings. Many of them had administered naloxone themselves.

One after another, those who had received naloxone thanked the people involved in this lifesaving program. I saw veteran law enforcement officers wiping away tears as business leaders hugged family members.

A man in his forties talked about how his near-death experience prompted him finally to get treatment. Through a local nonprofit, he was able to get his criminal record for drug possession expunged. He was now working as a janitor while taking night classes at the community college. Most important to him, he had reconnected with his children and had a relationship with them for the first time in their lives.

"I've seen death too many times," he told the group. "I was wasting the life that I have. Because of you, because of the person who saved me, I have my life back. Living this life, figuring out who I am, and now being there for my family—it's a beautiful thing. Thank you."

There were those who criticized my primary focus on naloxone as being shortsighted and nothing but a stopgap solution. They said that the better priority should have been addiction treatment. In some ways, they are right. The ultimate aim needs to be to increase treatment, and we have to do much more to address the underlying factors that fuel ill health and despair.

But I am also a strong believer in doing what we can now. We have to start somewhere and do what we can with the position we're in—we cannot wait for someone else to step up first. Naloxone was the entry point to gain attention and galvanize political will for public health in Baltimore. Even as we worked toward longer-term change, this was what we could do first. And what we do has inherent value: we have to save lives today for there to be a chance for a better tomorrow.

8

Treating Addiction as
the Disease It Is

Naloxone was the first step to combating the much larger issue of securing addiction treatment. My team and I changed the narrative around overdose: we showed that it was not random people who were dying but our family members, friends, and neighbors. We demonstrated the power of saving lives and started the conversation there instead of fighting about NIMBYism.

The next frontier was to identify and then remove the barriers to accessing care, ideally to get to the point that anyone seeking addiction treatment could access it when they needed it—as should be the case for any life-threatening disease. I began by asking a simple question: How do people know where to get treatment? How can patients and loved ones find out how to get in the door of the dozens of treatment centers spread across the city, all with different treatment options and accepting different forms of insurance?

One of my predecessors, Peter Beilenson, sought such answers by posing as a potential client. Some twenty years earlier, he would don a hoodie and sweatpants, go to treatment centers, and ask to be seen. Many of the centers turned him down. Peter would then call the center director, as himself, and be told that there were in fact treatment slots available. "You can find out a lot by doing your own investigation," he advised me.

I took his advice, and certainly, I found out a lot. When I asked hospital nurses and social workers how they got their patients connected to treatment, they gave me a list of phone numbers that they would call, hoping that one of them could help their patient. My outreach workers also had a list of numbers to call. Between these two sources, there were six phone numbers.

I called them all. One number was disconnected. Another required that you know your insurance information before connecting you to a human being. Three others had limited hours of operation during specific daytime periods; one of them was for mental health issues only, one was for addiction but specifically could not handle mental health concerns, and the third, by the time I finally got through, was closed for the day—at 1:00 p.m. The sixth number connected me to a representative who told me that there was a two-month wait for a treatment slot and that I should go to the ER if I needed urgent assistance. Since this was a number given to me by the ER social worker, the advice was particularly unhelpful.

As I made these calls, I became increasingly concerned. If I couldn't get through, with all the time and resources available to me, then what hope was there for a patient on the brink of withdrawal, who needed help immediately? From my ER experience, I knew that the majority of patients with drug-related issues required help after hours, and many didn't have insurance or would not know what their insurance was without additional assistance. Many of them also had mental health conditions like depression or anxiety that may have driven the substance use in the first place or resulted from it. They would hit a brick wall if they tried calling these numbers.

What we needed was one number that anyone could call, any time of the day. Because substance use and mental health issues were so closely tied together, the call-in center needed to handle both concerns. It needed to search people's insurance information and help them get insurance, if necessary. And it needed to be a resource not only for the patient but also for anyone trying to get help for another person: family members should be able to call, as should hospital employees and out-reach workers trying to assist someone who came to them.

I started having conversations with the existing phone line opera-tors, treatment center directors, and nonprofit organizations working in behavioral health treatment, crisis response, and health insurance access. Everyone agreed with the concept of the "one-stop shop." The question was how we would set it up.

It took months of coordination by my team, working shoulder-to-shoulder with three partner organizations to launch our centralized 24/7 "Crisis, Intervention, and Referral Line." The phone number was featured prominently in our "Don't Die" advertising campaign and printed on our naloxone materials. Word of mouth quickly spread. Within a few months of the launch, the phone line was receiving a thou-sand calls every week.

We also had to supply the operators with the most up-to-date infor-mation about the city's treatment centers: which treatments they offered, which insurance they accepted, and, most critically, what open-ings they had. My team and our partners came up with a plan for a high-tech dashboard that would display open slots in real time.

The mock-up was impressive. However, my chief information offi-cer, Mike Fried, estimated that it would take years for the technology to get up and running and to get all the providers to use it. We didn't have that kind of time; our patients needed the best that we could pro-vide to them, now. Two people in particular understood the urgency. One of my special assistants, a Baltimore Corps fellow, was a brilliant young man named Evan Behrle. He was a recent philosophy graduate from Oxford, where he had been a Rhodes Scholar. Another was Mark O'Brien, the health department's opioid overdose prevention director. Years before, Mark was driving intoxicated when he crashed his car. His fiancée died in the wreck. He went to prison, and after his release he dedicated his career to addiction treatment and reentry support.

Evan and Mark agreed with my motto to not let the perfect be the enemy of the good. While the tech and legal teams worked on long-term plans for the dashboard, they set up an Excel spreadsheet and called each of the few dozen treatment centers themselves, every week. They'd get the necessary information and give it to the phone line operators, who would update the spreadsheet based on the appointments they made. They also provided feedback to Evan and Mark to improve the process the following week.

This was not an ideal system, and it was pretty low-tech. But while we waited for the high-tech dashboard to be complete, we could at least get patients the help they needed when they needed it.

EVAN, MARK, AND THEIR SUCCESSORS, Matthew Stefanko and José Rodriguez, would help with a similar work-around when we faced the challenge of fentanyl. Fentanyl is a synthetic opioid that is one hundred times stronger than morphine and dozens of times more potent than heroin. It is also cheaper than heroin, and in Baltimore, fentanyl was getting mixed in with heroin such that people who were using heroin wouldn't realize they were getting a much more dangerous mixture. In some cases, users were receiving pure fentanyl without their knowledge, and it even got mixed in with cocaine and other non-opioid drugs.

As a result, even though our naloxone program was saving thousands of lives, the number of overdoses continued to escalate. Deaths involving fentanyl went from 12 in 2013 to 573 in 2017—a nearly fifty-fold increase in four years.

I was on the board of the Maryland office of the chief medical examiner, which performs autopsies and certifies cause of death. The rise in fentanyl fatalities was so precipitous that the medical examiner's office was placed on emergency diversion. There just weren't enough staff to take care of all the additional deaths. It was taking nearly a year for data to be processed and a cause of death finalized—a timetable that was incompatible with the urgent public health goal of intervening rapidly to prevent additional fentanyl deaths.

I needed a way to identify where fentanyl overdoses were occurring, in as close to real time as possible. That way, we could dispatch outreach teams to those affected areas and educate people on the existence and danger of fentanyl. As with our work in needle exchange, our focus was harm reduction. We didn't condone or promote drug use, and we offered resources to get people help with addiction if and when they were ready. In the meantime, our job was to save lives and prevent people from overdosing and dying. Our message in areas seeing fentanyl-laced drugs was to alert people that fentanyl was in their neighborhood, explain why it was so dangerous, ask that they not use drugs alone, and equip everyone with naloxone.

By order of Mayor Rawlings-Blake, I had convened an emergency citywide fentanyl task force that consisted of city, state, and federal law enforcement and social services personnel. Every month I chaired a meeting with senior representatives of the police and fire departments, local hospitals, the state's attorney's office, the attorney general's office, and the federal Drug Enforcement Administration. All of these entities were working on fentanyl, and all of them had crucial information. Though they were authorized to share their data under a new Maryland law, many were loath to do so unless it was final and confirmed data—which could take up to a year, like the medical examiner's data. Another case of the perfect being the enemy of the good. Lawyers at all levels were mired in various data-sharing agreements, and our tech and legal teams, led by Mike Fried and Gabe Auteri, worked through the intricacies of these cross-agency agreements.

In the meantime, Evan, Mark, and our department's epidemiologists came up with a much quicker work-around. We knew that individual entities had access to real-time information, because they already called us informally with these alerts. The fire department would call when there were multiple calls for service in a two-block radius. The nurses keeping track of ER capacity would let us know when they saw several overdoses in quick succession. An outreach organization would alert us to what they were hearing from their clients that day. These were not "confirmed" fentanyl overdoses—such confirmation required autopsy data that was taking months to obtain—but these were data we could use immediately to give people real-time, lifesaving information.

Our team once again relied on the tools at our disposal: an Excel spreadsheet, a phone, and our existing relationships across agencies. We worked with leads from the fentanyl task force and other local entities, who knew to call us when they identified a possible overdose cluster. We would then dispatch outreach workers through a rotation of employees and volunteers with the needle exchange program, Behavioral Health System Baltimore (a regional quasi-governmental organization whose board I chaired), and other community groups—in real time, that day, to prevent additional overdoses. And then we'd send an alert to hundreds of other groups in the city who could help us spread the word about these overdose spikes.

While Evan and Mark spearheaded this low-tech fentanyl response, Mike Fried pitched to me a higher-tech version through a program we were starting called Transforming Engineering for Civic Health (TECHealth), whose purpose was to bring together local entrepreneurs like software developers and architects to collaborate with the health department to solve pressing challenges. I loved it. Our agency had many talented people, but they had many competing priorities and simply did not have the time or the technical expertise that others in the community had. Engaging the private sector allowed us to jump-start projects that we otherwise wouldn't have the capacity or expertise to get off the ground.

Within a few weeks, there was a group working on the treatment dashboard. Another worked on health resources for individuals who had just been released from incarceration, and additional groups devised tech solutions to assist our programs in food access and childhood asthma prevention.

One group volunteered to help with the fentanyl rapid response. Our collaborators were high school students from a nonprofit called Code in the Schools that taught coding to inner-city students. These students came up with a program, "Bad Batch," that would work in concert with our real-time, in-person deployment response. Community members could sign up and receive alerts when there were overdose spikes in their areas. The app showed nearby pharmacies where naloxone was available and the locations of real-time training sessions. It also prominently featured the 24/7 treatment phone line.

Just like our Excel spreadsheets, Bad Batch was far from a perfect system. The alerts were sent based on imperfect data, and they were not a complete answer to the problem but were rather an adjunct to our education and naloxone distribution efforts. It was the best that we could do, rapidly, with the resources that we had.

I've received criticism that we launched these programs without evidence that they worked. This line of thinking is exactly what holds us back from innovation. Fentanyl was a new and emerging problem. There was no evidence that our programs would work because they had never been done before. It's not that we ignored other evidence-based programs and implemented our own instead; it's that we were not willing to wait for others to develop and test programs while people in our city were dying.

In government (and in other sectors), it's easy to hide behind bureaucracy and say that things can't be done because there are too many barriers. The technology isn't there yet; there are too many legal roadblocks; agencies just won't work together; there isn't enough staffing or other resources; the evidence doesn't exist yet; and so on and so forth.

Waiting for others to try first is the safest route. Following the status quo doesn't draw the potential punishment and condemnation that a public failure might. But if we all take the safe and easy route, how will progress ever be made? Innovation has to start somewhere, and we as a society need to not only be tolerant of bold actions but also to actively encourage them. Failure is a necessary part of progress. We should be committed to producing evidence to test and better refine our programs, but this does not mean that we should stifle initiative. When there is a crisis, we need to do what we can with what we have, then gather data, iterate, and improve.

Despite the initial skepticism, our rapid integrated citywide response would save hundreds of lives. We garnered national attention for these innovative collaborations, which in turn galvanized support for our opioid work across the city, with many partners asking us what more they could do to step up.

WHEN I FIRST SPOKE WITH Mayor Rawlings-Blake about the health commissioner role, I mentioned how committed I was to continuing my medical practice while serving as the city's doctor. I loved seeing patients. Doing so helped me understand their daily struggles and the challenges of the health-care system, and it would keep me grounded in what's most important to be a more compassionate and more credible health commissioner. She agreed completely, and I began volunteering once a month at a local health center that provides care for uninsured and underinsured patients.

Every clinical shift for me began and ended with a singular dream: What if we had a dedicated ER just for addiction and mental health treatment? So many patients were like Jessica, who came to existing ERs with a substance use disorder but were not best served there. Often, they were intoxicated or under the influence of drugs. They needed to be examined to make sure there wasn't another physical health issue, and then they needed a place to rest and sober up. Ultimately, they needed to consult with a social worker, an addiction counselor, or a case manager to connect them to long-term treatment, ideally with treatment that began that same day.

But in practice, when these patients came to the ER, they'd often sit in the waiting room or lie on a stretcher in the hallway for hours. The social worker who saw them might be overwhelmed with other needs and only have time to send them on their way with a piece of paper with a phone number to call. These patients were not getting ideal medical care tailored to their specific needs. When the ERs were busy, which was nearly all the time, they were also taking space away from other patients who did have acute issues that only the ER could address.

If only there were a separate emergency facility tailored to the needs of patients with addiction and mental health! It would help the patients in need and the hospitals they would otherwise have gone to. As it turned out, there were others in Baltimore who shared my dream. Yngvild Olsen is an addiction medicine specialist who happens to be married to one of my predecessors, Josh Sharfstein. Years before, she had written a concept paper on a "Stabilization Center," which she'd shown to a state delegate from Baltimore, Pete Hammen, who became a major proponent.

Yngvild and Pete were thrilled that I wanted to have the Baltimore

City Health Department spearhead this project and establish the first Stabilization Center in Maryland. It would also be one of the first in the country. With my deputy, Olivia Farrow, as the point person, we began to lay the groundwork from all sides. Drawing on her background as a lawyer and her deep knowledge of how to run complex projects in the city, Olivia identified an unused building, the old Hebrew Orphan Asylum, and navigated the terrain of city planning, housing, and developers to convert this space for medical use. She led a competitive bid process to identify the operators for various components of the center.

Olivia and the other members of our team participated in numerous community meetings to work through the concerns of residents and business owners. After a yearlong process that could not have succeeded without the vocal support of local elected representatives in the city council and the state legislature, we received the unanimous agreement of the community association to proceed.

In the meantime, we worked with members of Congress to ensure passage of federal legislation that allocated $10 million of opioid funding to the state of Maryland, $2 million of which would be designated for the Stabilization Center. Delegate Hammen was able to secure an additional $3.6 million from the state legislature. Yngvild was instrumental in getting the state and local emergency transport systems to agree to a protocol for sending patients who otherwise would have gone to local ERs to this center instead. Shelly Choo, Joneigh's successor as my senior medical adviser, worked with the hospitals' ER leadership to develop contingency plans for when seriously ill patients would be sent back to them.

It took a highly dedicated group more than three years of daily coordinated effort, and while there were many setbacks along the way, the Stabilization Center finally opened in April 2018. I stood at the ribbon-cutting alongside the people who turned this project from an idealistic dream to a hard-fought reality. It was an additionally poignant moment because Olivia had just announced her retirement from the city after thirty-three years of service. She had seen through every part of the project from conception to implementation. It was one of the innumerable contributions she made in her career, and she exemplifies so many other hardworking and dedicated people I had the honor of working with in Baltimore.

That day, Olivia and I watched as the first patients came into the Stabilization Center. One of them couldn't believe it when he found out that he could get treatment that same day. "You're telling me that I don't have to go through all them hoops and wait weeks and weeks?" he asked. When we told him that we had the staff to help him right there and then, he cried.

I thought about all the community members who would now be receiving compassionate medical care tailored to their needs, at the time they were seeking it, right in their city, with the specialists to tend to them. Addiction was finally being treated as the disease that it is.

Our progress on the Stabilization Center propelled other efforts to further normalize addiction and integrate it within the mainstream health-care system. When we held the first meeting with the city's hospital leadership in early 2015, not even one ER was distributing naloxone to patients who came in for overdose. By 2018, naloxone training and distribution were standard of care and done across all city hospitals. Six ERs had begun to offer buprenorphine to patients, and eight hospitals were working with us to pilot new initiatives, like having an "overdose survivors" program where people in recovery would talk to someone who had recently experienced an overdose to help connect them to treatment.

We found that the hospitals making the most progress were those with internal champions pushing for change. It also helped when we could supply additional incentives, such as grant funding, to help get a pilot off the ground.

Recognition was another powerful incentive. Rhode Island had launched a "Levels of Care" designation that I thought was brilliant. The idea was that hospitals already received a trauma center designation: a Level I trauma center can handle the most complex patients, followed by a Level II, then a Level III center for lesser emergencies. At a time of crisis for addiction and overdose, why shouldn't hospitals also have designations for their capacity to treat this urgent issue?

Our team followed the Rhode Island playbook. By this point, Evan

Behrle had agreed to stay on for an extra year to be a special adviser on opioid policy, and this became one of his focus areas. He and Shelly Choo met with all of our city's hospitals and worked with them collaboratively to develop the rating criteria. They then rated each hospital and helped those that wanted to reach the next level to do so. We also borrowed lessons from Vermont by starting a "hub and spoke" model to increase community addiction treatment and implement additional ways of bringing care to patients, such as telemedicine.

In May 2018, Baltimore became the first major city, and the first jurisdiction after Rhode Island, to implement Levels of Care designation for all of our acute care hospitals. We made the announcement in the mayor's ceremonial room, surrounded by the CEOs of all the major hospitals.

"Despite the national opioid crisis, the response in too many hospitals across the U.S. when patients come in for addiction treatment is, 'We don't do that here.' But not here. That's not what our hospitals in Baltimore are saying," I said to the press. "We in Baltimore do not take a back seat to public health, and our hospitals are leading the culture change within medicine. Our hospital CEOs are here today because 'We don't do that here' is not an option for us. We cannot stand by when we know that treatments work, and our only limitation is our ability to make them available."

It was a historic moment, one that I could have only dreamed of when I took on the job three and a half years earlier. The medical establishment in my city was embracing its role as a key part of the solution in the opioid epidemic. These hospitals were proud to be known as the place where patients could go to receive treatment for the disease of addiction. They were proud to be a model for the city, and for Baltimore to be a model for the rest of the country.

DURING MY TWO YEARS OF service in her administration, Mayor Rawlings-Blake supported every one of my public health initiatives, including the critical sense of urgency around the opioid epidemic. She understood that everything I was doing was for the residents of the city, and that every success of my agency directly reflected the strength of her leadership.

Our strong relationship didn't mean that I always agreed with decisions coming from city hall. I suspect that all cabinet members, at all levels of government, have had their share of disagreements over budget and resource decisions. My duty as an agency head is to advocate for the resources my staff needed to deliver services for our residents, while also knowing when to stand down to the city's other pressing needs.

I always knew, though, that I had the ear of the mayor when I really needed it. Those instances were infrequent: I can count on one hand the number of times I exhausted other methods and went to her directly to settle an issue. In every case, she heard me out before making her decision—sometimes it was the result I wanted, sometimes not, but she was always fair and clear as to her reasoning. I always knew that I was heard, and now my job was to execute her decision.

When Mayor Rawlings-Blake decided not to seek reelection in 2016, I was disappointed and worried. I admired the mayor and knew that she was a woman of principle who woke up every day to do what was best for the city. My team was hitting our stride, and there was no guarantee that a new mayor would support our proactive approach to public health. Twenty-four candidates entered the Democratic primary to succeed Mayor Rawlings-Blake. Some had a track record of supporting public health issues; others were known to hold views that ran counter to evidence and science. Many announced platforms in which public health was nowhere to be found.

As public servants in a government agency, my team and I couldn't support a particular candidate, but we could do our jobs and educate all the candidates on our issues. That education was critical, as public health is not top of mind for most people. We could sit around and bemoan why this is the case, or we could do what was in our control—and it was our responsibility to advocate for the necessary work of our agency.

To do this in a politically neutral way, we published and made publicly available a white paper titled "State of Health in Baltimore City," in which we laid out the top health problems facing our residents, what we were doing about them, and what more needed to be done. Every candidate had equal access to this document. Many of them adopted the white paper directly into their platforms and talking points. We held an open house for every candidate for every office to hear from us about our work.

At every meeting, I emphasized to each person how all the issues they were campaigning on—jobs, crime, housing, education—were directly related to public health. I was most concerned about the issue of addiction: our naloxone work was well known throughout the city, but these candidates were surely hearing from the NIMBY contingent at every turn. By this point, we had laid so much groundwork for the Stabilization Center and other points of treatment access. It would have been devastating if a new mayor were to order this work to be stopped because of community pressure based on misconceptions and misinformation.

In April 2016, State Senator Catherine Pugh won the Democratic primary, and she would go on to a convincing general election victory in November. I had met her previously and was aware of her views on public health issues. As a state senator she had voiced concerns about vaccine safety, and during her campaign she frequently linked addiction treatment to crime and neighborhood nuisance. These were worrying signs.

But the good news was that Senator Pugh saw herself as a champion for health. Years before, when I was first introduced to her in her Senate office, she showed me a series of children's books she had written that encouraged kids to exercise and eat vegetables. When she became mayor, she asked if the health department wanted to purchase copies of her book to distribute at community meetings. I declined, citing budget issues. (I could never have predicted that less than three years later, she would resign as mayor in the midst of federal investigations around a bribery scheme. The vehicle used to solicit the alleged bribes? This same *Healthy Holly* book, a copy of which I still have from that initial Senate visit.)

If the health department wanted to continue our opioid work under her leadership, I would need to take a different approach. I knew from working with her in the state legislature that medical experts citing scientific studies wouldn't sway her, so I needed to find credible messengers whose voices she listened to. The constituency she valued most was the business community. They formed the base of her support. She was the cofounder of a clothing shop and prided herself on being a small business owner. She also talked about how she "walked the streets" and asked for people's opinions; we needed to make sure that whatever we did had ample opportunity for community input and that business and community leaders shared our language and carried our messaging to her.

Soon after the primary, I enlisted two leaders I greatly admired to cochair a new advisory group we would call the Workgroup on Drug Treatment Access and Neighborhood Relations. One was Don Fry, the CEO of the Greater Baltimore Committee, the convening entity for major businesses in the Baltimore region. He was a former state senator known for his moderate, pro-growth approach. I had previously enlisted Don to help me begin several collaborations with businesses in Baltimore, and I saw how effective he was in representing his organization's interests while he pushed the businesses toward shared, citywide goals. The other was Bill McCarthy, the executive director of Catholic Charities of Baltimore. A former banker who had left a lucrative career for his true calling, Bill was also widely respected across the city and state as a bipartisan power broker. He was already very sympathetic to the public health approach to treating addiction, and Catholic Charities had been one of our first partners in naloxone distribution.

I knew that Don and Bill would be trusted messengers to the new mayor and to constituencies to whom our health department otherwise would not have access. Together, we assembled a diverse working group that held a series of community meetings throughout the city. Over the next six months, we invited medical experts and neighborhood leaders to testify, and we provided space to hear from community members from all walks of life. Small business owners and neighborhood association leaders aired their concerns about treatment centers, while people in recovery and their families attested to the continuing need for treatment.

After hearing the testimonies, the working group synthesized the recommendations and presented them back to the community members for input. Don, Bill, and I then gave the consensus recommendations to Mayor Pugh. Many of the recommendations were for projects that were already in progress; the formal process provided the cover my team and I needed for when they were ready to launch publicly. The process also ensured community buy-in, and Don and Bill's leadership as key inter-mediaries was instrumental to ensuring the mayor's ultimate approval.

Still, we hit some rough patches. One day not long after Mayor Pugh took office, I received a phone call from a reporter asking if I agreed with the mayor that patients seeking help for addiction shouldn't receive treatment in the city, but should instead be given a one-way ticket to Timbuktu and not be allowed to come back until they're "clean." She'd given several other interviews that day, including to the *Baltimore Sun*, and repeated similar comments.

I'd spoken to local media outlets countless times before about my views on addiction, and I knew that the reporter was looking for me to distance myself from Mayor Pugh. What a juicy story it would be if the health commissioner engaged in open debate with the new mayor. I was getting e-mails and texts from angry advocates who wanted me to go even further, to denounce the mayor's words as harmful and stigmatizing.

"How can you work for someone who would say this?" a leader of an advocacy group texted me. Another person called me, in tears. "This goes against everything you say you stand for," she said. "How can you look at yourself in the mirror if you don't come out and say how wrong this is?" Two other community leaders called on me publicly to resign over the mayor's comments.

The reporter and these advocates all knew that I strongly disagreed with Mayor Pugh's characterization of addiction. But they were mistaken if they thought that I would publicly call out my boss and the duly elected leader of my city. For one, what would it have accomplished? The story would have gotten much bigger and would have shifted into an internal political fight instead of being about the importance of addiction treat-ment. I would probably have irreversibly destroyed the mayor's trust in me. My success and my agency's success depended on my relation-ship with the mayor, and an open disagreement this early in her term would have been the death knell to my agency's ability to deliver on our mission. I saw the demand for my resignation as even more extreme; it was throwing in the towel before I even tried.

If my goal was to get the mayor to change her language, there were far more effective ways to do so. Pete Hammen had stepped down from the state legislature to serve as one of the mayor's three closest advisers. Building on our preexisting relationship, I called him. Over the next several weeks, he and I made sure that all of the mayor's talking points contained language that directly mirrored mine, speaking about addiction as a disease for which treatment exists—and about the need for more treatment and why. We worked with the mayor's communications and advance teams to get her to as many events supporting drug treatment as possible. At every event, we made sure she met people in recovery who could tell her their stories. I always introduced her by thanking her for her leadership on this crisis in Baltimore.

Within a few months, Mayor Pugh and I coauthored an op-ed on the importance of addiction treatment. I secured a keynote for her at a medical conference and wrote remarks that received such high praise that the reporters at this conference commented to me how lucky we were in Baltimore to have such a progressive mayor supportive of addiction treatment.

There were still plenty of people who did not agree with my decision or my strategy. Some have told me that not speaking up publicly was cowardly. To me, this was not about showing courage—it was about playing it smart. Speaking up loudly would have been the easy thing to do, but it would not have been the most effective. At every decision point, we need to recognize our role and where our voices are most needed. At that point and in the position I was in, my voice was most needed to push from within. Our approach also has to change depending on the circumstances we're in. My relationship with Mayor Pugh was different from the one I had with Mayor Rawlings-Blake, whom I could call directly and have a frank conversation with. With Mayor Pugh, I knew that my voice would not change her views on this topic. But I could use other methods to influence her actions. The method that worked was not overt aggression, but behind-the-scenes positioning.

This incident solidified one aspect of my approach to leadership. No

matter which public official or organization one works for, there will
be areas of policy disagreement. Inevitably, there will be circumstances
when employees are asked to do something they don't agree with and
defend opinions they don't share. In my role, I was a direct report to
the mayor and part of her administration. My job was to defend the
mayor and carry out her vision. Whatever disagreements I had with her,
I would have in private. Any public disagreement or backdoor leaks to
the media would only distract from the work of the city and sow distrust in the institution I worked for.

I see this as a necessary part of governing, though certainly there are
critics who may regard my philosophy as "selling out." This was a criticism I'd heard back in the AMSA days, and here was my counter: ideological purity is a luxury that those of us on the front lines can't afford.
I have colleagues who joined administrations in order to spearhead a
governor's efforts to expand health coverage for vulnerable families. The
elected official may have views on other topics that they don't share.
Maybe they disagree with their boss's policies on reproductive health or
criminal justice, but they can advance the work on, say, expanding health
insurance. Their job isn't to denounce these other views—it is to deliver
on what they signed up for, work behind the scenes for better policies,
and focus on the bigger picture of serving people.

This was also my expectation of the people who worked for me. I
was proud of recruiting superb team members who were so committed
to our vision of improving health and reducing disparities in Baltimore.
I expected my staff to be bold and innovative, to come up with new
ideas, and to constantly challenge me. They would not agree with me on
everything, nor should they. I hired them because of their unique per-
spectives, which I wanted to hear and learn from. But we were a team,
and a team speaks externally with one voice: my voice, as the head of
the agency.

To be sure, we all need to draw our lines. My lines were clear. There
were only three things I was not willing to do. I would never agree to do
something that's illegal. I would never provide public comments that
contradict science. (Who would want a top doctor in the city who goes
against science?) And I would never, ever throw my own staff under the

bus. I knew that the trusted members of my team always had my back, and they knew that I always had theirs.

IN TIME, MAYOR PUGH WOULD publicly stand behind all of our overdose prevention and addiction treatment initiatives. She came to the launch of the Stabilization Center, which she heralded (rightfully so) as one of her signature achievements. She hosted in her ceremonial room the recognition of the hospitals participating in Levels of Care and handed out certificates personally to each hospital CEO. She became a key champion in the Law Enforcement Assisted Diversion (LEAD) initiative, a pilot project started in Seattle that we brought to Baltimore in collaboration with the state's attorney's office and the police department, under which individuals caught with small amounts of drugs were offered treatment instead of incarceration.

The mayor's change reflected the broader cultural shift occurring around us. In 2014, in Baltimore and around the country, addiction was widely regarded as a choice and a moral failing. Law enforcement was the entity to deal with drugs, and the medical system and pharmaceutical industries had not accepted their complicity in the crisis. When I first testified to Congress in 2015, I received questions about whether naloxone encouraged drug use. One member even asked me what I thought about imposing Singapore's death penalty as a solution.

By 2018, the landscape was completely different. Naloxone distribution was widespread, with dozens of states implementing a standing order like mine. Police chiefs and prosecutor's offices were touting programs to address addiction treatment. The Centers for Disease Control and Prevention (CDC) had established guidelines to encourage judicious prescribing of opioids, and the pharmaceutical industry was being held to account for its role in fueling the epidemic. More and more obituaries explicitly mentioned overdose as a cause of death, as loved ones decided to come out and fight shame and stigma. When I testified to Congress again that year, members from both sides of the aisle started with the premise that addiction is a disease and that more treatment is needed. The questions they asked were about what kinds of treatments were best and what the cost of those treatments would be.

There is still a great deal of work to be done. There are more resources available to address the opioid epidemic than there were just a few years ago, but they are far from what is needed. Those on the ground continue to be frustrated: they do so much exceptional work on shoestring budgets and could do so much more if only they had the resources. Payouts from drug companies' settlements can help, as can philanthropic resources, but ultimately the federal government needs to provide sustained funding, proportional to the severity of the epidemic, directly to local jurisdictions that are the most affected.

When the Trump administration first started, there was hope that it would allocate this funding through the declaration of a state of emergency. This declaration came, but with funding of exactly $57,000 in total. This is an amount that's laughable for any other emergency; imagine if a hurricane struck and only $57,000 were available for the entirety of rescue, recovery, and reconstruction! In 2018, Congressman Elijah Cummings and Senator Elizabeth Warren introduced legislation that would achieve the requisite scale. Their Comprehensive Addiction Resources Emergency (CARE) Act was modeled after the Ryan White Act, which was successful in stemming the HIV/AIDS epidemic. Now that the rhetoric around addiction has finally changed, and now that local leaders across the country have stepped up, the federal government needs to do its part.

And we, as a society, must see drug addiction as the symptom of a larger problem: we must identify the cause of addiction and treat the poverty and despair, the trauma and unemployment, and the homelessness and hopelessness that are inextricably intertwined with this epidemic.

9

Unrest and Recovery

In April 2015, a twenty-five-year-old African American man named Freddie Gray was taken into police custody in Baltimore. A week later, he died from injuries that included a broken neck.

The morning of April 27 was his funeral. That evening, the world saw Baltimore burn—thousands of cars on fire, hundreds of stores being looted, and crowds of angry youth rioting in the streets.

Baltimore's unrest, and similar uprisings around the country, would prompt long-overdue soul-searching around issues of police brutality, structural racism, and widespread inequities. First, for those us in charge of the city's health and safety, we had to deal with the erupting crisis on our hands.

In the early afternoon, my team began hearing reports of a citywide "purge"—supposedly, activists had disseminated a plan over social media to gather the city's youth to disrupt the city's infrastructure through violence and arson. Media reports were wildly inconsistent, as more and more stories emerged of possible violence in specific areas across the city.

One of the health department's clinics was located in the area thought to be at the heart of the purge. Our top concern was the safety of our clinic staff and the safety of the hundreds of other health department employees scattered across the city. My agency had nearly a thousand people on staff, most of whom worked in locations outside our headquarters, in more than 180 schools, twelve senior centers, three clinics, and the WIC center that provided services for women, infants, and children. Many were in the field that afternoon, providing care in clients' homes, doing developmental screens for toddlers, examining houses for lead, conducting restaurant safety inspections, and responding to calls about animal neglect and abuse.

At what point should we recall our staff, given the potential danger to their well-being? It was nearly impossible to determine rumor from reality. I made the decision to close our operations in areas deemed likely to be affected, starting with arranging the safe transport of patients and staff out of the clinic, which did end up being in the epicenter of the unrest.

Soon after the first reports of violence, Mayor Rawlings-Blake activated the city's Emergency Operations Center (EOC). She asked for the health department to be a lead agency, along with the fire, police, and other key departments. I was glad that we were involved from the outset, since public health tends to be a function that's often overlooked. I knew that there would be a lot for us to do as the events unfolded. So much would require coordinated efforts with other agencies, and it was critical to be on the same page during this chaotic time.

An immediate priority was to ensure that hospitals could continue treating patients. Every hospital had a security plan, which included getting staff to and from their shifts and helping discharged patients get home. Implementing these plans was difficult, given the constantly shifting safety reports. In the early evening hours, I began convening hourly phone calls with each of our twelve hospital CEOs, with representatives of fire, police, transportation, and other agencies so we could provide updates at once and address the hospitals' concerns. It was not unlike what I knew from the ER when we cared for a gravely ill patient: there needed to be centralized leadership, with clearly established roles at the outset and regular check-ins to ensure coordination.

Our staff was also being inundated by calls from people who wanted to know if their doctors' offices would be open for business the next day. Most had appointments that could wait a day or two, but for others, getting to their care was a matter of life or death. We triaged these situations and arranged transportation for patients with the most critical needs like chemotherapy and dialysis appointments.

In this quickly evolving situation, many clinics hadn't decided whether they would be open. Like us, they were weighing the risk to staff versus the necessity to their patients.

The health department staff were adamant that they did not wish to stay home. I heard over and over again: "I live in this community. These patients are my neighbors. I am here to serve." Many other city employees must have felt the same, because a surprising number of service agencies were open the next day. Carla Hayden, the CEO of Baltimore's library system (who would later be appointed the librarian of Congress), decided to keep all the libraries open and even extended their hours. The libraries, like our schools, health clinics, and senior centers, were a safe haven for so many in the community.

Collecting information about openings and closings was no easy task. Our health department's emergency response team, led by Jennifer Martin, was calling every medical office, often a dozen or more times, as the events unfolded. We finally had the list for the next day, but then we needed a way to make the information publicly available. We also had to keep the list continuously updated.

The easiest method was to post the list on the health department's website. Unfortunately, the city's Web server went down during the night. There were rumors that we were the victims of a cyberattack, though later the cause turned out to be a technical failure attributed to the overwhelming number of visits that day. The city's IT staff was scrambling to get the server back, as every other agency also had urgent information that needed to be posted.

There was no time to wait for others to solve our problem. We had to do what we could, with the resources we had.

I looked around the EOC. It was after ten p.m. My senior team was working at maximal capacity, coordinating with hospitals, clinics, and other city agencies. I knew that they would be up all night, staffing the city's EOC and leading the health department's own EOC.

I called my executive assistant, Shirli Tay, and told her that she was in charge of figuring out the website and getting out the messaging about clinic openings.

"Have you ever built a website before?" I asked her.

"No . . . but I'll Google it. I'll figure it out!" she assured me.

And she did. Within an hour, she had set up a website for what we called the Baltimore Healthcare Operations List. She worked with the city's communications officer to publicize the website on social media, and I gave interviews on the four local television stations to spread the word. The city's server was still not working, so Shirli came to the EOC and helped other agencies post their information on the website she'd built. It was a very basic website, but it was what we needed to achieve our purpose in that crucial moment.

This was how our team worked. Coming from the ER where team-work and agility are paramount, I have no tolerance for people who say that a particular duty is "not my job." In an emergency, you do what-ever is needed. You need to be the "Swiss Army knife" for every situa-tion. If you've never done it before, now is the time to start. If you don't know how to do it, look it up and figure it out.

To be sure, preparation is key to emergency response. We put in place protocols for emergencies that we could predict. Some were rou-tine events that happened every year. For example, the health depart-ment participated in multiple weather-related emergency activations. We knew exactly what to do for extreme cold and hot weather, and we knew our role in snow emergencies. We ran drills for mass casualty events and outbreaks, often with community partners. A particularly memorable prep session involved the Girl Scouts as part of a drill for an anthrax outbreak, where boxes of Girl Scout cookies took the place of antibiotics!

No matter how much you prepare, there will be some emergencies for which there is no guidebook. Civil unrest is one of them: What exactly is the health department's role in this situation? This is not dissimilar from work in the ER. You know what to do for a typical patient who comes in for a problem you see over and over again. Many patients fall into the usual pattern, but some don't. For those, you rely on standard operating procedures to establish leadership and central- ized command. Then you need to quickly assess the situation, adapt, and respond. You stay nimble and flexible, and you adjust on the spot to the best of your ability.

I've been fortunate to work with many people who thrive in the pre- dictably unpredictable environment that is local public health. One summer, a Rhodes Scholar named Katherine Warren came to work with me between her first and second years at Oxford. She was supposed to research an academic project related to the opioid epidemic, but right after she arrived there was a suspected case of measles in Baltimore. My only communications specialist—the public information officer—had just left, and I needed someone to help me with media outreach and coordination.

"Katherine, can you step in and be our PIO?" I asked her as I gath- ered my papers to speak to the gaggle of reporters outside.

"Absolutely," she answered, without hesitation. "Before we go out there, can I just ask you—what's a PIO?"

That's the attitude embraced by every member of my core team. We have our areas of interest and expertise, but we will always step in and do everything to serve the needs of the team.

Over the years, I've also worked with other people, particularly recent graduates, who do not share this approach. They turn down projects and reject assignments because the work that's needed is not precisely what they signed up for. Not only are they refusing to con- tribute to the team's work, but these young people are also turning down invaluable opportunities to challenge themselves and to grow. Many of my most formative experiences came from diving in and doing the work, no matter how different it might have been from my initial expectations.

Shirli and Katherine are both completing medical school now, and some of their most memorable times at the health department were when they stepped up to assist at moments of great need. They and so many people gave their work their all and never said, "That's not my job."

THE UNREST AND SUBSEQUENT RECOVERY clarified the health department's role—and my vision for our work. When you are in charge of the health of a city, everything that impacts people's health *is* your job. It's also your job to identify ongoing needs and convince others to take action in the short term and to sustain the momentum for the long term.

There were many short-term needs to tend to. The day of the unrest, thirteen pharmacies in the city were looted, burned, and closed. We began receiving reports that people who lived around these pharmacies didn't know where to get their medications.

We got a call from a woman in her sixties who had had a heart attack a year earlier and had run out of her blood pressure pills. She lived across from the CVS on North Avenue and Pennsylvania Avenue that was in the eye of the storm and had burned down. How long could she go without her pills? she asked our health department operator. She had chest pressure and was scared that she was having another heart attack.

Another patient, a middle-aged man, had diabetes and was out of insulin. He called us two days after the unrest started. He hadn't eaten in two days, because he thought that the best way to hold off on needing insulin was to stop eating. By the time he called, he had blurry vision and was throwing up.

An elderly woman called us, who was out of her medications, too. She wasn't sure what they were called, only that she needed them because of her breathing problems. On the phone, she was so short of breath that she could barely get out two words at a time. Did she need an inhaler? No, it turned out she needed a blood thinner. She had a pulmonary embolus—a clot in her lungs—that would have been fatal if left untreated.

These patients needed emergency treatment, and we sent ambulances to bring each of them to the ER. Many others who called didn't have an emergency, but they needed ongoing care and a way to get their prescriptions filled at another pharmacy.

When I first brought up the issue with pharmacy representatives, they were less than sympathetic. "There are hundreds of pharmacies in the Baltimore region," I was told. "They can just transfer their prescriptions to a different store."

That might be easy for some people to do. But was I going to tell a patient who was in a wheelchair and used an oxygen tank to walk fifteen blocks to the nearest pharmacy? What if that pharmacy was part of a different chain, a Walgreens instead of a CVS—she'd have to get her doctor to call in her prescriptions, but what if she couldn't reach her doctor's office?

"Can't they drive, or ask a family member to bring them?" I was told. Again, that assumes a level of privilege that many of our residents did not have. Even basic safety wasn't a guarantee. News coverage showed ongoing riots. There was a curfew in place, and people were told to stay in their homes.

My team was responding to each request one at a time. Our staff were calling doctors' offices, troubleshooting insurance problems, and driving to get prescriptions filled and bringing the medications to people's homes. The emergency operations team drew in everyone who had extra capacity, and we enlisted students from local medical, nursing, and public health schools in our efforts. We set up a twenty-four-hour phone hotline that was linked to our city's "311" system, so that anyone could call us with their prescription needs and we would work with them to get what they needed.

Soon, all those who called us were being taken care of. My concern turned to the residents who were not calling but also needed our help. Now that we had a system in place to provide medication assistance, how would we get the word out to the community?

My special assistant, Gabe Auteri, was not due to start work for another month. He was finishing his law school coursework and studying for the bar. I needed an extra pair of hands to coordinate this community outreach, and I called him to see if he could start early.

"Of course. Anything you need," he said. As a result of his initiative, Gabe is probably one of only a few people whose first day at work began in the EOC! He helped me to organize door-to-door outreach plans and went with me as we canvassed senior-citizen buildings and provided information to more than 150 churches. (And much to his—and my—relief, Gabe would also go on to ace his exams and pass the bar.)

Our staff and volunteers would make more than two hundred prescription deliveries. During our canvassing, we heard from people who needed more than medications: they also needed food and basic supplies like Ensure and adult diapers. We began connecting residents with emergency food assistance. Local and state partners helped us to establish new shuttle and bus routes particularly for seniors to get groceries and go to the bank.

Another consistent request was for mental health services. Within two days, we had set up a Mental Health and Trauma Response Plan. First, we ensured that there was a 24/7 crisis response so that anyone who called with a mental health need would be connected immediately to the assistance they needed. Then we partnered with local behavioral health organizations to set up healing circles for community groups. We also made mental health counseling available at every one of our over 180 schools. Over time, we began providing trauma-informed care trainings to all frontline city employees as an additional step to helping our city heal and develop resilience.

None of this work was part of the routine duties of a health department. No one told us that this is work we had to do. There was so much else happening in the city, and the mayor led extraordinary efforts so that not one person died during the days of protest and unrest. My fellow city agency heads also worked around the clock and stepped up in every way that they could to deliver additional services and keep our city safe.

This is not to say that our efforts were always embraced. Nearly every initiative was met with resistance on many fronts. Staff were already overburdened with additional responsibilities and operating on little sleep; I could hardly blame them for not being excited to take on more duties. We also had to overcome the resistance from other partners, who were also working at their limits and whose first response to every request was no: they didn't have the resources, staffing, and time to assist. Then there were some who questioned whether we needed to do anything at all. For those of us on the ground who saw the urgent needs of our residents, this was the most frustrating response of all.

I always tried to understand where these points of resistance were coming from, but it was also my job to keep pushing ahead: to identify needs and meet people where they were. If our residents are telling us that their health is at risk, it's my job to figure out how to help them. It's my job to make the case that health cannot be forgotten.

THERE WAS ONE INCIDENT DURING our intense period of door-to-door canvassing that will always stay with me. My team and I were knocking on doors in a building that housed mostly senior citizens. We were dressed in health department shirts, and we gave our standard pitch about our prescription access program as we passed out flyers with the information.

We got two questions. First, people would ask: *What candidate is this for?* Cars were still burning on their street, and people really thought we were campaigning! Second, they asked, *What survey is this? Because we filled out a survey last week.*

Our residents weren't trying to be sarcastic or unfriendly. They were expressing that they always saw us there to serve our own needs, not theirs. They'd seen this before: they were used to seeing "drive-by compassion."

At Freddie Gray's funeral, Congressman Elijah Cummings looked around at the huge swarm of people who filled the church and streamed out onto the street. He asked the thousands of people assembled if anyone actually knew the man they were there to commemorate: "Did anyone recognize Freddie Gray when he was alive? Did anyone see him? Did anyone hear him?"

Public health's moral imperative is to see the people that society prefers not to see and media choose not to portray. While everyone focused on the "rioting youth," the police in military gear, and the state's attorney's press conferences, we turned our attention to the people who couldn't get their basic health needs met.

"Acute-on-chronic" was how I described the situation. In the ER, a patient with acute pneumonia who already has the chronic condition of emphysema will likely be much sicker than someone who only has pneumonia. Our residents already faced many disparities and inequities. They were already living in food deserts and had limited access to transportation. They were already struggling to make ends meet. The unrest unveiled just how many disadvantages they had stacked against them, and their acute needs were made that much more pressing.

Freddie Gray himself was an example of someone who had many odds against him, from early in his life. He was born prematurely and spent months in the ICU. Before he turned two, he was lead-poisoned, with blood lead levels seven times the amount that could lead to permanent brain damage. His mother was addicted to heroin. The neighborhood where Freddie grew up had the lowest average life expectancy in Baltimore, with an unemployment rate over 50 percent and a median household income of just over $24,000 a year. Freddie and other children in his neighborhood, as in mine growing up, were robbed of decades of their life before they even started. And then his life was taken away from him in an unjust, cruel, and inhumane way.

In the days and weeks that followed, my challenge turned from solving urgent problems to maintaining the momentum to address ongoing inequities. "Don't let a good crisis go to waste," the saying goes. Our city's wounds were laid bare for the world to see, and we needed to take advantage of the moment to rally local energy and bring in federal resources to catalyze lasting change. We needed to address the acute problems and quickly pivot to tackling the underlying chronic conditions.

In the immediate aftermath of the unrest, the city received many offers of assistance. No doubt all were well-meaning, but most had the effect of adding work to our already overburdened staff. A charity delivered thousands of pounds of food. We had to figure out the quality and safety of the food, then come up with a way to rapidly distribute it (and to dispose of what we could not). Doctors, nurses, and students from neighboring states heard of our residents' medical needs and contacted us wanting to help. A group from Virginia showed up and said they could set up a makeshift tent to see patients—even though they didn't have medical licenses in Maryland and there were no patients for them to see. It took additional time for us to figure out why they were there and to say "thanks but no thanks."

News cameras flooded the city, stopping traffic and drawing the condemnation of the community who said (rightfully) that the media only wanted to show one story of Baltimore—the city in decay amplified by chaos—rather than the one we knew and loved, with all the incredible people who are trying their best every day.

We also received a lot of attention from the federal government. President Obama instructed his cabinet secretaries to have their key designees reach out to local counterparts. The most helpful action they delivered was their physical presence in Baltimore, which provided us with additional momentum to push forward our long-term priorities.

For example, this was the opportune time to fuel our fight against the opioid epidemic. This was not a problem caused by the unrest, but the unrest brought the devastation caused by addiction to national attention. In the remaining year and a half of the Obama administration, the "drug czar," Michael Botticelli, came to Baltimore three times. His visits, and visits by the Food and Drug Administration (FDA) commissioner Robert Califf and National Institute on Drug Abuse director Nora Volkow, were instrumental in highlighting our addiction work and securing the commitments we needed from hospitals and local funders.

The unrest also brought to the forefront issues of mental health and trauma—another "acute on chronic" condition that I knew needed additional momentum to sustain. There was no one better to call attention to the issue than Vivek Murthy, the U.S. surgeon general and a colleague I'd known since my residency in Boston. My special assistant at the time, a medical student named Cooper Lloyd, organized Vivek's visit, which included meetings with key community and business leaders on the importance of mental well-being. His presence provided the impetus to form a Business Advisory Group on Health, one of the first times the business community in Baltimore publicly collaborated with the health department on shared priorities. These visits from Obama administration officials provided additional momentum to our work and allowed me to convene new partners in the city around our ongoing priorities.

In the meantime, Mayor Rawlings-Blake worked with the Maryland congressional delegation to put forth a list of funding requests for the city. I had given her my wish list, most of which did not end up on the city's overall proposal. I was disappointed by this, but as always, I knew that the mayor had many priorities to weigh. In the end, we received nearly $7 million toward our Mental Health and Trauma Recovery plan. This funding helped us expand mental health services to more than 120 schools and to pilot a telepsychiatry program.

We also received funding to specifically address trauma. Our staff organized a meeting with community leaders to share the good news, but the response was lackluster.

"More money for your agency," one person said. "That's good for you. But what's in it for the community?"

Our staff tried to respond that the entire purpose of the grant was to help the community. A national expert was going to come and bring best practices for healing trauma and developing resiliency.

"Does this person know anything about Baltimore?" someone else asked. "We who live here already know what works. We have community groups already doing this work. What we need is for our work to be respected, funded, and lifted up. This *is* the best practice, for Baltimore."

Over the next few months, my team engaged in challenging conversations like this. I came to a couple of meetings myself and saw the visible frustration on all sides. It was clear that we were at a turning point. The unrest had changed the dynamics, and the way things had been done wasn't going to work anymore. This community was saying that they were sick of having things being done *to* them rather than *with* them. Even if we had good intentions, it was time that we came to a different understanding of how our work was going to be done.

The health department would work with the community group to change the parameters of the trauma grant. The community elected a council to oversee the grant. The council would decide what the goals were, what metrics would be selected, and who would provide the services. We still had an oversight role—the city, as the recipients of the grant, needed to make sure that the council abided by the federal guidelines. And the health department had the technical expertise and provided the administrative backup to finalize budgets and submit grant reports. But the dynamic had completely shifted: this was a grant given directly to the community in a way that respected their leadership, expertise, and dignity.

THE ATTENTION TO MENTAL HEALTH and the reconfiguring of the trauma grant are examples of how the Freddie Gray crisis changed the trajectory of our work moving forward. I also began concerted efforts to lift up the inspiring work being done around the city. The health department started a newsletter and a monthly podcast that highlighted the "public health heroes" in our agency and in community groups who were making a difference every day. To counteract negative perceptions of the city, we shared stories of Baltimore's innovations and successes through local and national media.

These efforts paid off in numerous ways. For one, more and more exceptional young people came to work with us, some for a few months, some for a year, and others for the duration of my time in Baltimore. Most were taking time off during their medical, law, or graduate school studies; some others were recent graduates. I initially envisioned these roles as a fellowship to focus on a particular field of inquiry. Someone with an interest in opioids could help us with research and data collection in that area, for example, or we could attract scholars doing dissertation work in HIV/AIDS or child health.

The unrest entirely changed the cadence of my work and therefore the scope of their work: now, writing papers took a back seat to helping with the critical work of rebuilding a city. Special assistants who thought that they'd be accompanying me to community health fairs were now also helping me to write congressional testimony and organizing meetings with cabinet secretaries.

With all the dignitaries coming to Baltimore and the high-profile requests coming our way, the staffers' duties were expanding to things like planning multiday events for hundreds of people and coordinating multimillion-dollar grant requests with a turnaround of a couple of weeks. Katherine Warren created an informal guide that would be passed on from one special assistant to another. It began with templates of e-mails for different occasions and instructions on preparing speeches, then grew more detailed with other things that they'd had to figure out on the fly. Once one person worked out how to plan for a visit by a federal official, for example, they passed on the knowledge to the others, so the next special assistant didn't have to start from scratch. The living document had guidance on how to work with advance teams, coordinate invitations, book space, and organize joint press conferences.

The special assistant guide would grow to more than 160 pages. This was one of the many efforts by my dedicated team to pass on knowledge to the next person who would fill their shoes. It was critical that we set up processes that would improve our agency's work and that would last long after we departed. Every person contributed to increasing our team's effectiveness and efficiency as they dedicated themselves to our work and our mission.

THE UNREST CHANGED THE TRAJECTORY of our work in another key area. My team was already working on a strategic plan for health in our city that we called Healthy Baltimore 2020. On the eve of the plan's release, I called my chief of staff, Kristin Rzeczkowski, and asked her to tell the team that we needed to hit pause. The metrics we had used to measure health in the city were the traditional metrics of public health: life expectancy, infant mortality, overdose deaths, etc. We had an opportunity—and with the unrest, a mandate—to do something that communicated another critical goal. We could put forth a vision for health with a relentless focus on equity.

Specifically, I thought it was time for us to call out racism as a public health issue. At the time I first talked about this, in 2015, I got a lot of raised eyebrows in response. People could see racial disparities as a public health issue. But racism itself? It was something that I had to back into by explaining the cause of health disparities. For example, African

Americans in Baltimore bore disproportionate harms from cardiovascular disease because one in three African Americans lived in food deserts, compared to one in twelve whites. And where they lived was directly related to the history of housing discrimination from redlining and other racist policies in the not-so-distant past.

Structural racism had a direct effect on public health. We had an opportunity to address this by embedding metrics of these disparities into our Healthy Baltimore report.

Understandably, my staff was not too pleased with the last-minute change in focus. Our operations staff had to put a hold on the printers; our communications folks had to redo the press announcements; and all the epidemiology, policy, and program staff who had worked so hard on the initial version were concerned about the process for revisions. I held a team meeting that morning to explain my thinking, and after some initial grumblings, everyone came to see why this pivot was so important.

Within a couple of weeks, our team rallied to identify a metric of disparity that accompanied every metric of health. We laid out an ambitious goal: that improving health alone was not enough unless we also reduced disparities. After all, disparities are not a zero-sum game. You don't subtract years of life from one group for another to have more. We can improve health for everyone while also recognizing the fundamental importance of caring for the most vulnerable.

The unrest also gave us an opening to use the voice of public health to call attention to underlying social problems. The world was seeing what activists in Baltimore had been saying for so long: That our policies of mass arrest and incarceration haven't worked and in fact have worsened poverty and injustice. That discriminatory housing practices and structural racism have bred distrust and disparities that destroyed hope and opportunity, that fueled trauma and unrest. We could finally talk about how poverty, violence, and racism are public health problems, and that public health can be a powerful social justice tool to begin to address these long-standing issues.

Opening the floodgates to such complex issues as racism takes time and the willingness to have difficult and nuanced conversations. When

I first declared a state of emergency around opioids, I received some pushback from the community. At a church event, a gentleman in his late forties stood up to ask a question: "Doc, I need you to explain to me why this is now called an emergency, when there have been people dying from heroin for decades. Why wasn't it called an emergency then?"

I knew where this question was coming from. I told him that he was right. When addiction affected poor minorities in inner cities, it was seen as a choice, a moral failing. If they ended up incarcerated or dead, it was their fault. But now that addiction was affecting white, affluent communities, now that the face had changed from inner-city minority youth to suburban white college students, it was understood as a disease.

This was unfair. This was unjust. It was wrong that addiction was viewed for so long from the prism of racism and stigma. It was wrong that generations of Black and brown people have been put into jail and entire communities have been decimated because of discriminatory policies that run counter to science and evidence. We need to speak out about structural racism and the deep-seated inequities that got us to where we are.

But this was also an opportunity to right the wrongs of the past, and to not let the energy of the moment go to waste. We must point out past injustices so they are not repeated, or else new funding will once again bypass the communities most in need, who have been in need and have been owed for decades.

I was also adamant that it would be a mistake to turn down the opportunities we have now because we are so angry with the past. Should a state of emergency have been declared long ago? Absolutely. But it didn't happen, so it is happening now. Taking that opportunity is not about ignoring history but about seizing the moment to do everything we can for our residents.

My philosophy is that pragmatism wins out over idealism every time, because my North Star is the patients and communities I serve. Public health is their lifeline. They need services now, and there's no time to wait for the perfect policy or the ideal cultural environment.

In this way, I have little tolerance for those who value purity over practical action. I once walked out of a gathering where activists considered boycotting funding for opioid treatment because the funding allocation occurred after panel testimonies that did not include any people of color. Perhaps those who brought in white families to testify knew that they were the most sympathetic faces to the funders. Perhaps they knowingly fed into long-standing bias. Perhaps they did wrong, and should be told (in private) that there are concerns about their actions. But to make that point by forgoing funding that would literally save the lives of the Black, brown, white, and all people we served was, in my view, unconscionable.

I'd have similar disagreements with those who took issue with my patient advocacy work. I once wrote an article about how, in times of rising maternal mortality, women can take matters into our own hands and advocate for better care. If doctors don't ask us certain questions, we can make sure to bring them up. If we are ignored, here's how we can speak up.

I was surprised by the criticism from activists, who said that my article was perpetuating the myth that women, particularly Black women, were to be blamed for the maternal mortality problem. That was not at all what I was saying. In my article, I specifically pointed to the deep systemic issues at fault, including racism in the health-care system and ongoing disparities in access to care. But it will take years for these entrenched problems to be addressed. A patient who needs care right now should be empowered with all the tools possible to get the best care. Empowering her with these tools doesn't take away from the activists' calls for structural reform, but depriving her of these tools in the name of political correctness can harm her health. As a doctor, I cannot make such a decision.

That was another lesson learned from the unrest: there are many who approach emergency situations with good intentions. Too often, people get in their own way with bureaucratic reasoning, impractical solutions, and purity tests. Crises are opportunities for all of us to challenge how we do things. My team began to adapt, grow, and lead differently, because we had to—and in so doing, we brought about change for the people we served.

10

Putting the Face on Public Health

The deeper I got into my work at the health department, the more I learned about the type of leader I wanted to be.

Three people taught me key lessons. The first was Mayor Rawlings-Blake, who taught me the importance of being true to yourself as you stand your ground. She led the city during an extremely challenging time, and no matter what she did, she was criticized. Some people said that she could have prevented the civil unrest by calling in police reinforcements earlier. These critics forget that the initial allegations were of police brutality, and that the initial hours of the unrest were filled with rumors and speculation. Had the mayor mobilized hundreds of officers in response to peaceful protests, there would have been a massive outcry that could have led to a far more violent standoff.

Others pointed to what they said was lack of action after the unrest. What about all those people who wanted to help—where did those resources go, and why is Baltimore still struggling and mired in the same problems as before the uprising? I experienced for myself the extraordinary difficulty of wading through the offers of assistance. The mayor was able to mobilize additional government and philanthropic resources, and we did make use of them to make tangible improvements. The problems Baltimore faced were decades in the making, and while the unrest gave the city the impetus to unearth and begin addressing them, it would be unrealistic to expect many years of inequities to be improved within months.

No matter what the mayor did, she would have received torrents of criticism, because it's easy to be an armchair quarterback. Are there things she could have done differently? No doubt, especially with the benefit of hindsight. Leadership is about making difficult decisions in the moment, during extremely challenging and quickly evolving situations. Inaction is just as much a decision as action is.

I also believe that Mayor Rawlings-Blake wouldn't have received half these criticisms if she were a man. As an African American woman, she was often singled out with comments that can only be deemed sexist, racist, or both. Reporters wrote stories about her weight, then speculated on her diet as she focused on fitness. They talked about her makeup and her choice of jewelry—some thought she wore too much of both, some thought she didn't wear enough.

I can't count the number of times I was with her at events where a well-meaning constituent would come up just to tell her to "smile more." I never once heard such a suggestion given to a male public official. I'd hear the commentary after meetings she chaired. If she was forceful and decisive, she was called overbearing. If she was deferential, she was labeled a weak leader.

I knew this struggle all too well. When I was interviewing for a residency in emergency medicine, I received feedback that a program was hesitant to take me on because I was judged to be too "bossy." This comment came from someone who didn't know me and hadn't interviewed me, but who had seen from my résumé that I had a record of leadership positions. To his credit, the program director asked this person if he would have made the same remark about a male candidate with the same experience. (I don't know the answer, and I didn't end up matching at that program.)

Another time, at a minority leadership conference, I was on a panel about subconscious bias with three male panelists. We were all either MDs or PhDs. The moderator addressed all of us in turn. My three fellow panelists answered questions first, and each was introduced as "Dr. So-and-So." When I was introduced, I was called "Leana." Coming from the ER, where male doctors were routinely called "Doctor" and female doctors were not, I was used to this—though the irony of it occurring during this particular panel did not escape me or the women in the audience.

I had worked to overcome implicit bias by being particularly explicit about my identity as a physician. This was not about pride but about effectiveness. I'd have a long conversation with a patient only to have them ask, "When is the doctor going to come in and talk to me?" When there were multiple providers in the room, family members and paramedics would automatically turn to address the white male in the room, even if the white male was a medical student or a tech. In my clinical work, I followed the example set by other female minority doctors, who always wore a white coat, and I always made clear to my patients that I was the supervising doctor.

My work in Baltimore was no different, and I took notice that Mayor Rawlings-Blake insisted that everyone call her by her title or "Madam Mayor." Over her career in public service, she had seen how much harder women have to try in order to be taken seriously as the leaders we are. She'd always call me "Dr. Wen" in return, which sent an unequivocal message. The mostly white, male hospital CEOs who were physicians were always referred to as "Doctor," and it was important for my effectiveness for people to understand that the city's doctor—a minority woman—is in fact a doctor.

I also learned from the mayor to navigate people's expectations and express my true self. Like her, I was also receiving constant "advice" about how to dress and how to act. At one point, a high-level city official told me that I was appearing "too happy" and needed to be more stern. This was followed by another city leader chiding me for not being "warm" enough when I introduced him. Mayor Rawlings-Blake knew that she could not be everything to everyone, and I learned from her as I became comfortable with my own public persona—one that was authentic to me.

To be sure, there were still some tricky situations. As a leader, I knew that I needed to be careful of my facial expressions, but I didn't know how much people were reading into them until I heard from a manager that one of her staff members was crying: she was convinced that she was getting fired after an encounter in the restroom with me. Apparently, I had not reacted with even a smile when she'd said hello and told me about what she was working on.

I apologized to her and told her a secret that few people knew at the time: I was newly pregnant and was in the bathroom trying not to throw up! It was a reminder of how much people observe the actions of leaders, and how challenging it is for women in particular to balance others' expectations of us with our own authenticity.

THE SECOND PERSON FROM WHOM I learned critical leadership lessons was Senator Barbara Mikulski, the head of the Maryland congressional delegation. Senator Mikulski was the first female Democrat to be elected to the U.S. Senate who did not succeed her husband. She had been a social worker in East Baltimore and then a city council member before serving in the Senate for thirty years. ("Politics is social work with power," she'd say about her background.)

I got to know her as Maryland's senior senator and then as an adviser and mentor after her retirement from public office. There was no question that she was unabashedly her own person with her own distinctive brand of authentic, passionate, and courageous leadership. One of her aphorisms is "Do what you're best at, and what you're needed for." This became a guiding principle in my life.

An important piece of advice from Senator Mikulski came at a time when I most needed it. I'd arrived in Baltimore knowing that I was going to give this job my all. One of my predecessors had told me that the only limitation to how much I could get done was my own ability to stay awake. Indeed, I found that there was endless need and limitless opportunity. If I just pushed myself a bit more, I could come up with one more project, get one more funder, and go to one more community event.

A year into my job, I was at neighborhood meetings, church gatherings, and community fairs every night and all weekend. The rest of my time was taken up with meetings and directing projects. The initial months were so busy getting to know the city. Then the Freddie Gray unrest happened, and there was even more to do.

At this point, Sebastian was still living in D.C. He was very understanding that this was what I needed to do, though it was a rare evening that we'd see each other—and even then, I'd be glued to my iPhone.

The problem was that I was running a hundred miles an hour with no end in sight. I was in for a marathon, but at sprint pace. Though I was energized by the work, I was getting more and more exhausted. My days started with seven a.m. meetings and easily went until midnight. I subsisted on energy bars and was eating out every night. Exercise had always been important to me, but when I got home after a long day, it was the last thing on my mind and the first thing to forgo.

Mine was far from a healthy lifestyle. As I went around town talking about the importance of physical and mental wellness, I knew that I needed to practice wellness for myself, but I just didn't have the time.

I knew that my well-being was at a low point when Sebastian and I went to a dinner party with two other couples and I suddenly became very tired. I excused myself to go to the restroom, where I apparently sat on the floor and napped until Sebastian came to find me, an hour later.

I was also beginning to see that my frenetic pace meant that there was no time for reflection. We were doing all these projects, but were they the best use of our resources? What was our overall vision, our plan, our strategy?

Most importantly, my team was exhausted, too. They'd been through numerous crises but were still running at full speed. They needed time with their families and to focus on wellness themselves.

It was time for us all to stop and regroup. My core team was finally in place. These were dedicated people who would never have complained about the pace or the amount of work. They also shared my commitment to leave everything on the field. I knew that I had to slow down myself to give them permission to do the same.

Senator Mikulski is known for her relentless work ethic. When she stopped me one day to tell me to slow down, I was shocked, and I took her advice seriously.

"You need to pace yourself," she said. "We need you here for the long haul."

She gave me tips on how she managed her brutal schedule: She asked her staff to be extremely protective of her time and limit evening and weekend engagements. When she went to events where food was served, she tried to eat beforehand. This was healthier and gave her more time to engage with others. She blocked out parts of her schedule for important things in her life, including time with family. Doing so was crucial for her well-being and necessary for her staff.

A year into my job, I asked Shirli to start blocking out time on my calendar for family, exercise, and reflection to think through strategy. We scaled back my commitments to events, delegating more to my senior team to speak in my place and represent me in meetings. We gave more careful consideration to starting new projects and held one another accountable for physical exercise and better diets. We started having regular retreats to develop longer-term plans.

Initially, I was worried that these changes would have a negative effect on our work, but I learned an important lesson: cutting hours actually increased our productivity, and allowing space to reflect made us all better leaders. Having my staff speak on my behalf gave them professional development opportunities, and since I didn't fill the time with additional work, we all had more breathing room. Keeping a more reasonable schedule myself also served as an example to others. Doing meaningful work is a great gift, but so too is being with the people we love.

Together, the team came up with many more innovative solutions than we would have had we continued at breakneck speed. And our steady, slower pace allowed us to ramp up speed when real crises occurred, as they always did.

THE THIRD PERSON FROM WHOM I learned many valuable lessons was Congressman Elijah Cummings. When I started, I knew him only by reputation, as someone who was revered in the community and regarded as a mentor to generations of leaders. I had received the advice, said somewhat jokingly, that I should talk to Congressman Cummings but make sure never to go after him.

I didn't understand what this meant until our first encounter, at a church in West Baltimore. It was an event to call attention to the city's health disparities, and specifically to urge action on HIV/AIDS. Congressman Cummings began to speak. His voice rose, his cadence peaked, and he preached like I'd never heard preaching before. He called on everyone to do the work and said that the work is so much bigger than us. This effort, he said, was really about children: "Our children are messengers to a future we will never see."

The audience was on their feet. They clapped. They cheered, amen.

Then the moderator announced the next speaker . . . the new health commissioner. There was polite applause. I quickly figured out why the new girl drew that speaking slot, and why no one ever wanted to go after him!

After the speeches, Congressman Cummings pulled me aside and wrote down his cell phone number. He leaned close and said, "Doc, call me. You hear me? I need you to succeed because this is about the health of my people. I will help you help the city."

And he did. When a federal grant stopped, threatening to end a home visiting program for mothers and babies, he stepped in. He would not take no for an answer. When we needed to secure funds for mental health and trauma, he fought for us and got us the resources. His highest praise was for people to be "effective and efficient," and as he got to know my team's work, he began telling others that we were effective and efficient and that they should support us in our quest to save lives. I invited him to speak at dozens of events, particularly about the opioid epidemic. I knew that his moral authority was what we needed to shift the culture to overcome stigma. He always came.

Whenever we were at an event together, I saw how the congressman connected with people. He'd always look right at a person and make them feel like they were the only person in the room. Every time, he'd make the effort to meet at least one member of my team, and a number of them came to me later, in tears, because they felt as if they had been truly heard by this great man. They felt that they were seen, that he understood them and loved them for who they were.

Congressman Cummings had a particular passion for mentoring young people. I heard him tell numerous groups of high school and college students, "I want you to replace me one day." No matter how busy, he was always available to his mentees. Whenever I hired a new special assistant, I tried to follow his example: I'd been the lucky recipient of opportunities and mentorship, and now it was my turn to give back.

To say that Elijah Cummings was dedicated to serving the city would be a profound understatement. More than anything, he wanted to showcase Baltimore for what it really was, a city of hope and opportunity, and I learned from him the importance of changing the negative narratives. The biased view that people have of Baltimore is not just hurtful and inaccurate—it also prevented us from getting resources we needed. If Baltimore is thought to be in decline, nothing will get better no matter how much money is spent. Based on that logic, the city will never receive the funding it needs. Businesses won't invest. Residents will give up and move out.

One day, a high-level state official came to one of our senior centers. He was supposed to thank the older adults for their volunteerism and caring for one another, but instead he spoke only about crime and grime, the failure of city government, and how he and the state of Maryland were stepping up to rescue us from ourselves. When he finished, I took the microphone and spent the next fifteen minutes channeling my inner Elijah Cummings. I talked about all the inspiring work I saw— including the great efforts of the people in that very room. I wasn't trying to pick a fight, but I had to do what the congressman would say was my job: not just to implement good programs and advocate for sound policies but to carry the torch as a champion for the city.

Congressman Cummings showed that city leaders have to be the biggest cheerleaders for their people. We need to celebrate the successes at every opportunity and tell the stories of resilience we see every day. Just as we need to deliver excellent services, it is our job to lift up fellow citizens and imbue the city with energy. To bring about real change, first we have to switch the pervasive narrative of negativity to one of hope and optimism, vitality and growth.

ANOTHER LESSON I LEARNED FROM my role models was the importance of highlighting the health department's achievements. I was proud of the national recognition we began to receive for our innovative work, including awards from the American Public Health Association and *Governing* magazine. Our agency was named one of the "Local Health Departments of the Year" by the National Association of City and County Health Officials.

It's been said that public health succeeds when it's invisible, since we are in the business of preventing bad things from happening. By definition, then, there is no face of public health. There is the face of the person who suffered food poisoning, but we don't see the faces of the millions of people who benefit from food safety through the work of health inspectors. There is the face of the person who overdosed, who was shot, who had a heart attack, but we don't see the faces of all those who avoided these dire outcomes because of public health efforts.

But if public health is invisible, nobody will make the case for our work. When it comes time to decide the budget, it will be the first item on the chopping block.

This was my constant struggle in Baltimore, and the struggle of my colleagues around the country. One of the most frustrating parts of our jobs was having to continuously make the case for programs that had already proven to be effective. In Baltimore, foundations and philanthropists often stepped up when government funding was limited, but private sources cannot make up for the government's responsibility. The private sector can help, but it can't fill all the holes left by the public sector.

Take the Zika epidemic. In late 2015, a mosquito-borne virus became linked to severe birth defects for women infected during pregnancy. Babies were being born with microcephaly, an abnormally small head, and associated brain damage such that they may never walk or talk. The virus began spreading throughout South and Central America. At its peak, it was estimated that 1.5 million people were infected with Zika in Brazil, with over 3,500 cases of infant microcephaly in less than a year.

The *Aedes* mosquito that carries Zika is found in the continental United States as well, including Maryland and as far north as Massachusetts. Public health experts sounded the alarm that we needed to begin Zika prevention efforts to mitigate the harmful effects. We needed to do surveillance of mosquitoes to check for Zika, spray for them and eliminate their breeding locations, and educate health professionals and patients about travel warnings and other precautions. If we didn't, the health effects would be dire, as would be the economic consequences: according to the CDC, the cost of caring for and educating one child born with severe defects from Zika would be as high as $10 million over their lifetime.

Even though the CDC and the World Health Organization declared Zika a global public health emergency, it took ten months for Congress to approve President Obama's $1.9 billion allocation to fight the epidemic. I joined other local and state health officials to speak to members of Congress about the urgent need for action. We pointed out that the delay made no sense. If thirty-five hundred babies with severe defects were born in the United States, that would cost our country $35 billion. Not to mention the cruelty of knowing that a lifetime of suffering could have been prevented, if only we'd acted sooner.

Practically, the lack of prompt action forced the CDC to shift funding from other aspects of local public health to cover the cost of Zika preparedness. In Baltimore, had we not secured additional resources, funding work for Zika would have cut our emergency response staff by a third. These were the same staff who prepared the city for hurricanes and bioterrorism, who were on the front lines to respond to civil unrest. What sense would it have made to cut their numbers, to reduce the staff working on some emergencies in order to respond to another? This extended beyond health and economic issues—it was also one of public safety and national security.

Public health fails if people don't see its value. We learned this at great cost, only a few years after the fight over Zika funding and action.

With the arrival of COVID-19, the struggle played out on a far more catastrophic scale. It's up to those in public health to make its case. We have to make the invisible visible.

AT THE END OF MY first year as health commissioner, the team came together to look at our progress and our goals. We reaffirmed our commitment to the three major areas from my initial listening tour: addiction and mental health, youth health and wellness, and care for the most vulnerable. We also took on the overriding mission that would help us achieve our goals: making public health visible.

Over the next few years, we used five strategies to deliver on the promise to improve health and reduce disparities while putting the face on public health every step of the way. First, we made use of every crisis as an opportunity to amplify and solve an existing public health challenge. When we received reports of suspected cases of measles in Baltimore, we held mass immunization drives and educated residents about vaccines, emphasizing their safety and effectiveness. The vaccination rate among Baltimore's public school students soon became among the highest in the country, at over 99 percent. When there were deaths reported from synthetic marijuana, we launched a public health education campaign and got the city council to pass legislation banning the sale of these drugs from corner stores. When animal control officers rescued dozens of emaciated puppies bred for dogfighting, we used the public outrage to drive awareness of animal abuse and enact a city law outlawing dogfighting paraphernalia.

All of these issues were important to public health, but each by itself was insufficient to draw wide interest. Every year, there were calls for immunization. Our website stressed the importance of immunizations and the dangers of synthetic drugs; plenty of articles described the link between animal cruelty and violence against humans. Still, it took inciting events to capture media attention—and thereby public attention. We took advantage of the moment and made something tangible come of the crisis through the three-pronged approach of service delivery, public education, and policy change.

Second, we set long-term goals while demonstrating short-term successes. The trajectory of public health is long. Typical metrics of health outcomes are life expectancy and rates of diseases that will take years to manifest and measure. As scientists, we need to use these metrics, but we also have to come up with more immediate measures of success that will give confidence to the community and shore up support for our efforts. Our Healthy Baltimore 2020 goals set these long-term metrics (and accompanying measures of disparities); we also laid out short-term actions to show that we were making good progress toward our desired outcome.

While we aimed to reduce cardiovascular disease, we also strove toward a goal that was more quickly attainable to increase the healthy food options available to Baltimore's most vulnerable residents. We worked with corner stores to help them provide healthy options and expanded our partnership with a chain, ShopRite, to deliver groceries directly. We then held community celebrations and invited local media every time a new corner store signed on or a new senior center or library became a food delivery site.

These "Baltimarket" programs were very popular. Addressing food deserts was something the city's residents had requested, and it meant a lot to them that we listened and delivered on our promises. Our food access programs drew international attention, with health officials from the World Bank and delegations from as far afield as Saudi Arabia coming to learn how to duplicate them in their locales.

Third, we spoke about our work in a way that was grounded in data but highlighted by stories. As Senator Mikulski said, "Data validate, they don't motivate." Data provide context and credibility, but it's stories that compel action. Every time we talked about a program, we shared a story and attached a face to it of someone who was a participant.

One of our programs was designed to prevent falls among the elderly. One in four people over age sixty-five will fall every year, resulting in nearly three million fall-related injuries seen in ERs across the country, including eight hundred thousand hospitalizations and more than twenty-seven thousand deaths. I've treated seniors who've broken their hips, cracked ribs, and suffered brain hemorrhages from falls. I've seen how someone working and caring for their grandchildren could lose mobility and independence after one slip and fall. Among the elderly, falls are also a major cause of social isolation, depression, and cognitive decline.

The program started by analyzing hospital data to map out where older adults were falling. When we found clusters, we started looking for commonalities. In one housing complex, a hallway lightbulb had gone dark directly over a shaggy rug. Multiple people were tripping and suffering injuries in the same hallway. In other cases, we found problems in the home, like out-of-reach light switches or overwhelming clutter. We also identified medication interactions that led to frequent falls.

The statistics alone helped funders understand the health and economic impact of our work. The stories and the faces of the individuals drew human interest. When a local TV station featured an exercise class for seniors, many people called us, wanting to improve their agility and take part in Tai Chi and dance aerobics. When two seniors gave testimonials about how home renovations reduced their risk of falls, dozens of others requested services in their homes, too. Data grounded the work; stories are what brought it to life.

Fourth, since people don't often think of public health, it's our job to connect the work of public health to whatever they prioritize. There is one degree of separation between our work and everyone else's, but we have to be the ones to proactively make the case. If the conversation is around education, we need to show how medical conditions like asthma correlate with chronic absenteeism and poor academic performance. A program to treat asthma in schools will thus prevent the child from missing school to go to the doctor—and the parent or caregiver from missing work. An investment in school health therefore is also an investment in education.

The same argument can be made about public safety, employment, housing, climate, and infrastructure needs. Everything is influenced by public health, and the public's health is influenced in turn by everything else. There is no such thing as a non-health sector. Those of us working in public health need to reach out, constantly, to those who don't yet know the impact of our work and demonstrate how we bring them value. We will encounter skepticism, criticism, and downright hostility along the way, but we cannot be afraid of venturing outside our comfort zone. If all we do is talk to people who think like us, we will never make progress or advance our priorities. In much the same way, we need to be at the table for strategic conversations about the future of our communities. If other officials neglect to invite us, then we must set our own table and bring everyone else along.

No one told me or my staff that the health department needed to convene the fentanyl task force. In other jurisdictions, law enforcement was the convening entity. We could have waited for someone else to invite us, but that would have taken time and cost lives (and if we'd waited, we might never have been invited). Furthermore, having law enforcement as the convener would have undercut my aim of having addiction be understood primarily as a health concern and not as a criminal justice matter.

No one told me or my staff that the health department needed to bring together tech and engineering companies. We saw an opening and started TECHealth. Not only did we gain invaluable technical expertise, we also engaged local start-ups that became even more invested in the city. No one had expected the health department to convene businesses around health priorities, but when I did, with Don Fry's help, all the major businesses stepped up. In time, they would become key contributors to our Healthy Baltimore 2020 goals, including spearheading initiatives on a citywide workplace wellness designation and leading a "Billion Steps" exercise challenge.

Partnerships can also engage stakeholders who may not agree on every issue. At the same time that I, on behalf of the health department and the city, was the named defendant in a lawsuit brought by the Catholic Church over a reproductive rights issue, I also worked with Catholic Charities and representatives of the Catholic Church on projects we all cared deeply about. Together we successfully advocated for the passage of state legislation on paid family leave. Together we championed increased funding for children's health and violence prevention and collaborated on delivering mental health and trauma care services. We transcended ideological differences in some areas to further the greater common good.

By developing and cultivating these partnerships, the health department was able to innovate, lead, and prove that public health should be at the table—and often at the head of the table.

There is one drawback when an agency chooses to place itself at the forefront of key issues. As our work became more prominent, people began to ask us to be responsible for things far afield from our work. I received letters from residents who argued that potholes were a public health issue. Not a day went by when we didn't get constituent calls asking what we were going to do about rat infestations. These were the responsibility of other agencies—the transportation department filled potholes, and the public works department ran the program for rat eradication. We politely declined and referred the responsibility to our partners.

Then there were other issues that didn't neatly fall to any particular agency, that the health department could have addressed but for which we simply didn't have the bandwidth. Another commissioner might have chosen to focus their work on environmental policy, homelessness, and chronic disease prevention.

But as Mayor Rawlings-Blake frequently reminded us, if everything is a priority, nothing is a priority. And so we chose to focus on the most pressing needs of the community, on where we could make the biggest impact, and on what would make the invisible visible. We knew that what may have seemed like incremental progress made a tangible and lasting difference to the people we served. Our focus was on the big picture, but we could not get there unless we started with what could be done now. And we never forgot that what mattered was not what we were fighting about but whom we were fighting for.

11

Hurt People Hurt People

One summer morning, in July 2016, I was awakened by a phone call from Kristin Rzeczkowski, my chief of staff. It was not yet six a.m. My senior team and I kept our phones on at all times for emergencies, and we knew never to call after hours unless something truly time sensitive needed our attention. And still the middle-of-the-night phone calls occurred with some frequency. Most of the time they came from elected officials with constituent requests. Sometimes they were medical emergencies: a traveler quarantined at a local hospital with possible Ebola, an outbreak of Legionnaire's disease at a nursing home, a dog-fighting ring that had just been uncovered.

"We've had a break-in," Kristin said. "Eastern got robbed last night."

"What? Again?"

I couldn't believe it. Eastern was one of our two main health centers that provided key services like childhood immunizations, reproductive health care, dental care, and HIV and hepatitis testing and treatment. That month, we'd already had two burglaries in the same facility. After the first, we requested security cameras to be installed; after the second, after-hours police patrols.

"Did the police catch them in action?" I asked Kristin.

"No. They just came around and found a broken window. We're looking through the cameras to see if there's any useful footage."

"What did they take? There's nothing left!"

During the first break-in, the burglars stole two TVs from the waiting rooms, along with laptops and a stash of bus tokens that we gave out to low-income patients. During the second break-in, their target was the medicine cabinet. They took all the medications, which for this clinic consisted primarily of antibiotics to treat STIs and birth control pills. My staff had made the macabre joke that if the thieves actually distributed these pills, this was just another way of reaching people where they were. Maybe we'd even see a dip in the rate of STIs and unintended pregnancies.

Kristin was silent for a moment. "They're still trying to figure it out, but I think it's worse this time," she said.

I told her that I'd be there in half an hour. When I arrived at the clinic, I saw what she meant. The previous two times, the burglars took valuables from the patient care areas. This time they targeted the workspaces of other staff in the building, which included the maternal and child health staff and the school health staff.

Staff belongings were strewn everywhere. The floor was littered with sweaters, broken photo frames, pens, and personal trinkets. Boxes of coloring books and dolls had been emptied, the remnants scattered across the room. Police officers were sweeping up crayons and markers as they took pictures of the wreckage.

The staff were beginning to arrive. I saw the shock on their faces as they came through the door. They needed to process what was happening. I asked Kristin and one of my deputy commissioners, Dawn O'Neill, to gather folks for a meeting in a conference room next door.

The room quickly filled. Everyone was standing and fanning themselves, as the lone air conditioner was not working. But nobody was looking to leave. We'd gathered there after the first break-in, too, but the emotions that day were different.

Many people expressed their frustration at the burglars. "We are the safety net," one person said, visibly agitated. "We are here to serve our community. They've already disrupted our services twice and we had to close down twice. Don't they see that they're hurting children and pregnant women with what they're doing?"

Others vented at me and the senior team. They asked about how we could allow a third burglary to occur. Didn't we care about their safety? "This is so traumatic for us," another staffer said. "And now what's the point—are we going to clean up today just so that they can break in again tomorrow?"

Kristin, Dawn, and our human-resources and facility heads began a conversation about the security measures we had already taken and what more should be done. Because we were in the process of moving Eastern to a new location, the city had balked on installing additional physical security. We had fought back, citing our employees' and patients' safety, and eventually we had received authorization from the city to install new locks, security cameras, and bars on the first-floor windows. But bars had not been installed on the second-floor windows, and it was through one of those that the burglars came in.

The city had also agreed to provide a uniformed police officer during work hours and to do intermittent patrolling after hours. The day of the burglary, though, there was a shooting not far from the clinic and the patrol unit was responding to that situation when the burglary at the clinic occurred.

"I know you guys have been trying, but it's not enough," someone said. "How can we work if we don't feel safe? Why don't we build a fence around the clinic? That way nobody can get through."

"Or at least a wall on the side with the accessible window?" another person chimed in. "And it can't be that much to install burglar bars on all the windows."

Others began saying that they wanted a police officer stationed at the front of the building with signs posted that the facility was under 24/7 watch. We also needed to get the word out that this was now a totally secure facility. They came back to the idea of the fence—if the city wouldn't pay for it, we should ask donors to chip in.

Then the door to the room opened. In walked one of the clinic managers, who'd been assessing the damage with the police.

She was carrying a plastic bag. "I want to show you something," she said, as she began taking out sandwiches that looked half-eaten and a half dozen empty Tupperware containers. "These were just outside the staff fridge. So far, food looks like the only thing the thieves took."

"They ate our old lunches?" someone said, incredulous. "Who knows how old this food is. They must have been real hungry."

The manager nodded. "So far, we don't think they took anything else," she continued. "They went through our drawers and tossed everything everywhere, then they ate the leftover food. From the security footage, it looks like it was a couple of teens. They came in looking for something to eat."

The room was silent. I thought about how desperate these kids had to be. They committed a crime by breaking and entering. They made a mess and ransacked staff belongings. But how hungry must they have been to go into a fridge and eat old leftover food?

"These kids—they are also our patients. They are the people that we serve," I said.

"We can't build a fence," someone else said. "What kind of message would we be sending to the community? The people we'd be keeping out are the same people we're trying to serve."

"It's not the first time we've been robbed, and it's not the last time," another person chimed in. "We need to keep our staff and our patients safe, but we also need to keep making our clinic the safe place for the community."

There were nods around the room. There was no more mention of a fence. Instead, the staff came up with the idea of a community gathering. Our patients and members of the community knew about the burglaries. They'd seen the police tape around the clinic, and they saw the break-ins on the news. They said they wanted to help, and we were going to give them a way to do that.

Later that week, we held a "Day of Service and Celebration" at Eastern. The staff cleaned up, painting over damaged areas and decorating the hallways with children's art. They also planted small trees. We provided games, healthy snacks, and music for members of the community, who stopped by to thank the staff for their service. Patients and their family members came to tell our staff how much their work mattered.

We stressed one of our core principles: that violence is a public health issue and should be treated as such. It is something that can be prevented, and it's our job to understand the root causes and make the changes that we can. And because this was yet another opportunity to reach people where they were with our messaging, we also trained people to administer naloxone, taught the ABCs of Safe Sleep, tested children for lead poisoning, and hosted other public health outreach activities.

"We know that the break-ins at Eastern have been unsettling and traumatic," I wrote to the staff afterward. "We have increased security procedures, but we stay true to our goal that we are here to serve the community. There are a few who have hurt our operation. But we do not stop providing needed services to our children and families. Eastern plays an invaluable role in our community, and today, the residents are celebrating the work that you all do every day."

Eastern is now in a new building. Thanks to concerted fundraising efforts and the strong support of the community, the clinic offers enhanced services to treat more children and families. The new building has additional security to protect medications and equipment, but no wall or fence. The health center continues to be a gathering place for the community, where all are welcome.

I'VE OFTEN THOUGHT BACK TO the moment when the clinic manager told us about the half-eaten sandwiches. It was a major turning point. The staff who were so angry at the thieves and denounced them as perpetrators suddenly saw them as people in need of care themselves. That realization completely changed their attitude.

As one of our staff said so poignantly, "It's hurt people who hurt people." This was the basis of the trauma-informed care training sessions that we began doing for frontline city employees. Instead of the first perception of someone as a problem to be dealt with, could we see that they are often victims of trauma themselves? Can we understand

the full cycle using public health principles, that violence perpetuates
trauma and trauma perpetuates violence?

At one of the first trauma training sessions that took place at the city's
War Memorial building, a homeless man walked in. He was directed
to leave but refused to, and he became increasingly agitated. He threatened that he had a weapon. Police were called.

Then the organizer of the session started talking to the man and
learned that he had a history of mental illness. He was a veteran, seeking refuge on a cold day in a building that celebrated military service
and doubled as a homeless shelter on extreme cold weather days. When
he was stopped and refused entry, he became angry and frustrated.

The attendees were initially upset that this interloper had interrupted
their day. But just as our staff had their lightbulb moment, when they
learned the veteran's story, they saw him in a different light. People who
were angry that the police weren't called sooner were now saying to the
officers that they could leave. They saw that this gentleman shouldn't be
handcuffed and arrested. He needed their compassion and support. The
organizer, together with the attendees (who were all city employees),
helped him find shelter and connected him with a mental health provider.

Understanding the links between trauma and violence helped our
staff approach their work differently. Many of them became aware of the
trauma that they experienced in their own work. Teachers spoke about
the difficulty of instructing children who couldn't pay attention because
they were hungry, scared, and didn't know whether they'd have a home
to return to. Police officers described the no-win position they found
themselves in, as they were told to stop using tactics they'd long known
but didn't have new ones. They talked about the difficulty of dealing
with mental health and homelessness—issues they hadn't trained for but
were now part of their job.

"When you're a hammer, everything's a nail" was a sentiment we
heard expressed many times over. Our employees' frustrations were similar to those I faced working in the ER. They could see that they needed
to do better for the people they served, but they needed the tools to do so.
For many of them, the trauma training gave them the opening to express
their long-pent-up feelings. This was a safe space to open Pandora's box.

They had to be able to talk about their problems in order to come up with solutions. The training also provided tools to assist city employees in de-escalating conflict and connecting to existing resources. In time, the city council would pass a bill to require trauma-informed care trainings for all city workers, making Baltimore the first major city in America to do so. The legislation was named the Elijah Cummings Healing City Act.

In the meantime, the conversations around trauma spurred agencies to pilot interventions to better equip their staff. Under the leadership of Commissioner Kevin Davis, the police department started homeless outreach teams, so that specially trained officers would respond to calls involving individuals experiencing homelessness. In the past, these people may have been arrested for trespassing; now they received specific services to help them with what they needed. Commissioner Davis, like his predecessor, also supported our programs to treat addiction as a disease and helped champion naloxone distribution and diversion programs like LEAD.

We worked with the school system to develop curricula that focused on developing resilience. As one of our trauma experts said, "Trauma is like a rubber band being stretched and stretched. We need to get the spring back and become more resilient. That's what will help people regain control." A number of schools started healing circles and instituted meditation programs. We obtained a federal grant to create a pilot program called Dating Matters, which taught students about healthy relationships as a way to build resiliency.

None of these programs is a panacea, but together they helped change the orientation of our city toward greater empathy and understanding. Baltimore is a city where so many have experienced trauma and violence. We can't change the circumstances of the past, but we can change how we face the future and treat one another.

VIOLENCE AND TRAUMA ARE INTIMATELY linked. That they are both health issues was never in dispute for me. Growing up, I saw neighbors and my own family who were the victims of violence and who suffered health consequences because of gunshot wounds and physical assault. I still have a paradoxical reaction to nice weather: sunshine and warmth means more violence and crime. I didn't have the words for it, but I certainly understood trauma and the gaping wounds it leaves.

In my medical training, I came to understand violence as the cause of the suffering I was there to ameliorate as an emergency physician. I got skilled at the medical treatment for broken bones, facial fractures, lacerations, and stabbings. I ran "code traumas" when patients came in with severe gunshot wounds. I knew the protocols to stop the bleeding, repair the injuries, and save lives.

This was what I thought was my role: to fix the damage of the injury inflicted by violence. Then two things occurred. One was a Florida law, passed when I was in my residency, that forbade doctors from asking patients about gun ownership. This was not a question that I routinely asked my patients, but it seemed to be a reasonable one, especially for pediatricians to ask parents. After all, pediatricians ask parents about the accessibility of other potentially hazardous substances, such as medications, liquor, and cleaning supplies. That the government would censor physicians was an egregious intrusion into medical practice.

The Florida law also made me think about the role that physicians could play in preventing gun violence in the first place. Of all women killed by firearms in the United States, half died at the hands of an intimate partner. The majority of gun deaths are due to suicide. Doctors screen patients for many risks and exposures; wasn't it also our job to ask about firearm safety? This wasn't about restricting people's right to own firearms but rather about providing education to prevent injury and death.

My second introduction to violence prevention as a public health issue was a pilot program of "violence interruption" at my hospital. The concept was that violence often begets violence, an idea very similar to "it's hurt people who hurt people." The same person who is a victim of violence today is more likely to be a perpetrator of it tomorrow. A patient who comes into the ER with an injury now may well be seeking retaliation once he leaves. Or he may be the victim of another violent injury later. But while this person is in the ER, we can intervene and offer resources to prevent or make less likely another violent injury.

I was fascinated when I learned about this program. I'd just treated a patient in his late teens with three gunshot wounds to the chest. When I examined him, I saw scars across his abdomen. He'd been to the same ER just a few months earlier for another gunshot wound. I remembered another patient who had been punched in the face and came back to the ER on my same shift with fractures in his hand for assaulting someone else. If we were to think about these patients in the same way as we thought about patients coming in for overdose and addiction, could we also intervene and offer them "treatment" that would prevent the subsequent acts of violence?

The pilot program was just beginning when I finished my residency in Boston. By the time I arrived in Baltimore years later, I learned that a physician at Maryland's Shock Trauma Hospital, Carnell Cooper, had started a similar initiative that "begins in the hospital and thrives in the community." Patients are approached to participate when they are still in the hospital. Once they are discharged, case managers continue to help them with the resources they need, such as mental health and addiction support, housing, employment, or other social services.

This program identified participants who were already the victims of violent injury. Going further "upstream" was to prevent people from injury in the first place. Such a program was being run by my own health department. Learning about the program and working with its employees would be some of my most treasured moments from my time in Baltimore.

Based on a national model called "Cure Violence" that was first started in Chicago, Baltimore's "Safe Streets" program began with the premise that violence is a contagious illness, just like measles or the flu. Just like these infectious diseases, it is spread from person to person. Its effects can be treated; it can even be prevented.

Instead of intervening only after a violent injury has occurred, Safe Streets employed outreach workers and "violence interrupters" to break cycles of violence and stop shootings before they happened. The program's staff came from the communities they served, and included many who had been recently released from incarceration.

Lamont Medley was an outreach worker in the Sandtown-Winchester neighborhood, where Freddie Gray lived, at a Safe Streets site that we ran in collaboration with Catholic Charities. Like many of his peers, Lamont had been involved in gangs and drugs from the time he was ten. He was trying to provide for his siblings.

"It was rough trying to take care of myself and provide stuff we needed," he told a reporter from the *Washington Post*. "The only thing that I saw was negativity: robbing, stealing. Selling drugs, that was the avenue that I took."

Lamont went to jail for eleven years for attempted murder, but upon his release he became a violence interrupter, delivering a message to young people in the community that there are alternatives to shootings.

The key to the violence interrupters' effectiveness is that they've walked in the shoes of the people they're working with and are perceived already as leaders in their community. If well-meaning health department employees were to walk the streets of Baltimore and try to do this work, they wouldn't know where to start. On the other hand, these Safe Streets men (and they were mostly men) knew their neighborhood. They knew who had a "beef" with whom. They already had deep relationships and could build others based on their own credibility and trust. If they saw a conflict brewing, they could work to de-escalate it, with the goal of breaking cycles of violence and stopping shootings before they happened.

This evidence-based approach was proving to be effective. In 2017, Safe Streets staff mediated nearly a thousand conflicts. An independent review found that 80 percent of those conflicts would otherwise have been likely or very likely to result in gun violence. Three of four sites had gone a year or longer without a firearm homicide, at a time when gun deaths nearly doubled in the city as a whole.

In the aftermath of a shooting, Safe Streets workers would organize community members to protest the impact of gun violence, changing the local norms of gun carrying and use. Safe Streets staff would also connect at-risk youth to a wide variety of services, including job train-ing, education, mentorship, housing, and family support. Researchers at Johns Hopkins University have called Safe Streets one of the most effective public safety interventions in the last decade.

Despite the evidence, Safe Streets faced continuous funding insta-bility. Like many of the health department's programs, it was initially started with federal grants and private philanthropy, with the under-standing that if it were shown to be effective, the entities that stand to benefit—namely state and local government—would take over the financial responsibility. However, when a federal grant was due to end in 2016, we had no commitment from the city or from the state govern-ment to sustain the program.

Our team had been trying to build the case for Safe Streets. We arranged for local and national reporters to shadow our outreach work-ers. News shows and documentary teams profiled the violence inter-rupters and helped to tell their inspiring stories. We also provided hard data from economic projections. A single gunshot injury would result in medical costs of at least $100,000. One involving the spinal cord would be at least $500,000. A fatal shooting would cost society at least $1 million in terms of lost economic productivity. The total cost of operations for one Safe Streets site was just $500,000 a year, but given the dozens, if not hundreds, of shootings that were prevented, surely this was a sound financial investment.

In the end, this argument helped to secure the funding we needed from the city, though it was a bruising fight. I put forward the eye-popping statistic that the entire amount the city budgeted to the health department was less than what was allocated just for over-time for police officers. Surely, our Safe Streets work should be consid-ered to be public safety as well—and what a cost-effective mechanism it is to prevent crime before it occurs!

We used a similar argument with the state, and after months of advo-cacy, the legislature set aside $1 million more to close the remaining gap as part of an $80 million budget deal. We thought we were in the clear. However, in the summer of 2016, Governor Larry Hogan vetoed the entire measure. Our program had just three weeks of funding left. If we could not find $1 million, we would have had to close all four sites and lay off sixty people.

I found out about the governor's decision the same way that our outreach workers did: through reading the *Baltimore Sun*. My team immediately gathered the employees for an emergency meeting. It was one of the most emotional meetings I'd ever attended. One violence interrupter described how he had just come from an intervention where he helped someone leave a gang. Another talked about the meaning of the work to him, how he was giving back to the community he once helped destroy.

For many of the men, this was their first and only job in the formal economy. They talked about the dignity of work. Some of them were yelling in frustration. Others openly cried. Here they were, out on the streets in some of the most dangerous jobs in the city, knowing that all around them were people with weapons. They were risking their lives every day, and they were making a difference—they could see it and feel it in the communities where they lived. Now everything they worked for could be gone, and they could lose their jobs.

"We've got criminal records, convictions, jail time," someone said. "What other job are we going to find? We're finally back with our families, paying child support and seeing our kids. What are we going to tell them?"

"Our work is more than a job," another person said. "It's changing the way of life for the community. It's a movement that's working. And now it could all be for nothing."

Some staffers wanted to know whether the money was being withdrawn due to recent controversies involving Safe Streets employees being arrested on criminal charges. This was not unexpected—one of the side effects of employing ex-offenders is the risk of recidivism. We had strict protocols in place to handle these cases, and our recidivism rate—just like the rates across the Cure Violence sites—was significantly lower than for other ex-offenders.

There had been some bad press coverage of the arrests a few months earlier, but I reassured our staff that this was not the main reason this time. I expressed to them my own shock and deep frustration, and I vowed that I would do whatever it took to secure the needed funding. "It's a privilege to work with you and to fight for you," I said. These guys were sticking out their necks every day; the least I could do was to stick out mine, too.

The problem was that my options were limited. The city budget had already been approved, and there was no appetite to reopen the process and find additional city dollars. Over the years, the private funders had chipped in so much for Safe Streets that they were at the end of their rope. The promise to them all along had been that once the program was proven to be effective, government funding would take over from the philanthropic contribution; we couldn't break that promise. The state legislators I called said they had already tried, and their main priority now was to get the entire $80 million budget back on the table, as numerous other high-priority programs were in jeopardy, too. The governor and the mayor had such a contentious relationship that a direct appeal from Mayor Rawlings-Blake was not likely to work.

There were no other options left. I decided to take an action that otherwise ran counter to my principles of working within the system: I chose to publicly call out the governor for this decision. With two and a half weeks to go before all of Safe Streets' programs had to stop, I wrote an op-ed for the *Daily Record* in which I called Governor Hogan's decision not to fund Safe Streets a "death sentence for a lifesaving program."

"What signal does jeopardizing this program send to our dedicated outreach workers, many of whom are former felons, about their value in improving our communities and about Maryland's commitment to supporting our neighborhoods?" I wrote. "What is our duty to support these credible messengers who come from the communities they serve, who are on the streets every day risking their lives to promote peace?"

My team sent the op-ed to our community partners and to local business leaders to urge them to contact the governor. Safe Streets workers and community activists organized rallies in Baltimore and Annapolis. They urged the governor to visit Baltimore, to walk the streets with the violence interrupters and see how effective the program is. They marched to the statehouse and rallied outside with impassioned pleas.

For a couple of media cycles, the news was dominated by public outcry over Governor Hogan's decision that would effectively end Safe Streets.

The backlash from the governor's office was swift. Through his surrogates, I heard that Governor Hogan took personal offense at the advocacy efforts, and he named me for directing them. I was accused of everything from hurting the governor's reelection chances to personal harassment for revealing the governor's "private home number." (During one of the rallies, someone gave out the number for the Office of the Governor—a publicly accessible number for citizen complaints.) I was told that I had irreversibly crossed a line, from being a doctor and public servant to being a partisan political figure. The governor's office called the mayor's staff and demanded a public apology from me.

All of this might have taught me the lesson to stay in my lane, except that I was certain in my conviction that this *was* my lane: to advocate for my staff and the people we served. And it worked. Governor Hogan must have heard from enough constituents that he realized this was a very small concession that could win positive publicity in the long run. At the annual meeting of state and local public officials later that week, his staff told me that he was going to be making an announcement that he would fund Safe Streets. "He'll be here in ten minutes with the cameras, and we expect you to thank him publicly," I was instructed.

The funding was not for the entire $1 million that we needed, but it was a win—and I was more than happy to offer my gratitude. Congressman Cummings, working with the rest of the Maryland congressional delegation, was able to secure the remaining funding from the Obama administration. Safe Streets would make it through another year. Our programs would continue. And our staff would maintain their jobs and their livelihoods.

Since then, I've spoken and written about addressing violence as a public health issue. There can be no doubt that it is a health issue, and treating it that way allows for treatment and prevention interventions to break the cycle of poverty, trauma, and violence.

To be sure, violence is not solely a public health issue. Stopping violence also requires collaboration with law enforcement. In the years that followed, I took issue with the "defund the police" movement because the terminology implied that law enforcement no longer had any role in public safety. Policing practices absolutely must be reformed, and police brutality itself is a public health issue, too. And I fully support reexamining the public safety budget so that programs like Safe Streets and other community supports can be funded in a way that recognizes their value in improving overall health and safety.

Yet I also knew how instrumental the police are in protecting the public. When our clinics were vandalized, our staff asked for police presence to protect them. When mental health outreach workers encounter patients who have firearms, they need the police to accompany them to do their work. Abolishing the police is not a practical solution, but reforming police work is—as is encouraging public health approaches to public safety.

In addition, much more needs to be done legislatively in light of mass shootings and other horrific acts. It is a travesty that for decades federal agencies had been prevented from doing research on gun violence prevention, and that widely supported measures like universal background checks are stalled by the gun lobby.

But just as with any other issue, we can all do what is in our power. Cities and states can reexamine their budgets to have a broader conception of public safety. Effective local programs like Safe Streets can thus receive the funding they need. Culture change within the police department can occur, as I saw for myself with our naloxone work, LEAD, and trauma-informed care training.

12

Going Upstream

On a hot summer evening, Wilbert Carter had five drinks before picking up his two-year-old daughter, Leasia. He strapped her into her car seat and drove home. A few hours later, around midnight, his friends came by to go back out on the town. They dropped him off at seven a.m. the next morning and he slept until four p.m. When he woke up, Leasia's mother asked him where their daughter was. Wilbert hadn't seen her since he first strapped her into the car seat, some sixteen hours earlier. He went to his car and found her there. She was unconscious. In the ER, she was pronounced dead from heatstroke and second-degree burns.

Zaray Gray was one and a half years old when he was brought to the ER with multiple injuries. His mother's boyfriend, Francois Browne, had taken him out to play and claimed that Zaray had fallen down a sliding board, bumping his head and back. In the ER, doctors found that the child had bruises across his face, chin, neck, and mouth. His left collarbone was broken, and he had multiple internal injuries including tearing of his bowels that was consistent with forceful blows to the abdomen.

Zaray died from his injuries. After Francois was arrested, police found that he had been charged and convicted for the death of another child, his seven-month-old biological son. He had been sentenced to fifteen years but was released after two years and eleven months. The death of Zaray was his second arrest for child abuse and homicide in five years.

One of the most important and difficult parts of my job was to chair a monthly meeting of the Child Fatality Review (CFR) committee. Established by state law to allow for interagency data sharing, CFR mandates a review of every child death in Baltimore. Some are accidental injuries: a house fire, a drowning, a stray bullet. Some are the consequence of neglect and abuse, as in the cases of Leasia and Zaray, which received public attention in the local news (CFR proceedings are confidential; all details provided here are from news reports).

CFR meetings began with introductions. Around the table were representatives from the health department, social services, city schools, police, juvenile services, state's attorney's office, medical examiner, and other relevant government agencies and nonprofit groups that may have been involved in the child's or the family's care. After reviewing the progress of action items from the previous month, I'd read the first case description: the circumstances of the child's life and where and with whom he or she lived, what happened on or leading up to the day of the death, how the authorities were notified, and what medical services were delivered. I'd then call on the other agency representatives who would provide, in turn, the information they had.

One striking theme was how, in nearly every case, multiple agencies had already been involved in the child's care. The health department and our partners may have provided home visiting services when the mother was pregnant with that child. Over the years, social services may have come to the family home. A student may have been struggling in school and counselors became involved. Parents and siblings, and possibly the child himself, may have had numerous encounters with the criminal justice system.

This is not to say that these agencies had been negligent in their care. CFR reminded me of the "mortality and morbidity" reviews conducted by hospitals to discuss cases resulting in patient harm and/or death. Very rarely was a single mistake responsible for the tragic consequence. Much more likely, a series of signs were missed by several individuals, and multiple decisions were made that, in hindsight, led to the unfortunate outcome. This is the "Swiss cheese model," where the patient fell through the holes and missed being caught by all the safety nets.

The purpose of mortality and morbidity reviews is not to punish or assign blame but to fix the system; similarly, in CFR our goal was to figure out what we could learn from these cases to prevent tragic outcomes in the future. As chair, I made sure that we spent the time to review each case but that we didn't linger on the circumstances of the tragedy. The point of the gathering was to identify specific action items and determine which agency would take the lead to implement them.

During my time as chair, we would identify dozens of interventions to prevent future harm. Following Leasia's death, we implemented a public education campaign about heat deaths in cars. We held a press conference where we parked a car on the pavement in front of the health department and placed a thermometer inside to demonstrate how quickly the temperature would rise. On a sunny 70-degree day, the temperature inside a car could reach 104 degrees within half an hour. If the temperature outside reached 100 degrees, a car parked in direct sunlight could heat up to 172 degrees. We broadcasted public service announcements about never leaving children or pets unattended in cars, and worked with local businesses to put up signs in their establishments. Because substance use was implicated in the circumstances around Leasia's death, we also raised awareness of our twenty-four-hour addiction and mental health hotline.

Through CFR, we also identified gaps in existing laws and regulations. Maryland law had required notification of local officials if someone is convicted of murdering a child. However, this notification was made only to local officials in the jurisdiction of the conviction, which meant that an offender who moved to another county would fall through the cracks. Advocates and lawmakers helped us to remedy this situation; a state law passed in 2018 now provides for the state health department and social services agencies to be notified if someone who has been convicted of murder, attempted murder, or manslaughter of a child becomes the parent of a newborn. This would flag more cases and allow social services to preemptively conduct home assessments and offer services.

Still, it would not have helped Zaray, because his mother's boyfriend was not his birth parent and the law only matches court records with birth records. To help identify such cases, we started an interagency program to share information about children deemed to be high-risk for abuse and neglect.

Another striking and heartbreaking theme from CFR was how the odds were already stacked against these children from the time they were born. Many had been exposed to substances in utero and came into the world experiencing symptoms of opioid withdrawal. They and their siblings often cycled through multiple households: maybe they initially stayed with their mother; then they went to a grandparent when the mother was deemed unable to care for them; then they went to their father, before being taken away due to concerns of abuse; then they went back to a grandparent and then back to the mother. For school-age children, this meant many different schools and poor academic performance as a consequence. Many children lived in households where multiple relatives had been arrested on domestic violence charges and where they witnessed assault, arrest, and death. Addiction and mental health issues in the immediate family were the norm, and some of the children themselves were diagnosed with depression and other behavioral health concerns from an early age.

These traumatic childhood events are called "adverse childhood experiences," or ACEs. Numerous studies have shown that children with high ACEs suffer not only from behavioral health issues but also from physical health problems. As adults, they are more likely to have substance use disorders themselves and to have higher rates of suicide. They are also more likely to have high blood pressure, diabetes, and heart disease and to die at an earlier age than those who were not similarly exposed to early childhood trauma.

In the cases of children we reviewed at CFR, I'd count the number of ACEs they had. Then, I'd count the number of ACEs their mothers had, and their fathers, and other caregivers. We wouldn't know all the circumstances of their lives, but even from what we knew, it was apparent that these children had been born into extremely challenging situations with multigenerational trauma—cycles of violence and trauma, addiction and mental illness, poverty and deep disparities.

It was our job to break these cycles and intervene wherever we could. The Swiss cheese model of medical error requires many component parts to go wrong and for the patient to pass through many systems where warning signs could have been detected. Of course, we can't fix every problem, and our interventions may still not work despite our best efforts.

There is a parable about public health that begins like this: Three friends are walking along a river with a very fast current. They see children floating by, screaming for help.

The first friend jumps in and tries to save the children one at a time. He rescues some, but many others stream past. The second friend runs upstream, where there is a dam. He starts to repair the dam. If he can fix it, the current will slow, allowing them to pull out more children. The third friend runs even further upstream. "Where are you going?" the first two call after him. "Come and help us here!"

"I'm going to see who's throwing in the kids in the first place," he answers.

This is the concept of going upstream, with the idea that the further you go to the root cause, the more problems can be prevented and the more lives you can save. It's a core principle of public health and one that I believe in deeply. Our field should be examining the causes of poor health, such as poverty and disparities; devoting our resources to focus on prevention; and transforming our sick-care system to a health-care system.

But I also feel strongly that if children are drowning, we have to try to save them now by fixing the dam. And when we come across children floating past, who desperately need our help, we have to do everything we can to pull them back onshore.

IN 2009, BALTIMORE HAD ONE of the worst infant mortality rates in the country. Babies born there were dying at the same rate as babies born in countries in the midst of civil war. Another shocking statistic is that an African American infant born in Baltimore was five times more likely to die in his or her first year of life than was the case for a white infant.

Under my predecessors Peter Beilenson and Josh Sharfstein, the Baltimore City Health Department had begun a public-private partnership that had grown to include more than 150 partners, from hospitals and insurers to neighborhood associations and churches. This program is called B'More for Healthy Babies and has multiple components. One essential component is screening and triaging every pregnant woman on Medicaid—fully half the pregnant women in the city. For those who are found to have the highest level of need, a nurse will visit them at home throughout their pregnancy and postpartum. Those with the next-highest level might have a social worker or community health worker check in on them and monitor their progress.

Participants in the home visitation programs receive resources tailored to their needs. Women with high-risk medical issues like preeclampsia and gestational diabetes receive home visits from nurses to monitor blood pressure and glucose levels. Because their job is to care for the woman and the family, the staff do more than just screen for the woman's physical health problems. When I accompanied the nurses on these home visits, I was struck by how many other needs they tended to. I watched one nurse point out that the flaking paint in the house could be ingested by the mother's two other young children. She got the kids tested for lead poisoning and enrolled the mother in a home lead remediation program. Another nurse recognized that the pregnant woman she was visiting was a victim of domestic violence. She was able to find safe shelter for the woman and her children.

When I started as health commissioner, we were experiencing an uptick in sleep-related infant deaths. Some of these cases were the dreaded sudden infant death syndrome (SIDS), where there is no clear cause identified. Others involved tragic but preventable circumstances. When we reviewed these cases in CFR, we found that what they all had in common was a consistently unsafe sleep environment. A baby suffocated between sofa cushions. Another died in a crib, facedown on stuffed animals. Yet another rolled beneath a sleeping adult.

We already had a program that taught the ABCs of Safe Sleep: Alone, on the Back, in a Crib, Don't smoke, no Exceptions. The program had been developed using national guidelines, with messages that were tailored to our communities in Baltimore. Now we needed to identify barriers to why the guidelines were not being implemented effectively.

One obvious barrier was a lack of awareness of the ABCs and how these guidelines often ran counter to existing cultural practices. I knew that in my own Chinese culture, co-sleeping is the norm and the expectation. As a baby, I was put to sleep on my belly, with the thought that if I were to gag, I'd throw up on the bed and not choke on the vomit. Many mothers in Baltimore shared this perception: it was common for mother and baby to sleep in the same bed with the baby facedown. If a mother did use a crib, she often loaded it with stuffed animals and padded it with crib bumpers, even though such practices have been correlated with SIDS.

The health department and our partners already had the campaign materials to teach the ABCs of Safe Sleep. We were already doing outreach in the community. But recognizing how ingrained these traditional practices were, we knew we had to do a lot more. Every interaction with a mother needed to become a point of education and intervention.

The B'More for Healthy Babies team attended grand rounds for obstetricians, pediatricians, family practice doctors, and internists at every local hospital. Our request was for every waiting room to display the ABCs poster and that the doctors show an informational video to their patients. We also emphasized that while this information was most relevant to expecting and new parents, it was also important to educate the extended family. Grandparents were often caregivers, and we wanted to empower other loved ones to speak up if they saw an unsafe situation.

We also worked with our outreach team so that every home visit included a review of the family's sleeping arrangements, followed by a conversation with the extended family to ensure that everyone understood the rationale. Outreach workers also went to churches, community fairs, and neighborhood block parties to spread the message.

It was critical for patients to receive this information from a variety of sources. Some patients might listen most to their medical providers. Others would find the most credible messenger to be someone from their community. One of our most effective campaigns featured a local woman whose baby had died. It was impossible not to be moved by her story and how the experience inspired her to prevent other mothers from suffering a similar loss.

Child health was one of Mayor Rawlings-Blake's priorities, and she lent us the power of her office to ask other city agencies to join us in promoting safe sleep. Our posters went up in social service offices, WIC locations, senior centers, and parks. We worked with the district and circuit courts so that while people were waiting for jury duty or to have legal matters processed, they would watch a video about infant safe sleep. (We also included the naloxone "Don't Die" materials, too—another public health practice that empowered community members to save lives.)

I was gratified every time I went to a medical appointment and saw these posters. The ABCs of Safe Sleep was one of my most memorable moments when I gave birth myself. Just minutes before the birth of my son, a nurse rushed in and told me that I needed to watch the video. It was part of the hospital's protocol, she said, and she was very sorry that she'd forgotten. She knew I was uncomfortable but could I watch it soon? I don't think she expected such a positive and enthusiastic response from her patient!

We also ramped up other support programs for new mothers. As I learned for myself later, breastfeeding is not an intuitive skill for many women. We increased our lactation support programs and made available lactation counselors, one of whom would be of immeasurable help to me when I struggled in the early days after my son's birth.

We also started a program to provide free cribs, which in turn taught us an unexpected lesson. Our home visitors did a survey after the cribs were delivered and discovered that there had been no change in sleeping habits: the baby was still co-sleeping or in another unsafe environment. When the home visitor looked for the crib, it was often found tucked away behind a couch or in a basement, in the box and unopened.

The reason? Each crib had been delivered in a flat pack and required tools for assembly. This was a solvable problem. Going forward, when we delivered a crib, we also sent someone to assemble it. It was a basic intervention, but it met people where they were and made all the difference to the family.

The result of these initiatives was dramatic: within seven years, the infant mortality rate in Baltimore dropped by 38 percent. That's equivalent to fifty babies each year that would have died in 2009 who were able to be alive in 2016. For three years in a row, we achieved record reductions in sleep-related infant deaths.

Because we had the additional metric of health equity, we also measured the change in racial disparities. We were particularly proud of this result: within that same time frame, we cut the disparity between African American and white infant mortality by more than half.

Other cities have come to visit us and ask about the reasons B'More for Healthy Babies succeeded. A key factor is the broad coalition of partners focused on the single goal of reducing infant mortality. Prior to this program, each of the 150 partners was working on their own initiatives. This program aligned them to one evidence-based strategy and one shared goal that's as objective as it gets. Though the strategy was set by the city, the delivery is not just by the health department or other city agencies: the expectation is that all partners are part of the effort together.

Another factor in the program's success is that although the initial strategy was rooted in evidence, leaders accepted the need to pivot when the frontline staff identified barriers to implementation. We established and embraced processes to troubleshoot and change the strategy along the way. What we did not change was the unrelenting focus on the public health principles of using credible messengers and going to where people are. But we were eager to solicit the ongoing input of our staff, our partners, and the families we served so we could be nimble and do whatever was needed to meet our goal.

B'More for Healthy Babies is a classic example of an upstream intervention. The focus is on starting as early as possible, at birth and even before a child is born. That way, we try to break the cycles of poverty and poor health and give each newborn every chance from the earliest age.

EARLY IN MY TENURE AS health commissioner, I had lunch with Bob Embry, the head of the Abell Foundation. Bob was in his eighties and a revered city leader, having served in just about every capacity from housing commissioner some forty years earlier to president of the state board of education. Bob, through the Abell Foundation, was a generous contributor to the health department's work and was a lead funder for B'More for Healthy Babies and various school health projects, along with many other initiatives.

Bob's reputation preceded him. He had requested the lunch, and I knew that he had an agenda.

We were shown to our table. Before I could sit down and unfold my napkin, Bob had started. "Glasses," he said. "Doc, let's talk about glasses."

And talk we did. Bob shared with me a study that his foundation had sponsored, which found that as many as ten thousand school-age children in Baltimore needed eyeglasses but weren't getting them. And why not? Maryland law requires children in public schools to get vision screening in prekindergarten, first grade, and eighth grade. There was a long gap in between when problems can emerge. Medicaid pays for eye exams, but many families were not taking their children for these screenings.

I remember my own struggles with vision. I must have already had vision problems in China but just didn't realize it. In fourth grade, I remember having to squint to see the blackboard. My spoken English wasn't great and I didn't want to get called on, so I sat in the front of the class only for math—the one subject where I knew I'd excel. For the other classes, I tried my best to listen to keep up. An astute teacher noticed this and brought it to my mother's attention. Learning a new language was hard enough; I could only imagine how much longer it would have taken me to catch up in school if I had an undiagnosed vision problem.

In addition to the gap in screening, the Abell study also found that fewer than 20 percent of those students who were screened as needing glasses were actually getting them. The report identified numerous barriers, including lack of transportation, caregivers not being able to leave work, and lack of insurance. Another major problem was that the information about the child's vision difficulties was not reaching the parents because the school did not have accurate phone numbers and mailing addresses for many families.

I was astounded. "Wow," I said. "I'm all for research, but I don't think I need a study to tell me that if our children can't see, they can't learn. Then they can't read, and may even be labeled as being disruptive and held back in school."

"They could end up in gangs and be in trouble, and it could all have been prevented with a pair of glasses," he said.

We both knew that glasses were no panacea for the panoply of other problems that these young people were facing. But this was a solvable problem, and one that was in our control to figure out.

"If you can get this program going," Bob said, "I'll help you find the money for it."

Not long after the lunch, the Freddie Gray unrest occurred. It took me several months after that to regroup and to come back to this, but Bob's words were never far from my mind—in part because Bob is omnipresent in Baltimore, and he'd remind me about "Glasses!" every time I saw him. By the fall of 2015, I found another fantastic partner in Ron Daniels, the president of Johns Hopkins University, who was eager to deploy the university's many resources to this effort.

The program began to take shape. The goal was straightforward: to provide vision screenings for every child in every grade, K–8, in every public school in Baltimore. If the screening turned up the need for additional exams, we'd provide the exam; if the child needed glasses, he or she would choose the frames and get the glasses. This would be done free of charge and, importantly, right in the schools through a mobile van, so that the students wouldn't have to miss school and parents and caregivers wouldn't have to miss work.

As with every new program, there were a number of bureaucratic hurdles to overcome. The health department already had vision screeners, but we needed to hire more to account for the greater workload—a daunting task given the city's antiquated human-resources bureaucracy. We needed to enlist additional partners to provide the eye exam equipment and the van. We had to work with Medicaid and private insurance companies to figure out reimbursement, and to connect students to insurance when they qualified but had not yet signed up.

Thankfully, there was a national nonprofit, Vision to Learn, that was starting to run pilot programs in other jurisdictions, and we brought them in as partners. Warby Parker signed on to provide the glasses. The Abell Foundation, Annie E. Casey Foundation, and Johns Hopkins contributed significant funding, and together we raised $3.5 million from local and national philanthropists and foundations to kick off the program.

Gabe Auteri was finishing his Baltimore Corps fellowship year when it came time to get this project off the ground. I assigned him to coordinate the work of the various partners, finalize the donations, and launch the program. He did an outstanding job. Within a year, we were fully operational in ten schools and had given out a thousand pairs of glasses. Gabe laid out the legal and partnership framework for the program so that it could be scaled up to provide eye screenings—and, if needed, glasses—to every student in every Baltimore public school within three years.

Gabe could always be counted on to lighten the mood. He and Mike Fried, our CIO, brainstormed names for the glasses program. A top contender was Glasses Half Full; another was Sight for Sore Eyes. Eventually, we settled on a less groan-inducing name, Vision for Baltimore.

Word of the program spread quickly, and a dozen other cities soon began similar initiatives. Vision for Baltimore was widely covered in the national media as an example of a replicable public-private partnership with a lasting impact on children's lives.

One of my favorite moments was when *PBS NewsHour* came to Baltimore to film the students receiving glasses for the first time. The producer was looking for the "aha" moment. How great would it be to capture the look on a kid's face who is seeing clearly for the first time!

I was with the camera crew when an eight-year-old girl came to be fitted for her new pink frames. She'd chosen the color herself and seemed excited to get the glasses.

She put them on, and the producer asked her if she saw a difference. The cameras turned to her. Maybe this was the moment!

She said no. The producer held up a book from about a foot away. She was asked to read a page, first without glasses. She read slowly, haltingly. She squinted, moved closer to the book, then tried again.

"Now, can you put on your new glasses and try again?" the producer asked her.

She donned her new glasses and read again. This time, she had no pauses.

"So, do you see a difference?"

The girl looked straight into the camera. "No," she said.

"Are you sure?" the producer persisted. "I think you read a lot better the second time."

She shrugged. She wasn't impressed.

This was not the made-for-TV moment the crew was hoping for. But off camera, to the side of the crew, was one of our employees, who had worked in school health for more than twenty years. She had tears running down her face. She could see the better future this girl would have—all because she got a pair of glasses.

That's the power of public health, when one small intervention can change the trajectory of someone's life. It doesn't have to be the most high-tech, complex solution; in fact, when there is low-hanging fruit, we can and should start there. It isn't solving the problem of who is throwing kids into a river, but it is repairing a part of the dam and giving students a life raft before they are swept up by a rising tide.

I WAS ONCE ON A panel where everyone was asked this question: If we were given millions of dollars, where would we invest it? I didn't have to think long before I gave my answer: I'd spend it all on school health.

In Baltimore, more than four out of every five public school students qualified for free or reduced-fee lunch, just as I had as a child. For thousands of children, their school meals are their only guaranteed source of food. This factor was top of mind for me when I declared weather emergencies: I knew that the consequence of school closures was that thousands of children would go hungry.

On any given day, hundreds of Baltimore's students experienced homelessness. I knew what it was like myself, and how hard it is to focus on school when you don't know where you will be sleeping that night. I recalled my mother talking about the difficulty of teaching students who were distracted by so many other life problems. Just as I felt in the ER, when I thought I couldn't open Pandora's box by asking certain questions, teachers also feel helpless when they simply don't have the tools to assist students with what they need.

School health is one way to address these problems. Every Baltimore public school had a school health clinic that provided a basic level of care, such as first aid and general health education. The health department provided a nurse aide or a nurse to staff every clinic. Fourteen schools had a higher level of care, with a nurse practitioner or physician on staff, who could diagnose and treat routine medical conditions.

There were huge unmet health needs among our student population. If there could be such abysmal numbers and many barriers to obtain something as basic as glasses, one can imagine how many other supports our children needed.

During my time in Baltimore, we started two additional school-based health centers that provided more comprehensive health services, including treatment for asthma and other chronic conditions. We began a pilot program in telemedicine, to see if this could allow clinics to have increased access to specialty medical services, without a child having to miss school. And recognizing the critical importance of mental health, we expanded mental health services to more than 120 schools.

While I'm proud of these innovations and program expansions, I wish we could have done more. Imagine if school health clinics were also staffed by a social worker to assist children and their families. Imagine if the school-based health centers were a hub for medical services not only for the student but also for the entire family. Imagine if every child could be screened for trauma and receive the care he or she needs, before there was the need for a serious mental health intervention.

Not every school district will have these needs, but in places like Baltimore, such services could have a transformative impact on the child, the entire family, and generations to come. Yet it was extremely difficult to raise funds for these additional services. Baltimore was not alone in this; around the country, budget priorities are tailored toward the end of the line instead of early upstream interventions.

Even finding funding to sustain existing programs like B'More for Healthy Babies was a struggle. One year, we had to use salary savings from vacant positions in order to backfill funding. Another year, we secured money from the state legislature, only to have the governor refuse the allocation when it was withheld for Safe Streets—and unlike Safe Streets, this funding never did come through. Luckily, our foundation partners stepped in to fill the gap in the nick of time. But this is not a lasting or sustainable solution, and I often think about how much more could be done for our children if only we had the resources to do so. What more could our staff be doing if they didn't spend all their time fundraising for a program that had proven many times over to be effective and efficient?

ALCOHOL HAS LONG BEEN A public health hazard, but not long after my arrival in Baltimore, we received notice of a new substance, powdered alcohol, that would soon be available for sale. Health experts across the country were sounding the alarm: this tasteless, odorless substance could be combined with alcohol to make it far more potent. It could even be mixed into soft drinks and given as a date-rape drug.

My team and I rallied state and local leaders to ban powdered alcohol in Maryland before it ever came to market. Two weeks into our public education campaign, the state comptroller used his authority to do that, and the state legislature followed by passing a bill banning the substance a month later.

We sounded a similar warning about synthetic marijuana, which was not marijuana at all but rather dried chemicals sprayed onto plants. "Taking these substances is like playing Russian roulette," I testified to the city council, which subsequently voted to ban the sale of these substances to protect young people in Baltimore.

We also convinced the city council to pass legislation mandating more stringent inspection for lead in toys and lowering the acceptable level of lead to protect Baltimore's children against lead poisoning. I joined my fellow health officers in Maryland to champion increasing the smoking age to twenty-one, which passed in the state legislature after several years of advocacy.

Then there were the battles we lost. One of the hardest-fought was to place warning labels on sugar-sweetened beverages. A number of advocacy groups like Sugar Free Kids Maryland and the American Academy of Pediatrics had urged this action to help combat childhood obesity. I saw the necessity in my clinical practice as well. It used to be that I treated obesity only in adults, but it was now routine to see eight-year-old children who weighed two hundred pounds, and young people suffering from diseases like high blood pressure and type 2 diabetes that used to affect only adults.

In Baltimore City, one in three high schoolers have obesity. One in four school-age children drink one or more sodas every day, which science has shown is the major preventable cause of childhood obesity. Physical activity is important, as is changing other food habits, but cutting down on the empty calories in soda is the single most consequential nutrition change that will improve children's health.

In 2016, my team and I consulted community groups to ask what intervention they would consider most helpful to reduce the consumption of soda. They suggested that we start with requiring warning labels to be displayed where sodas are sold. The city couldn't mandate labels directly on the bottles or cans, but we could require small labels on vending machines and store refrigerators. The idea was to "nudge" consumers to make healthier choices. Similar legislation had already passed in San Francisco.

Parent groups were particularly motivated, because they wanted to counter the disproportionate soda advertising targeted to communities of color and poor neighborhoods. For us, it was about fairness and public education. Why should our children be the only ones to see advertisements featuring sports stars and celebrities drinking soda, without being given the facts about the medical problems attributed to sugary drinks?

The beverage industry came out in force to lobby against the bill, spending more than $3 million, according to one independent estimate. The Baltimore City Council hearings were packed with workers from nearby Pepsi and Coke plants who claimed that they would lose their jobs should the bill pass. The lobbyist talked about how this bill was a waste of time in a city that should focus on its homicide problem. (This was a classic argument: don't look over here at this problem, look over there.) The beverage companies contacted community groups and offered sizable donations in exchange for withdrawing their support. They mobilized local businesses, who initially expressed no opposition to the bill but then began to submit testimony about the impact on their sales.

This was my first time facing the lobbying power of big moneyed interests. I admit I was naïve. I vastly underestimated the opponent and thought we could win because of community support and because the facts were so clearly on our side. I also thought this bill wasn't that big of a deal. What we were pushing for wasn't a tax or a ban—it was a type of public education campaign to level the playing field of information. And it was just in Baltimore City. I should have realized that the industry would push back hard because they feared a slippery slope, but I had not anticipated that our grassroots volunteer educational campaign would be met with a sophisticated and extremely well-financed operation.

Despite the vocal support of more than two thousand community residents, public health leaders, and doctors, the bill failed. It never made its way out of committee. On the day of the committee hearing, most members didn't show up. They were made various promises by the beverage industry, so they did what they could to make sure the bill didn't see the light of day without having to cast a "no" vote and anger their constituents. I understood the position they were in, but I was disappointed by their lack of courage on such a clear-cut issue.

I learned a lot from this failure. Two years later, the health department would introduce another bill about sugary drinks, this time to make the default drink in restaurant meals a healthy drink. Previously, kids' meals had soda as the default drink, and parents had to pay extra if they wanted their children to have milk or some other non-sugary drink. This bill would ensure that the default drink would be milk, pure fruit juice, or bottled water. Parents could still buy soda if they wished, but this would make the healthy choice the easy choice.

This time, our team knew what we would be up against. Kelleigh Eastman, who had helped drive our legislative campaign the first time around as a special assistant and Baltimore Corps fellow, stayed on as director of special projects and served as our lead again. She and my legislative director, Jeff Amoros, made sure that we spent months putting the pieces in place before our plans became known to the beverage industry. We had already implemented a policy for city agencies to start healthy vending, which included non-sugar-sweetened drinks, and received no pushback or decrease in sales. We had already worked with major restaurant chains and small businesses to change their default drinks, voluntarily, and they were ready to testify that this had had no negative impact on their bottom line. We had secured public commitments from key legislators and community leaders, and the mayor and key city council members were ready to stand behind the bill.

This time, our bill passed out of committee and through the city council with minimal drama. The beverage industry still came out in opposition, but the companies could see that they weren't going to win.

At the bill signing, I thanked the mayor and the city council. "Thank you for doing the right thing this time around," I said. "This legislation is about the public's health. It's about our children's health."

It was also about recognizing what I had seen through our work in Baltimore many times over: that choice is predicated on privilege. While I believe in empowering people and all of us doing what we can to improve our own health, personal responsibility is not the only factor that determines health and well-being. As policy makers, we have a societal responsibility to break systemic barriers and provide the information and the access that will enable all people to make the best choices for their health.

Our legislative, educational, and service work to improve children's health demonstrates the necessary role of local government: to go to where people are, to bring the community together, and to respond to residents' needs. Young people are not problems to be solved; they are why we do what we do. We go upstream, and we intervene midstream and downstream, too, wherever we can.

13

New Beginnings

In 2017, the landscape shifted in three major ways. Each had a profound impact on the health department's ongoing work.

One was the start of Mayor Catherine Pugh's tenure. My team and I quickly figured out the new mayor's priority issues, and we focused our attention on framing how public health tied to those areas and finding the best messengers to deliver the message to her. We worked with her transition team to call attention to how public health was instrumental in every aspect of their work.

I had anticipated that the mayoral transition would be the most significant change from the 2016 elections, but I was wrong. Like many others, I did not anticipate Donald J. Trump's victory over Hillary Clinton in the presidential election. I was looking forward to the prospect of an immensely experienced woman, the first, becoming president of the United States. I felt certain that a Clinton administration would support the public health policies to which I was committed.

Just as I did for the city transition committees, I contributed my perspective on the needs of urban public health throughout the presidential campaign. I testified at the Democratic National Committee's platform drafting session on the opioid epidemic and maternal and child health, and I made it clear that I would have just as happily contributed to any candidate's working group or testified to the Republican National Committee if I had been invited.

This, I thought, was the right role for me professionally: leading policy, aware of the political landscape, but clearly nonpartisan and willing to work with everyone. When Trump won the general election, I still had hope that the new administration could be convinced about the value of local public health. I gathered fellow health commissioners from around the country to write a letter to the presidential transition committee outlining a public health vision for the new administration. We made the case that public health was integral to national security and that upstream investments were more cost-efficient.

We never received a response. In the days after Trump's inauguration, we saw that his election was indeed earth-shattering, when one policy after another slashed our funding, prevented us from delivering key services, and negatively affected our residents' health and well-being.

REPRODUCTIVE HEALTH CARE WAS FIRST on the chopping block. The administration withdrew funding for the health department's program to prevent teen pregnancies, a withdrawal that would have removed access to sex education for twenty thousand young people in Baltimore. Our teen pregnancy prevention program had been successful in cutting teen birth rates by 61 percent, to its lowest point in decades, and its continued progress was being threatened.

Then there was the Trump administration's proposed change to the Title X program. Title X is a public health program established in the early 1970s, during the Nixon administration. Its purpose is to provide affordable reproductive health care like birth control and Pap smears to low-income women.

My health department oversaw the distribution of Title X funds to nearly two dozen clinics, including three we operated ourselves. When we learned that this program was likely to be dismantled, I asked all the local grantees to come together and discuss our next steps. The potential impact on our city was significant: one in three women in Baltimore depended on publicly funded health-care services to receive contraception and reproductive care. Of those served by Title X, 86 percent had incomes at or below the federal poverty line.

When my team and I reached out to the other Title X grantees, several had a common concern: they were hesitant to come to our meeting if Planned Parenthood was going to be there. We explained that nationally, Planned Parenthood health centers served 40 percent of all Title X patients; surely a conversation about Title X should involve the local affiliate. But leaders in hospital systems and community health centers pushed back.

"We need to have a nonpartisan health-care conversation," said one of the administrators, a respected local leader who was personally pro-choice. "The moment Planned Parenthood shows up, it's immediately about abortion and politics."

This was deeply concerning. Already, I was troubled by how women's reproductive care was increasingly singled out, stigmatized, and attacked. If Planned Parenthood was seen as too controversial—even in a city steeped in liberal politics like Baltimore—then reproductive health was at risk of becoming even more cut off from the rest of health care. I thought about my own patients in Baltimore, and the millions of women around the country who would lose their access to low-cost services for their health care.

Then there was the Trump administration's policy toward immigrants. In addition to the harsh rhetoric and actions directed against undocumented people, a new "public charge rule" targeted legal immigrants: if they were to use government-funded services like Medicaid and food assistance programs, their ability to remain in the country could be put in jeopardy. These were the services that my family had depended on, that had helped us get on our feet and enabled my parents to find permanent employment and my sister and me to pursue our education. I thought about what we would have done if this rule had been in place during my childhood. When my father had a hemorrhaging stomach ulcer, would we have gone to the hospital to save his life, knowing it could risk our future? Would we have chosen to go hungry, or to forgo our public education, if we thought it would hurt our chances of staying in the country? I couldn't help but imagine if family separation had been in place when we were going through our asylum application. Would I have been one of those children in cages, ripped away from my parents and denied basic care?

In the summer of 2017, the administration issued a "conscience clause" that was purportedly to protect the religious liberties of health professionals. But its true effect was to permit health professionals to deny care to specific groups of patients if they had objections to who they were. Patients could be denied surgery for a broken arm because they are transgender, or children not given vaccinations because they have same-sex parents.

This was tantamount to giving legal cover for discrimination. I worried about what it meant for those who already faced the greatest barriers to care. Women, minorities, and LGBTQ individuals, particularly those living in areas with few providers, could lose their sole source of care and be forced to forgo health care altogether.

I also worried about what these changes would mean for the nature of the healing professions. In medical school, I learned that a doctor's primary duty is to the patient. When there is a conflict, physicians are instructed that "the health and rights of the patient, who is in the more vulnerable position, must be given precedence." We doctors, nurses, and other health care professionals chose our field. Our patients can't choose when and how they become ill and, often, in which doctor's hands they might end up. It is our job—and our privilege—to take care of patients. We don't judge the people we serve. We don't allow our beliefs to override their needs. And we certainly don't deny lifesaving care.

When I was in medical school, I worked with an attending physician who consulted for the prison system. They would send him medical records to review for inmates seeking a transfer to a specialized medical facility. The transfers were highly coveted, as the medical facility had fewer restrictions and better amenities than the prison. My attending asked me to take a first pass at reviewing the records to determine which inmates should have this higher level of care based on medical necessity.

At first, I had a lot of trouble with this project. The records included descriptions of the reason for each inmate's incarceration. Many of them had been convicted of horrific crimes, from sex trafficking of children to multiple murders. It was hard for me to look beyond these descriptions to the medical circumstances—how could someone who raped children find any sympathy to transfer to a more comfortable facility, even if he did have leukemia or liver failure?

I spoke to the attending about my internal struggle. He asked me what I would do if someone showed up to the ER who was a convicted murderer. If the person were about to die from a heart attack, would I refuse to treat him because of his crime?

"Of course not," I said. "We don't turn anyone away."

"That's right. It's our duty to treat everyone. We are not here to judge the choices they made and what they may or may not have done. That's for the court of law. It's our duty to treat their medical condition, regardless of who they are."

This was how I learned to practice medicine, to treat all of my patients based on best medical standards, regardless of who they are, where they happen to come from, and whether they can pay. My job was to regard all people with humanity, dignity, and compassion. That this ethos of medical care was being threatened really shook me to my core.

As these policies accumulated, I thought about my obligation to the patients I served. In my medical training, I'd wrestled with this and decided that my duty as a physician was not only to provide care but also to strive for a better system. Now, I wondered if I should reevaluate my responsibility as the doctor for my city and become more vocal about the impact of these policies on the communities I served. I had tried hard to stay nonpartisan and to focus on policies and not politics, but if the health of my residents was being threatened by partisan politics, was it also my duty to be speak up?

To be sure, I had been an outspoken advocate on many public health issues in Baltimore. It was different, though, to draw attention to a problem where the culprit was a disease, or even a systemic problem, as opposed to a specific government policy resulting from a politician's ideology. The most significant time I had stepped outside of this zone was to speak out about Safe Streets. I had learned from that experience the danger of singling out a particular politician. My actions helped to save Safe Streets, but to some, they branded me as a partisan who was opposed to a Republican governor.

This was an outcome I'd always tried to avoid. Someone told me once of a study that looked at the credibility of physicians and activists. Physicians started off with much higher credibility than nonphysician activists. That credibility is maintained if the physician sticks to facts and science. The moment a physician begins using partisan activist language, their credibility drops below the activists'. The study was consistent with my experience as the city's doctor: I drew trust from the community because I was seen as being motivated by caring for people rather than electioneering politics.

But if the direct cause of poor health of Baltimore's residents were the policies of a specific administration, did my approach need to be retooled as a result?

My decision—and my approach—became clear when I saw a patient in the urgent care clinic where I volunteered. She had been receiving treatment at the clinic for a couple of years, though it was my first time to treat her.

When I walked into the exam room, she was crying. She had seen the news that the Affordable Care Act was being threatened, and she was among the forty thousand people in my city who were newly insured because of it. Through her tears, she told me that it was because of health insurance that she finally got her diabetes under control, and she was able to get treatment for her long-standing alcoholism and depression. Now she had a job as a home health aide and was able to provide for her family.

"Health insurance is my rock," she said. "I don't know what I'll do if that's taken away from me."

For her, the politics had a personal price. What was political strategy for people in Washington was about life and death for the people I cared for.

I made the decision that I was not going to comment on the partisan politics, but I was going to speak up and be vocal about the effect of the new policies on my constituents. I was not going to denounce Trump by name or rail against any party, but I was going to talk about how the administration's specific policies, like its efforts to repeal the Affordable Care Act, would hurt the patients I treated. And I was going to do that by leaning into my experience as a physician and my vantage point as the city's doctor.

I began speaking at town halls and then rallies about what it was like to practice medicine before and after the Affordable Care Act. I talked about the children receiving vaccines and the women receiving mammograms, thanks to the Affordable Care Act. I recalled the patients I took care of in the ER who had been priced out of health insurance because of their "preexisting conditions" like high blood pressure, migraines, and asthma, and how they were finally able to get their medical conditions under control. And I tied this to the impact of reversing these policies, and the harm of other policies that took away services from those who already faced the greatest barriers to care.

"Access to health care is access to life," I said, harking back to my AMSA days. "And health care has to be a human right guaranteed to all, not just a privilege available to some."

I also worked with the city's law office to take an unprecedented step: the city of Baltimore sued the Trump administration for its "arbitrary and capricious" decision to cut funding for our teen pregnancy prevention program. To our surprise, the judge ruled in our favor and we won the lawsuit. Our program continued and we were able to keep providing evidence-based health education for young people across the city.

THE DISCUSSIONS AROUND THE NECESSITY of health care became even more personal to me for another reason: I was pregnant.

Sebastian and I had discussed starting a family from the time we first met. We knew that we both wanted children at some point. But there was a setback. Right before we got married, I was diagnosed with early cervical cancer. It was caught early enough for treatment to be curative, but the treatment made it harder for me to carry a pregnancy. When we weren't successful in conceiving naturally, we consulted specialists and found out that even with advanced medicines and technologies, it would be a struggle for us to have children of our own.

For several years, we didn't spend too much time thinking about this, because we were both busy with our careers. When Sebastian moved to Boston to be with me, he had transferred to the U.S. office of Thomson Reuters and then went to IBM to work in the company's mergers and acquisition practice. I was busy with my patient advocacy work and then with my responsibilities in Baltimore.

About a year into my job, when I started planning with my team around longer-term priorities, Sebastian and I also did our own soul-searching. He was already in his forties. We knew that there would never be a perfect time. So we started trying again, in earnest.

On Christmas Day 2016, I found out that I was pregnant. It was the best present that we could have hoped for. We couldn't wait to tell our family and friends. Still, so much could go wrong, given my health issues. I knew that I'd have a high-risk pregnancy.

Indeed, my obstetrician advised that I see him every two weeks for a physical exam and ultrasound. Closer to delivery, I was to see him every week. I didn't hesitate to follow these recommendations. I had excellent health insurance with no co-pay for doctor's visits and a minimal cost for tests.

But what would have happened if I didn't have health insurance? My pregnancy happened to coincide with the numerous attempts to repeal the Affordable Care Act and to roll back Medicaid, through which half of Baltimore's pregnant women were insured. What would happen if these women lost coverage and were forced to pay out of pocket for services, and what would happen if others who had private insurance were no longer guaranteed maternity coverage?

I looked up what these costs amounted to. At that time, on average, an obstetrician visit would cost $150. With an ultrasound, it would be $400. A Pap smear would cost $53. One set of blood tests would add another $300. All told, my prenatal care with all visits and tests included would be over $10,000. This is not counting labor and delivery, which in the Baltimore area was estimated to be up to $30,000 for a vaginal birth and $50,000 for a caesarean section.

Facing these astronomical costs, would I be forced to pick and choose care based on my ability to pay rather than my doctor's recommendations? Would I choose to pay for the ultrasound that could detect a problem now, or buy food for my family? Would I forgo bloodwork and monitoring, if it meant I didn't have to scramble for rent?

I thought a lot about how fortunate I was that I didn't have to make these unthinkable trade-offs. Every time I went to a community event and people commented on my growing belly, I thought about my mother hiding her pregnancy under my father's big sweaters because she feared her boss firing her if he knew. Every time I went to a medical appointment, I wondered how many appointments my mother skipped because she couldn't miss work, and how appalling it was that many women today still have this concern.

All mothers want what is best for our children. Every politician talks about family values, and it seems that the least our society can do is to provide a level playing field at the very beginning of life. The consequences of not doing so aren't just poor health but also higher costs passed down to taxpayers. Women who do not have prenatal care are seven times more likely to give birth to premature and low-birth-weight babies who require more intensive medical care. The average medical cost for a baby with problems of prematurity is $79,000, compared to $1,000 for a healthy newborn. Hospitalizations for a preemie can be upward of $500,000; intensive care can cost in the millions. On the other hand, studies have shown that for every dollar spent on prenatal care, there are expected savings of nearly $5.

My pregnancy gave me an additional vantage point to advocate for health-care access. It also made me a better leader in a way I hadn't anticipated. When I first became pregnant, I struggled with how I'd tell my colleagues. My boss, Mayor Pugh, frequently spoke of her decision to remain childless as a sign of her devotion to service and the city. I didn't want my colleagues to think that I was any less dedicated to the work. I also worried about being absent at critical decision points, with a new mayoral administration that had not yet defined its commitment to public health and new federal policies that could significantly reduce our funding.

I held off on telling my team for a couple of months. When I did, my deputies Dawn O'Neill, Olivia Farrow, and Heang Tan, all mothers themselves, laughed and hugged me.

"We knew it!" Heang said. "We were just waiting for you to give us the official news."

News in Baltimore travels fast. Or maybe I wasn't as good as keeping this secret as I had thought.

"You'd turn every shade of the rainbow in one meeting and then go out and throw up," Dawn said. "We're just so happy for you!"

Our other team members were just as thrilled. Kristin Rzeczkowski teared up when I told her and didn't hesitate when I asked her to step in for me as the acting commissioner when I planned to go on maternity leave. Gabe Auteri's wife was pregnant, too, and we'd soon share stories about being first-time parents.

The most memorable reaction came from my special assistant at the time, Kathleen Goodwin. Kathleen was about to start medical school at Columbia University. She was one of the most reserved of my special assistants, and I didn't know her as well personally as I knew Gabe, Shirli Tay, and Katherine Warren before her.

That's why I was surprised when she became visibly emotional at my news. Kathleen would tell me later that my being a mother and a leader was important for her to see firsthand. Like so many young people, she envisioned having a family and a career, too, and she appreciated being there with me as I made this choice and learned to grow into a new identity.

Speaking to Kathleen, I remembered that in graduate school and residency training, I had always paid special attention to the working mothers around me. Since I was far from having children myself, it was less that I needed their specific advice but more that I wanted reassurance that they could do it. When I became pregnant and later as a mom myself, I would continue to seek out the company of other working mothers. I saw myself in them, as they saw themselves in me. And even if we were hardly close to "figuring it out" (whatever that means!), all of us had an obligation to be role models for the young women who were similarly wondering about how they would navigate their identities, responsibilities, and futures.

THE MOMENT MY SON ELI was born, everything changed.

For all the tests and monitoring, I had a fairly uneventful pregnancy. I went about my daily work, which wasn't so different in pregnancy except that I was asked about it at every event. Before I became pregnant, I couldn't have imagined strangers touching my belly and asking very personal questions, but I quickly began to appreciate the opportunity to bond with my constituents in a different way. Mothers and grandmothers were not shy about giving me advice on birth and child-rearing. I found my pregnancy to be a great conversation-starter, and I learned a lot about my constitutents' families and daily lives in a way that I wouldn't have otherwise. My pregnancy was also an excellent advertisement for the health department's services. I used every opportunity to speak about our B'More for Healthy Babies programs and successes, and to recruit new families to join.

My due date was at the end of August 2017. As the hot summer went on, I always made sure that I had a staff member with me who could fill in at events if I went into labor. Before one keynote address, I needed to find the restroom before I started speaking, but the closest ladies' room was two floors down on the other side of the building. By the time I came back, the event had started—and my staff member was giving my remarks! We were good at contingency planning and had pretty seamless teamwork.

As it turns out, I went into labor that very night. We knew it was a boy, and Sebastian and I had a name picked out. We'd call him Eli, after a man we both deeply admired, Congressman Cummings. We wanted Eli to be courageous and kind and to work toward a just and compassionate society.

When I told Congressman Cummings about his namesake, he cried. Every few weeks, I would receive a text or a call about Eli. "How's my Eli doing?" he'd say. "What's he doing—changing the world yet?"

Eli certainly changed my world. My identity had always been shaped by my career—I thought of myself first as a physician and a public health official—but suddenly I thought of myself first, second, and third as a mother.

To be fair, the startling identity change was in part because I had no idea what was involved in caring for a newborn. Sebastian and I had gone to some baby care classes at the hospital, where we practiced putting on diapers and I learned the positions most conducive to breastfeeding. After I gave birth, the nurses taught us swaddling and gave us some idea of how often to feed and change (in those early days, it seemed like every hour). They made sure we properly installed our car seat and could safely transport Eli home.

But then we got home, and it was a whole different ball game. Initially, Eli lost nearly 20 percent of his body weight and became so jaundiced that he was almost readmitted to the hospital. It turned out that I was having trouble breastfeeding, which was compounded by mastitis, a breast infection, that I developed soon after delivery.

Once we were both back on track, there was still a mountain more to learn. Our families were many thousands of miles away. I sought advice initially from the Internet and found a community of mommy bloggers from whom I learned a whole lot more about babies than I ever did in medical school. I also started attending various mommy-and-me activities, where I met other new mothers in my neighborhood. Being a mother dominated my thoughts and consciousness in a way that I could have never imagined before I had Eli.

Everything I did in my professional life was also suddenly shaped by my new perspective. During my maternity leave, Kristin would come to my house a couple of times a week and review key decisions. When she brought over the minutes from an overdose meeting, I saw the victims for the first time as somebody's child. When I chaired the next convening of the Child Fatality Review, I saw in every case of child death the face of the mother and her grief.

It wouldn't be accurate to say that I had more compassion for these families than before, only that my worldview became dramatically different. I wondered if this had also happened with my mother. I thought about her all the time. There was so much about motherhood that I wish I could have discussed with her. And I know that she would have fallen in love with Eli.

My changing perspective made me acutely aware of workplace policies that were needed to better support pregnant women and parents. Before I had to navigate the day care drop-off, I didn't understand the impact of early morning meetings on my staff who had childcare needs. I didn't appreciate the panic of finding last-minute babysitting when a fever or a snow day came unexpectedly.

Mayor Pugh didn't have children, and I saw that she was doing what I had inadvertently done myself: she'd set early morning and late afternoon meetings at the last minute, without knowing the consequence that it would have on working parents. Her (and my) subordinates would not want to create a problem, so they'd show up dutifully to the meeting. All the while, they'd be frantically texting to make alternate arrangements, with half a mind to the meeting and the rest to worrying about their families.

This was a solvable problem. From time to time, there were still meetings that were urgent and matters that needed our attention at odd hours, but we could set the default in-person meetings to take place at reasonable times and do our best to convert other meetings to conference calls. With the support of my executive assistant, Jacki Anderson, a mother and grandmother herself, we restructured all of our senior team meetings, and in so doing, we gave my deputies the room they needed to signal to their teams that we supported their time with family.

In addition, becoming a mother sharpened my focus on needed legislative changes. There wasn't much I could do about the federal government's policies, but there was plenty to be done in the state and in the city. Though I had previously testified before the Maryland legislature in favor of paid family leave, I didn't fully understand its necessity until I experienced trying to go back to work six weeks after Eli's birth. I had an uncomplicated delivery and a healthy baby. We were lucky to find a very competent nanny who would care for Eli during the day. And I was returning to a job that I knew well and loved. Still, it was excruciating to leave my son, and I worried about him constantly and wished that I could have been home with him longer.

Despite enormous amounts of literature showing the benefit of extended maternity leave to both mothers and infants, many women have no choice but to return to work just days after delivery. I recalled that my mother, after a C-section with my sister, had to go back to work within two weeks, when she could barely walk. What kind of society proclaims that we value women, children, and families, but we cannot do something as basic and humane as supporting new mothers at their most vulnerable time?

My team and I worked with a coalition of partners to advocate for paid sick leave legislation, which finally went into effect in 2018 after the state legislature overrode Governor Hogan's veto. We also worked on legislation at the city level and secured the passage of bills to mandate that public buildings and businesses of a certain size offer diaper-changing tables and employee breastfeeding accommodations.

Two newly elected city council members had babies around the same time as I did. At our press conference announcing family-friendly legislation, we were all carrying our infants. Remarks were interrupted by cries, and there were a couple of dirty diaper incidents. But the fact that we were there to announce pro-women, pro-children, and pro-family policies was a testament to the fact that the life experiences of people in leadership roles really do matter.

Embracing my identity as a mother was made even more poignant with the national rhetoric around women. I used every public opportunity to highlight that being a mother was a choice that made me a stronger and better public servant. I began to talk about my own immigrant experience and attended gatherings to support people whose own identities—like mine—were under attack.

The world in 2018 was very different from that of 2016. The country's circumstances had changed, and so had my own. I developed new strategies and shifted my voice to be a more effective advocate for the times we were now in.

The work of local public health had become more important than ever. At our all-staff meeting in 2018, I quoted Congressman Cummings: "The work that we have in front of us is bigger than us—it's so much bigger than us. It's about our children who are messengers to a future that we will never see. It's not enough to look for common ground. We need to aim for higher ground."

Our aspiration in Baltimore was to strive for that higher ground: to be the model, the bright spot that others in the country would look to. Federal policies may have threatened the city's services, but we would continue to serve our residents and communities—to improve health, reduce disparities, and strive for a world where poverty does not translate into lost years of life.

PART THREE

Transforming

14

Decisions

For all the joy that came with motherhood, I had been struggling more than I realized. When I came back from my short maternity leave, I couldn't figure out a cadence that incorporated the many new parts of my life, from waking up at dawn to feed the baby to finding time and space to pump milk during the day to trying to finish up work at night while comforting a newborn.

One day was blurring into another, and I couldn't shake the feeling that I was just not myself. I burst into tears at the slightest provocation and snapped at the people closest to me. I had dreams about Eli suffocating in the crib, then rushed to the nursery in the middle of the night to make sure he was breathing. I had recurring visions of Sebastian and me both dying in a car accident and leaving Eli an orphan.

I was also drinking more and more. As soon as I came home from work, I poured myself a glass of wine. I'd have another with dinner and another before bed. If I couldn't drink, I didn't think I would get through the night. I looked forward to weekends because it was my license to start drinking early in the day, which I'd continue to do for the next forty-eight hours.

There was something wrong, but it took time for me to muster up the courage to call my doctor and admit to her that I needed help. She put her finger on it instantly and referred me to a psychiatrist specializing in postpartum depression. At my first appointment, I went through extraordinary lengths not to identify myself as a patient. The appointment was in a medical building, and I came up with what I would say if someone recognized me and asked why I was there.

"I'm here to meet someone to talk about a research project," I might say. Or, if they saw me as I headed into that psychiatrist's office, I'd say that I was looking into postpartum depression as part of my work for the B'More for Healthy Babies program.

Then I felt guilty for coming up with these excuses. I was the city's doctor. I regularly spoke about the stigma of addiction and mental illness and the need to treat mental health with the same compassion and urgency as we treat physical health. Why couldn't I just say that postpartum depression is normal and that I was getting treatment myself?

Working with the psychiatrist and then a mental health counselor helped me understand my own thought distortions. I learned that so much of what I was feeling was common—the anxiety of something bad happening to me and my family, the exhaustion, even the alcohol dependence. It took me several months of regular therapy, but I was finally in a place where I almost felt back to myself.

IT WAS AROUND THIS TIME, in May 2018, that I was first approached about a new job: to be the new president of Planned Parenthood. I didn't respond to the search firm that contacted me because the prospect was laughable. I already had the perfect job, and by this point, I'd recruited an exceptional group of people who came from all over the country to implement our shared vision for health in Baltimore. Also, my work was in public health, not reproductive rights. And I was finally finding my footing again; I couldn't imagine going through another major life change.

A close friend thought I should at least dip my toe in the water by attending a book talk given by the outgoing president, Cecile Richards. I decided I could do that much, and anyway, I wanted to meet someone I'd admired for years. Halfway there, I realized I'd forgotten my breast pump. Taking it as a sign that this meeting was not meant to be, I turned off at the next exit on the highway, back to my baby and my job.

It was around this time that the Trump administration announced its changes to the Title X family planning program, and clinics in Baltimore were faced with potential closures. I was shaken to my core when health-care leaders in the city refused to come to a strategy meeting if Planned Parenthood was going to be there. Planned Parenthood was part of the safety net that provided essential care. In the ER, I'd treated countless women who had delayed preventive checkups because they didn't have health insurance. I remember a single mother of three who waited more than a year to have a lump in her breast examined. By the time she came in, the cancer had spread to her bones and her lungs. She died not long after I saw her, leaving her young children orphans.

For millions of women, Planned Parenthood made preventive care possible. My mother, my sister, and I all depended on the organization at different times in our lives for health services like Pap tests and birth control. If Planned Parenthood was considered too polarizing even in Baltimore, then the state of women's health care was more dire than I'd thought.

The people who had qualms about being in the same room as Planned Parenthood told me that a major reason for that was the organization's advocacy on abortion. There was a way around this problem, I thought. Instead of leading with the language perceived as the most controversial, we needed to start with points of agreement.

With this in mind, I invited leaders to join me at a community forum to talk about the role of Title X health centers in serving low-income women and families, and the impact of losing this care for tens of thousands of people in Baltimore. It was important to have these champions—some of whom were leaders at major hospitals—support our advocacy, and a softer, nonpartisan tone allowed them to do so.

After the forum, an African American pastor came up to me. She supported Planned Parenthood but hadn't found a way to talk about it to her congregation. "If I went to my church and talked about abortion,

people would shut off." Now, she felt, if she "talked about why women
need health care, they'd be interested."

I began to imagine what it could be like if Planned Parenthood were
to be repositioned as a mainstream health-care organization rather than
as an activist political one. Could that allow more people to support its
work openly? Such a repositioning wasn't just about optics. A woman
in 2018 was more likely to die in pregnancy than her mother. Black
women had nearly three times the maternal mortality as white women.
Women weren't dying only because of what happened during birth—
they were dying because of poor health before their pregnancies and
their ongoing unmet health needs.

Many patients depended on Planned Parenthood as their only source
of care. Why shouldn't the organization expand its services to provide
primary care and mental health care, too? Planned Parenthood was
one of few health-care providers with a presence in all fifty states—why
shouldn't it aim to extend its care to millions more women and families
in rural and urban underserved areas?

When I looked at Planned Parenthood's annual reports, I saw that
it seemed to be going in the opposite direction. Because the Affordable Care Act incentivized comprehensive treatment, more doctor's
offices were offering non-abortion reproductive services. At the same
time, abortion providers were closing because of restrictive state laws
around abortions. As a result, Planned Parenthood clinics were providing proportionally more abortions and fewer other health services. If
that trend continued, Planned Parenthood was going to be even more
closely associated with the most controversial part of its identity. The
result? Abortion access would be even more imperiled and abortion care
further stigmatized.

THE DEEPER MY RESEARCH, THE greater was my concern for the future of
Planned Parenthood. I was convinced that urgent change was needed,
although I had neither the desire nor the hubris to lead the change myself.
Still, I felt an obligation to share my thoughts with the people deciding the organization's future. When the search firm reached out to me

again, I agreed to speak to the committee to air my concerns and present my vision for the organization.

I talked about what I had seen in Baltimore, how Planned Parenthood was increasingly associated with divisive politics. I also talked about its health-care operations. There was a danger to limiting services to sexual and reproductive care. Planned Parenthood was seen as a charity, I added, not as an innovative health system that patients choose for top-quality care.

"In ten years, I want Planned Parenthood to be on the list of leading health-care systems," I said. "When the CEO walks into a medical conference, she should be treated no differently than the CEO of the Mayo Clinic. If Planned Parenthood is truly understood as a mainstream entity, then reproductive care will be normalized as the standard health care that it is."

This approach, I believed, would strengthen the organization's advocacy work by helping it to reach a broader audience. I had seen that in divisive times, partisan messages end up canceling each other out. The more Planned Parenthood could speak with a doctor's voice, the voice of medicine and science, rather than with a voice of partisan advocacy, the more effective it could be to grow its coalition and its influence.

The search committee was intrigued by my vision. I, too, started to imagine what it would mean if it could be translated into action. The idea of leading Planned Parenthood still seemed far-fetched, but so was my entire journey up to that point. I loved my job in Baltimore, but perhaps this was an opportunity to translate all that I had learned to make a difference nationally. Providing health care and fighting to protect access to that care—that was the same mission I'd been on throughout my career.

OVER THE NEXT TWO MONTHS, I had individual discussions with each member of the search committee. In particular, I spent time talking to the CEOs of the Planned Parenthood affiliates who were on the committee. Planned Parenthood is a federated model, with the local affiliates—fifty-five at the time—as its members, who vote for a national board that then selects its president. Each affiliate has its own president/CEO and board. Affiliates vary by size, from those that serve several small rural counties to those that span multiple states. The affiliates are the entities that run the over six hundred health centers and provide health care and education across the country; the national organization oversees that care and sets a shared vision.

Every person I spoke to mentioned tensions between the local affiliates and the national leadership. This was natural and would always be the case in any federated system. Local entities have to prioritize the interests of the people they serve, which will invariably differ from national interests. There are inevitably disagreements over fundraising and divisions of resources between local and national.

As I spoke with the affiliate CEOs, I felt that I knew where they were coming from. In many ways, I was one of them—a clinician who understood that health care is local and has to be tailored to the needs of each community. If I were to come on board, I'd want to spend as much time as I could visiting the affiliates and learning from their staff.

When the search committee let me know that I was their choice, I made a request of my own: to meet with the board members and make sure that my vision aligned with theirs. The committee couldn't grant my request because the board was too large and they didn't want my identity leaked to the press. In lieu of this, they agreed to arrange a meeting with Cecile Richards. Sebastian had an ask, too: to speak with Cecile's husband, Kirk.

Sebastian and I drove up to New York, dropping Eli at a temporary day care there that morning. This was the first time Eli had gone to day care and there were a lot of tears, from him and from me. He had terrible stranger anxiety, and I couldn't stop worrying about him. Just as we were leaving, Eli threw up on me. Try as I might, I couldn't get rid of the large stain down the front of my dress. I was nervous as it was to meet this icon who had done so much for women. The best I could do with the stain was to wrap a large scarf around my chest. It was July, and I began sweating through the fabric.

Cecile arrived looking elegant and perfect. She was gracious in answering my pages of questions. Kirk was equally kind. We talked about the impact of travel and the security concerns, and Kirk's answers reassured Sebastian. We had a lot to discuss on our drive back to Baltimore. (Eli survived his day care experience without incident, and we received his first-ever fingerpainting as a souvenir.)

On Planned Parenthood's end, the search firm hired investigators to do a background check on me. They read through all of the articles and blogs I'd written and reviewed my years of social media activity. They interviewed people from different points in my career, asking questions ranging from temperament and management style to ideology and values. Eventually, the firm produced a report that was over two hundred pages long.

I was also interviewed and asked about things that might be embarrassing to Planned Parenthood should they be made public. I revealed that I was receiving treatment for postpartum depression. Even though I felt far better and was thankful to have found the help I needed, I still saw my depression as a source of shame. When the investigators began digging, I realized that my shame was the liability, not the actual diagnosis. Rather than leaving it for adversaries to discover and use against me, I decided to tell my story my way.

I spoke at a conference for Unidos US, an advocacy group for Latinos, about the stigma of mental health treatment. Part of overcoming the stigma is being open about our own struggles. I spoke about my shame and guilt—I loved my son so much, how could it be that I felt depressed? I also mentioned the cultural demand to embody certain notions of motherhood, which I saw resonated with the audience. And I talked about the importance of treatment and my goal in speaking up, which was to encourage others to do the same and help end the stigma.

Afterward, dozens of women came over to thank me and tell me their own mental health stories. So many of them had struggled in silence, and some had not yet sought treatment. Though my reason for sharing was spurred by external factors, I was relieved and very glad to have opened up about this challenge I was working through. It helped me to talk about other parts of my past that I'd locked away out of shame and fear.

In my final meeting with the Planned Parenthood search committee,

I was asked if I had any remaining concerns. I had only one. It turned out to be not quite the right question and posed to the wrong audience.

I asked the committee if they shared my vision. "Do you see yourself as an advocacy organization first, with medical services that are necessary to strengthen your impact, or do you see yourself as a health-care organization first, with advocacy as a necessary vehicle to protect rights and access?" Only the latter made sense to me. Other entities could have advocacy and activism as their primary mission, but for a provider that people depended on for care, serving patients had to be its core mission. The meeting ended with the committee giving strong affirmation to my vision and where I believed the organization should go.

STILL, I FELT TORN. PROFESSIONALLY, I did not want to leave the job that I loved, and I knew that this new role came with great risk. I consulted my longtime mentors, and they gave conflicting advice. Most cautioned me against it. Planned Parenthood was seen as too controversial, and being the head of the organization could mean losing the impartial doctor voice that was core to my identity. A few thought that the controversy around Planned Parenthood was exactly why I needed to try to depoliticize women's health care. Everyone warned me that this huge undertaking was a tremendous gamble.

Personally, I worried about what this would mean for my family. Planned Parenthood's national headquarters were in New York, with secondary offices in D.C., San Francisco, and Miami. Sebastian and I decided that if I were to do this, we wouldn't move, since his work was now in Baltimore and I would be on the road much of the time visiting affiliates. Still, this would be a dramatic change in our lives. My job in Baltimore was demanding, but I was almost always home in time to pick up Eli. Most after-hours commitments were community events, and I took him along. Could I really go from seeing Eli every day to only on weekends? Was it fair to Sebastian for him to take on the role of primary caregiver?

Sebastian had mixed feelings, too. Mostly, he was anxious about my safety. Abortion providers had been gunned down and killed, and we knew that I would become a visible face and the target of protests and death threats. As he had always been, Sebastian was patient as we debated the decision over and over. Then it came to a head.

We had a routine of walking together every day after work. Our neighborhood had many young families, and we'd push Eli in the stroller and wave to the children riding their tricycles. We often went to the playground connected to our local preschool.

That day, we sat on the bench and watched Eli crawl across the park to the sandbox and pull himself up on the slide. He had just mastered a very speedy crawl. I was again going through my list of all the challenges this would present to our family.

Sebastian stopped me midsentence. "You know that I've always supported you, and I always will," he said. "But we can't talk about this anymore."

"But this is a huge decision for us," I said, surprised. "It's a huge risk."

He put his hands over mine. "For as long as I've known you, you've never shied away from taking big risks. Don't do this job if it's not the right thing, but don't *not* do it because you're afraid of the risk."

That night, I thought of all the opportunities I'd been given, from medical school to the Rhodes Scholarship to health commissioner. I thought of all the mentors who had invested their time and energy in me because they believed in what I could do for those I'd one day serve. I thought of Dr. Garcia, who had passed away from cancer a few years before, and how he'd say, "Girl, you can do anything you put your mind to." I thought of Senator Mikulski's call to action—"Do what you're best at, and what you're needed for." And I thought of what I frequently said to my students, that they shouldn't wait—they needed to do what they could, now. How could I ask this of them if I wasn't willing to do so myself?

After talking to Sebastian, I called the search committee chair. I was in, all in.

The day of the announcement was set: September 12, 2018. That morning, the search committee was to present to my candidacy to the board, which was expected to approve it unanimously. The *New York Times* had an embargoed story that was due to run just after the official vote. There just one thing left for me to do, something that broke my heart. I had to tell my Baltimore team. Kristin was the only person who knew in advance. Once I'd made my decision, I had asked her to come with me. I had heard from search committee members about the restructuring needed at the national office. Kristin had helped me set up systems in Baltimore and I wanted her help once again. In keeping with her no-nonsense, let's-get-it-done attitude, the first thing she said was "What do you need—how can I help?" When I broke the news to the whole team, I expressed my deep gratitude to every person and told them how difficult this decision had been. While I felt an obligation to serve on this national stage, my greatest regret was leaving such an incredible group of people—we'd done so much together.

There was no time to dwell on my departure, however: even as the board was still voting, the *New York Times* story broke. I was quickly ushered from the board to a meeting with the Planned Parenthood national staff and then to a conference call with the affiliate CEOs. In the blur of the rest of the day, calls were made and received from legislators, donors, and the media. In the thousands of messages that poured in, physicians and public health leaders conveyed excitement at this new dawn of Planned Parenthood: with a physician at its helm, there was no question that this organization's mission was health care.

It was a message I repeated throughout the day. "This is my mantra, and you will hear me say it many times," I told the board, the staff, the CEOs. "Reproductive health care is health care. Women's health care is health care. And health care is a fundamental human right."

15

The Courage to Try

After a sleepless night, I was off to an intense media day. First up was an appearance on ABC's *The View*, followed by an interview with CNN's Christiane Amanpour.

In Baltimore, I was used to working with local media. Most weeks, I'd take part in a couple of press conferences, a few local televised events, and some radio interviews to talk about heat or cold warnings, the flu, or health screenings. Over time, as our opioid work and other projects gained wider attention, the national press came to Baltimore to interview my team and me about our programs.

That felt very different from what I faced on my second day in the job: introducing myself and my philosophy of Planned Parenthood to a national audience.

I spent hours rehearsing. One of the main points I wanted to get across was that health care shouldn't be political. Getting cancer screenings and medications shouldn't be political. I had to come to this job as a doctor, and my charge was patients' lives.

I was pacing and practicing my key messages in the greenroom when Whoopi Goldberg walked in. If I wasn't anxious enough, meeting

Whoopi right before I had to step on the live set took care of that. Of course, she was kind and funny, and I could see that she was very supportive of Planned Parenthood.

The interview was seven minutes long, although it seemed to be over in seconds. I felt such pride speaking on behalf of the doctors, nurses, and patients I now represented. I was exhilarated to hear the audience cheering and applauding as I made my case for how women's health care is health care. This was a major validation that my message—my whole reason for coming to Planned Parenthood—had resonance. I left the studio with a big smile and a deep sigh of relief.

MY ELATION LASTED LESS THAN an hour. I was on the way to the CNN studios when the messages started coming. Most were positive, but some threw me off guard.

"Good job on *The View*," a board member texted. "Next time, make sure you talk about abortion." Two people on the national staff let me know that back in the office, there was a lot of worried chatter. Did I leave out abortion on purpose? Was this a signal that I didn't want to defend access to abortion?

"Next time, just say the word," one of them counseled. "You need to talk about abortion at every media interview. You're the president of Planned Parenthood. People expect that from you."

This was the first sign of trouble. Until that moment, I'd thought that the overriding reason Planned Parenthood was equated with abortion instead of its other health-care services was the anti-choice opposition. The more they could associate the organization with its most controversial provision, the easier it was to convince legislators to take away its funding. That goal becomes harder if the attempted delegitimization is aimed at a general provider of health care. Even those who oppose abortion may not want women in their communities to go without cancer screenings. So I was taken aback to see that it wasn't just the anti-choice side that wanted to brand Planned Parenthood with abortion.

I tried to understand the perspective of those who raised this issue. "Not saying 'abortion' sounds as if you're ashamed of it," I was told.

"Many of us would call ourselves pro-abortion. We're proud of providing abortions and leading abortion advocacy. We don't need to sanitize abortion with other services."

I still wasn't getting it. "Of course I'm pro-choice and agree that abortion should be safe and legal," I said. "But that's not being an advocate *for* abortion. It's more accurate to say that we're advocates for all aspects of reproductive health, including birth control and sex education to reduce the need for abortion, right?"

"No, that's trying to cover up abortion again. If we don't talk about abortion openly, loudly, and proudly, as a positive moral good, then we are further stigmatizing it and the people who need it."

I would have some version of this conversation at least once every day with people on the board or national office staff. Intellectually, I could see the basis for their position, because there was indeed stigma around abortion. I just didn't agree with the way to combat the stigma. There were already too many who thought that women who had abortions were careless and resorted to abortion as a form of birth control. Some people have even gone so far as to accuse Planned Parenthood of profiting from abortions, or of being part of an "abortion industry" recruiting women to meet an "abortion quota."

I was concerned that the terminology of being "pro-abortion" gave fuel to this anti-choice opposition. The phrase also ran counter to my experiences with many women who had sought abortions. I'd cared for women who had much-desired pregnancies and were given the devastating diagnosis of fatal fetal anomalies and for women who were so ill during pregnancy that abortion was the only way to save their lives. I'd known women who had abortions because they couldn't afford another child, because they'd have to drop out of school and give up their dreams, because they were the victims of abuse and couldn't bear to bring a child into a world that they themselves longed to escape. These women felt fortunate to have had access to abortion care, but they would much rather never have had to go through any of it.

Yet when I described the heart-wrenching decisions of patients such as these, I was told that I was once again stigmatizing women. "Not all women who go through abortions think the decision was difficult," I

heard. "For some, it's an easy one. Abortion is one of the safest procedures, and you can't make it sound so dramatic."

This didn't give the full picture. In my new role, I was meeting women
every day who'd tell me their abortion stories. They had often faced the
most difficult decision of their lives, and it took great courage for them
to share with me the details of an incredibly vulnerable time. How could
we ignore their feelings, their soul-searching, and their very real lived
experiences? And wouldn't doing so also alienate people who were
already on the fence about reproductive rights?

I BECAME MORE AWARE OF the complexities of the reproductive health
landscape as I began my listening tour of the affiliates. Under the direction of a superb young woman, a Rhodes Scholar named Emily Mediate, who'd come with me from Baltimore, I visited twenty-six affiliates
in seven months.

I particularly wanted to see the health-care innovations that succeeded in expanding care to vulnerable women. I knew that such innovations existed, because frontline providers are always scrappy and
creative. They know the needs of their patients and come up with whatever it takes to help them. I wanted to hear their stories and observe
the programs they had implemented and find a way to replicate them
across the country.

In every location, I watched the affiliates draw on core public health
principles to provide the services their communities needed. Many of
the programs reminded me of those in Baltimore. In Ohio, I learned
about Healthy Moms, Healthy Babies, an initiative that reduced maternal and infant mortality through home visiting and public education.
In Colorado, I spoke to outreach workers who performed HIV testing
in bars and at drag shows. In New York, I went on a mobile van that
offered Pap smears and connected uninsured patients to Medicaid. In
Rhode Island and Connecticut, I talked to care coordinators who linked
patients up with food, housing, and other social needs.

Some affiliates were beginning to provide mental health services,
and centers in New Hampshire and Vermont had started to screen and

refer people for opioid addiction treatment. In California and Florida, I met *promotores*, community health educators who conducted outreach in migrant farms, barber shops, schools, and supermarkets.

I also visited health centers that faced extraordinary hardships. There was a twelve-hundred-mile stretch between Idaho and the Dakotas that had no abortion provider. The Planned Parenthood in South Dakota, in Sioux Falls, was the only place to access abortion care in the entire state. It was not uncommon for women to drive four or five hours to get there. Additionally, South Dakota, like five other states, had a mandatory waiting period of seventy-two hours, which meant that a woman had to find childcare, get time off from work, and drive several hours each way for her first appointment. Then she had to repeat the entire process and return three days later for her procedure. If her employer wouldn't grant her another day off, or if she ran into any number of barriers such as car trouble or a sick family member, she would have to come back the following week and start the clock ticking all over again.

This system depended on a single doctor, an obstetrician-gynecologist, who saw patients in Sioux Falls. She was based in Minnesota and flew in twice a week. If her flight was canceled or if she had personal issues of her own, the patients in South Dakota simply wouldn't get seen. Because of the early gestational age cutoff in South Dakota, it could well be too late for the patient to return the next week.

All this was complicated by the need for the doctor to keep switching up her flights for security reasons, to prevent her from being targeted at the airport. I was struck by so much that the staff had to do that was second nature to them, but would be unthinkable to other health professionals. They regularly changed their daily routines. They watched for cars that might follow them from work. They kept limited social media profiles and were particularly guarded with information about their family. They did this and showed up to work with the abiding knowledge that if they didn't serve their patients, no one else would.

The same affiliate operated clinics in Minnesota, where the state began requiring doctors to read a long script, one that contained grossly inaccurate information, such as "abortion causing breast cancer and infertility" (when it doesn't). Doctors have to say things that they know are untrue, which is a direct violation of the oath they took to serve in their patients' best interests. Such intrusions are the definition of political interference with the practice of medicine. The American Medical Association and other major medical bodies uniformly denounce these demands as an affront to the doctor-patient relationship.

The clinics coped with the onslaught of restrictive laws as best they could. "Whenever they pass a law, we have to comply with it," I was told. "But we find a way to do so that we can keep serving women and preserve their dignity to the best of our ability." Some doctors would preface the script, saying that it was a government-written document they were required by law to read and the information contained was not all medically accurate. Once they finished reading, they'd answer questions and explain the actual medicine and science. That way, they complied with the law and upheld their oath to their patients.

Similarly, when a South Dakota law was passed that required patients to receive an ultrasound test to hear the fetal heartbeat, the clinic staff complied—but also gave their patients an option. "We offer them an eye mask and earplugs, if they wish," one staff member said. "That way, women make the choice, not the government."

THROUGH THE AFFILIATE TOUR, I gained a better understanding of Planned Parenthood's protective hold on its identity as an abortion provider. Well-funded opposition groups spent millions of dollars every year to prevent women from accessing abortion care. As a result, Planned Parenthood was compelled to defend it. As one affiliate leader told me, "You get pretty tired of people asking you why Planned Parenthood doesn't stop doing abortions. They say they'll support you if only you didn't do abortions. But we will never trade away our patients' rights."

I learned to reframe my talking points. I stopped saying that "only 3 percent" of Planned Parenthood's services were abortion and instead spoke about how over 90 percent of the organization's work was in prevention. I wouldn't say that I was "pro-abortion" or use the more political language of abortion rights, but I'd talk about the danger of increasing maternal mortality if women didn't have access to safe, legal abortion. And whenever I could, I spoke about the affiliates' health-care innovations.

The first national initiative I launched was "This is Health Care," a campaign intended to showcase all the exceptional care provided by Planned Parenthood. The program made the daily reality for affiliates visible. At a staff meeting in Texas, one manager had explained that he wore a golf shirt with the Planned Parenthood logo everywhere he went.

He'd often get stares, snide comments, and questions. Once, he was in a Home Depot store and a large, imposing man came up to him. After confirming that the manager worked at Planned Parenthood, he demanded, "So you go to work every day and kill babies?"

"Planned Parenthood performs abortions, yes," he replied. "But let me tell you what else Planned Parenthood does." He went on to recite the litany of services: cancer screenings, STI and HIV tests, contraception, and annual checkups.

"Men can also get health care there," he added. "We do vasectomies, too."

"Huh, I had no idea," the man said. "Thanks for telling me."

The affiliate staff applauded when the manager finished talking. One after another, they told similar stories. They were all passionate about defending access to safe, legal abortion, but they saw that the best way to do this was to contextualize rather than emphasize it. The more we highlighted all of our services, the more we could protect Planned Parenthood—and access to abortion care.

TRYING TO CHANGE THE MESSAGING of a behemoth organization was a daunting challenge. It was nothing like Baltimore, where I spoke for the health department and as long as the mayor was on board, we could change our language. At Planned Parenthood, there were many more stakeholders. As well as all the affiliate leaders and staff, there were national board members, affiliate board members, national office staff, donors, and partners. Many disagreed with my attempts to de-emphasize abortion.

A few months into my tenure, BuzzFeed published an article describing my broader vision of comprehensive women's health care, titled "New Planned Parenthood President Wants to Focus on Nonabortion Healthcare." Although the headline actually reflected my vision for the organization, the article prompted such ire that the executive committee of the board met to discuss it.

In response, I agreed that the media team could issue a statement from my personal Twitter account to affirm that abortion was Planned Parenthood's core mission. This was a dramatic departure from what I'd previously said, and it didn't go unnoticed. The anti-choice opposition seized upon this social media statement, and numerous state bills were introduced in subsequent months directly referring to my quote. This was one of the few times in my career that I conceded on such a crucial point in conflict with my convictions, and I regretted the decision.

Another growing point of contention was my desire to engage people with nuanced views about choice. Poll after poll shows that most Americans have complex views on abortion. They may identify as pro-life while still opposing extreme bans outlawing abortion in the case of rape, incest, or danger to a woman's life. They may wish that abortion did not have to exist, but also not want to force families into cycles of poverty. They may regard abortion as a tragedy, but believe it needs to remain legal in order to be safe. They may oppose abortion altogether, but support Planned Parenthood's work to reduce abortion through providing birth control.

My efforts to bring these individuals into an expanded coalition drew substantial consternation, with land mines at every turn. Once, I invited a renowned, pro-choice public health expert who spoke about the goal of abortion being "safe, legal, and rare." She didn't know that activists saw that phrase as the third rail. To them, the word "rare" stigmatized women who have abortions; whereas for her, from a public health standpoint, it was a way to emphasize prevention.

It was just as controversial to express any doubt about abortion, even those done later in pregnancy for nonmedical reasons. These are exceedingly rare and are opposed by the vast majority of Americans. The small percentage of those who support such procedures is comparable to the number of people who oppose abortion under all circumstances. As I learned, concern about a slippery slope drove abortion rights groups to resist all restrictions. They feared that allowing limits to third-trimester abortions could open the door to the same for the second trimester, and so forth. (Ironically, these groups dismissed gun rights advocates for using a similar slippery-slope argument against implementing background checks for gun purchases.)

I realized it was a mistake to take on these internal culture battles so early in my tenure. Planned Parenthood had been under attack for all of its existence and was deeply suspicious of anyone who didn't fully share its views. It was no doubt jarring for many to meet the new president and find that she thought differently and encouraged others who did to join the coalition.

Board members had growing concerns, I heard. Some had been unhappy about my hire from the start because they didn't like the search process: they didn't think the board should have been presented with only one candidate. Why hadn't they also been presented with a "Cecile Richards Part Two," a dyed-in-the-wool activist, so they could have had a choice? I was in a restroom stall when I heard two people talk about me. "I thought we'd get a rock star rabble-rouser, a congress-woman or a senator," one of them said. "Instead, we got a doctor." The other woman agreed and expressed her frustration that I'd continued seeing patients, albeit in a very limited capacity (I'd reduced my clinical hours to one morning every month); surely, my time was better spent lobbying legislators and attending donor events.

I thought the problem was that I couldn't give the full-throated defense of abortion the board needed, or that they rejected my broader health-care vision, but neither was exactly it. They, and I, struggled to put our finger on the source of friction, though it was becoming increasingly clear that where I was trying to take the organization was a sharp deviation from where many believed it should go.

WHAT KEPT ME GROUNDED DURING these internal conflicts were the visits to affiliates and their health centers. My travels were made possible by my trusted deputies. While Emily traveled with me and coordinated day-to-day matters on the road, Kristin oversaw work in the national offices. I also brought on Lyric Chen, a lawyer and a brilliant classmate from Oxford; Julia Frifield, Senator Barbara Mikulski's longtime chief of staff; and several other trusted colleagues from Baltimore.

My new team began the painstaking work of developing processes for project tracking, strategic planning, and budget development. As this work was underway, I discovered an aspect of the organization that was far more fundamental than process changes. This was symbolized by a section of the Planned Parenthood website labeled "Tracking Trump." The section documented, month by month, the numerous actions taken by the Trump administration, those that involved reproductive health but also extending far beyond. With frequent use of words like "attack" and "assault," the web page appeared to have only one goal: to make the case for Trump's inhumanity and the need to vote him out as president.

Even as I personally agreed with much of the content, I was stunned by the tone. This was not a medical voice, but an activist political voice. I worried about its divisive impact on the many millions of Americans—including Planned Parenthood patients—who supported President Trump. What if they went to our website for health information and saw this targeted, hyper-partisan criticism? I feared that it would make them doubt the impartiality of the medical information they'd find and discourage them from seeking care at our clinics.

I also learned that Planned Parenthood had taken public positions on a number of legislative issues that seemed remote from health care. Some, like rent control, could arguably affect health directly. But others, like net neutrality, were harder to justify. One major area of focus for the organization was democracy reform. While I could see the role that Planned Parenthood might have in voter registration and the census count, it was unclear why it needed to take positions on D.C. statehood and expanding the size of courts. Similarly, defunding the police, banning assault weapons, and stopping Trump's border wall were issues not directly related to reproductive health care. A vocal position on these hot button topics could be alienating to many patients and health center staff with different political views.

I was beginning to understand the source of the friction. During the search process, I thought there was tension between the missions of health care and advocacy. But that wasn't exactly right. The work I had done in AMSA, in patient-centered care, and in Baltimore, was also advocacy, intended to influence public opinion and push legislation so our system could better serve patients.

Planned Parenthood did this, too, but it did something else as well. What I hadn't grasped was that the organization's advocacy wasn't restricted to reproductive health: it was fully aligned with progressive politics. By the time I joined, Planned Parenthood was firmly ensconced within the base of the Democratic Party and considered itself to be a leader of the anti-Trump movement. Many of the younger staff, in particular, took pride in the organization they devoted themselves to being the vanguard of anti-Trump activism. They felt that sexual and reproductive health was inextricably intertwined with all the other issues they cared deeply about, such as income inequality, the environment, criminal justice reform, and LGBTQ rights.

Thus my efforts at bipartisan collaboration were never going to take off. When I first arrived, I tried to identify areas where we might be able to draw Republican support, such as mental health. As I had in Baltimore, I thought that partnering with Catholic hospitals and religious institutions could help reposition the organization as a mainstream entity. But Planned Parenthood was at war. It was a partisan war, because they saw Republicans attacking them on every front. The Affordable Care Act was under threat. Republican-led legislatures were introducing abortion bans at alarming speed. Trump was appointing a record number of anti-choice judges. It was time to fight, not to build bridges.

I knew that I could speak passionately about the Affordable Care Act and protecting health care for my patients. I could certainly talk about the importance of family planning and the medical consequences of outlawing abortion. But I was having trouble shifting to the unequivocal partisan voice that was increasingly expected of me. I questioned whether this was the right role for Planned Parenthood. Should an organization that runs health centers be at the forefront of broad ideological fights? Planned Parenthood was legally divided into two entities, one that provides health care and one that does political advocacy, but this distinction was probably lost on most. I wondered whether Planned Parenthood could center its health-care mission and cede more of its political advocacy to partner organizations like NARAL Pro-Choice America. I had also met incredible leaders, primarily women of color, who had started reproductive justice organizations. These entities deserved far more recognition and funding, and I thought that it would help the entire movement if these other organizations took the lead on advocacy and Planned Parenthood were to focus more on patient care.

As the months went on, my questions about Planned Parenthood's identity became more sharply articulated. It wasn't possible to be a leader in both progressive politics and mainstream health care, so which would it choose?

In the meantime, Sebastian and I were trying to get pregnant again.

The timing wasn't ideal. I was already missing out on much of Eli's life. My schedule had me so frequently on the road that I'd often leave on Sunday evening and not return until Friday night or Saturday. When I was home, I ran around trying to do errands and was so glued to my phone that although physically present, I was unavailable to my family.

I had been so consumed with the job that I hadn't—and couldn't— process the toll of my absence on those around me. One weekend, my best friend from medical school, Kao-Ping Chua, drove down from Michigan to visit with his wife and two girls, who were just a bit older than Eli. We were all together as the children played with Legos when Sebastian left the room to get snacks. The moment he was out of sight, Eli started crying. There was nothing I could do to console him. It struck me that I had become a stranger feared by my own son.

Eli had just turned one when I started at Planned Parenthood. He was still crawling and could do little more than babble a few words. Now he was a toddler, full of energy, running everywhere and constantly asking, "What's this?" I realized that I couldn't remember when he'd transitioned from baby to toddler.

While I was gone, Sebastian and I would try to video chat every night. Many times, I was at meetings or donor events during the time when he came home from work and Eli went to sleep. We'd try to sneak in a few minutes of FaceTime, but often I couldn't get away and Sebastian would end up leaving me a video message. I accumulated many such messages that I'd watch from different hotel rooms night after night.

Sebastian never indicated that my absence was a burden to him. We made this decision together, he'd remind me when I felt overcome by guilt. Only later did I learn of the effect my job had on his emotional well-being. He worried about my safety constantly. There were many nights when he'd dream that I'd been gunned down and he was left to raise Eli alone.

We had always talked about our desire to have a second child. At that moment, our lives were ill-suited for the one child we had, much less two. But we also didn't want to wait. I was already thirty-six and Sebastian nearing forty-five. There was no sign that my schedule was going to get any easier. So we were both thrilled when the pink line appeared on a pregnancy test. I began having the familiar symptoms: the nausea, the bloating, the fatigue.

We started making plans. One weekend, I unpacked all of Eli's baby clothes. We bought another crib and started shopping online for double strollers.

AROUND THIS TIME, IN MAY 2019, two new board chairs were voted in. They made their request of me clear: I needed to become much more political, fast. With the existential threat to abortion access and 2020 elections on the horizon, a nonpartisan doctor voice wouldn't do. No more with the softer tone of "This is Health Care." This was the time to work with progressive allies and focus on abortion advocacy.

I was given a choice: change, or leave. The board chairs also took issue with the team I had brought in. They were part of the ultimatum. For me to stay, they had to go. I felt strongly about the work of the organization, but feared that were I to agree to these demands, more would be asked of me further down the line. And how could I choose my own career and push my team—the people I'd brought with me—under the bus?

I was struggling with this ultimatum while away on an affiliate visit when I got the awful feeling that I'd lost the pregnancy. Just as suddenly as my symptoms had started, they had vanished. The fatigue, the nausea, and the bloating had stopped. However uncomfortable they were, their disappearance was far worse.

Maybe this pregnancy was different from the last one. I frantically searched the Internet. Other women had had symptoms wane, too, and everything was fine. I tried to calm myself.

But it wasn't fine, and I knew it. The day I got back to Baltimore, I went to my doctor. He ordered bloodwork and an ultrasound, which showed what I suspected. I'd had a miscarriage.

My pregnancy loss was devastating in a way that I couldn't have anticipated. I cried for many hours and could not be consoled. In the ER, I had counseled dozens of women in my situation. I tried to tell myself what I always told them: About one in four pregnancies end in miscarriages, and those that occur early are likely due to genetic abnormalities. There is nothing you did to cause this and nothing you could have done to prevent it. But I knew that stress could be a factor. I couldn't help but wonder if the escalating conflict contributed to the pregnancy loss in some way. Also, what if I'd traveled less and gotten more rest?

Over the Fourth of July, Sebastian and I took a week off. It was my first break since starting the job, and the first week I'd been able to see him and Eli every day.

We spent a lot of time talking about the ultimatum. Then a bombshell went off. I had confided in someone at Planned Parenthood about my miscarriage, who told others without my consent. People began suggesting that I should use it as a reason to explain my departure. This was offensive and hurtful on so many levels that I began writing an op-ed about my miscarriage so as not to have this deeply personal experience stolen from me. I could not fathom the additional trauma if this news were made public by others who wished to use it for their own purposes. It was important that I tell my story with my voice, in my words.

Writing about the miscarriage helped me to make sense of my inner turmoil. It clarified for me that like so many other women, I held nuanced and complex thoughts about pregnancy. I could mourn my own miscarriage as the loss of a potential life while also supporting another woman's decision to terminate her pregnancy. It gave me an avenue to express my commitment to women's health in concert with my identity as a mother and my respect for both life and choice.

In the days after the op-ed appeared, I heard from thousands of women, including friends and colleagues, who told me their stories of pregnancy loss. Many thanked me for being willing to share something that for them was also a raw and painful experience.

The op-ed surfaced a lot of vitriol, too. I could tune out the anti-choice extremists who said that I deserved what had happened to me. It was harder to ignore the criticism from people who accused me of stigmatizing abortion by talking about miscarriage. I had implied that miscarriage should elicit sympathy while abortion shouldn't, they said. They asked if I would have been so open to talk about my experience if I had an abortion instead.

By this point, I was too tired to fight this battle. Instead, Sebastian and I took a lot of long walks. I cooked dinner every night. Eli began calling me Mommy again and seeking me out for cuddles.

I asked the board chairs for more time to come to a decision, citing my need to recover and be with my family. This was denied. That made my decision easier. I was not going to change who I was to be the person that others wanted me to be.

It was the words of Congressman Elijah Cummings that came to me over and over again during this time. At the end of the day, he'd say, all you have are your morals and your integrity. You can't control what happens to you, but you can control how you choose to live the life that you have. Your conscience should guide your conduct. And your family must always come first.

MY LAWYERS WERE IN THE midst of negotiating a mutually agreed upon departure statement when I heard that a board meeting was underway to vote on my ouster. I learned of the result through a breaking news alert on my phone. Just as they had with my appointment, the *New York Times* released an embargoed story about my departure.

That week in July 2019 was one of the worst I'd lived through. I felt that I had let down so many people: my team, who gave up their jobs to join me, and who were out now, too; all those I'd met along the way who believed in my vision; all those who saw themselves in me, as the first Asian-American to lead the organization, as an immigrant, a doctor, a mother. What gave me strength were the many people who reached out to me during that period. Friends, colleagues, and total strangers told me their stories of losing a job, of how professionally difficult and personally tragic circumstances had seemed at the time like the very worst thing to happen. They reminded me that we are not defined by a particular setback but by what we do when that happens.

For days, I was bombarded with media inquiries. I chose not to answer any of them. I didn't want to be seen to be picking a fight with the organization, and I wanted to talk about my departure in my own way. I decided to issue one statement and write one op-ed, for the *New York Times*. I wanted to frame my leaving as something bigger than about me and Planned Parenthood: it went to the heart of the divisive discourse in our country.

"Can we put aside partisan differences to do what is best for the people we serve?" I wrote. "Will the conversation continue to be dominated by a vocal minority from both ends of the spectrum, or can there be space for those of us in the middle to come together around shared values?"

ONE OF THE PEOPLE WHO got in touch was Pam Maraldo, an advanced-practice nurse who had served as Planned Parenthood's president in the early 1990s. She told me that she had also tried to reposition the organization toward mainstream health care. Indeed, I found an article that announced her appointment with the headline "Moving 'Beyond Abortion': Planned Parenthood President Pamela J. Maraldo Says Her Mission Is to Re-emphasize Health Care and Birth Control."

Dr. Maraldo was also asked to leave after a short tenure because, as the *New York Times* reported, she "aroused opposition with her emphasis on reshaping Planned Parenthood into a broad health organization that could compete in the era of managed care—a focus that some of the group's affiliates felt would inevitably diminish their role as advocates for abortion rights."

Pam drove to Baltimore to see me. Over lengthy conversations, I came to see that our experiences, separated by more than two decades, had much in common. Perhaps our approaches could have been right for another organization, but not for Planned Parenthood and not at the times in which we served.

I learned, too, that the board had made a key process mistake, as had I. The job had been offered after I had given what I thought was an explicit statement of who I am and where I thought the organization should go. I believed that I had the mandate to dramatically reposition Planned Parenthood. As it turned out, the search committee didn't fully represent the view of the board, and there was no consensus among its members, the affiliates, the staff, and its supporters on the organization's vision, strategy, and identity. Indeed, many thought that things were fine as they were.

People are often surprised when I say that despite the pain around my departure, I have deep empathy and profound appreciation for all those involved with Planned Parenthood. During my time there, I met some of the most dedicated people I have ever encountered. A CEO who spent her entire career working her way up from clinic assistant to running an affiliate. A patient who received care then went to nursing school and is now a clinical supervisor. A teen mother who took part in a Planned Parenthood program that helped her finish school and now works at a health center, as does her daughter.

So many devoted their lives to Planned Parenthood. They saw their work as a calling, their cause as a reason for being, and their colleagues as a family of kindred spirits. A passion that borders on fanaticism has been the key to many successes, although it also bred an insularity that became only more exclusionary as external pressures built. These were all people who bore the battle scars from being constantly under attack.

That Planned Parenthood is still in existence, over one hundred years after its founding, is a testament to the courage, ingenuity, and resilience of those who put themselves on the line for its mission. The bunker mentality is the result of always being at war. But it also means that short-term, urgent priorities will always take precedence over long-term investments that may be just as important. The attendant suspicion of outside people and distrust of new ideas could also perpetuate the siloing of the organization and of reproductive health care.

I'd like to think that my work there changed the focus in some way, and that some of the approaches and programs I started will continue. It was wonderful to see lasting evidence of the health-care-first language I introduced and to know that some affiliates continued to expand their non-abortion services.

Nothing could shake my gratitude for the care that my family and I received at Planned Parenthood. It is a community of courageous people who provide lifesaving, life-transforming care in extraordinarily challenging circumstances. They are heroes, and it was a privilege to serve alongside them.

16

Preventable Harm

In early 2019, my longtime mentor, Dr. Fitzhugh Mullan, was diagnosed with end-stage lung cancer. He had suffered through metastatic cancer once before, in his thirties, but had survived to spend the next forty years serving vulnerable communities and training generations of physician-activists to strive for health equity.

To recognize his accomplishments, George Washington University created the Fitzhugh Mullan Institute for Health Workforce Equity. The week after my tenure ended at Planned Parenthood, Fitz asked if I would join the institute as its first distinguished fellow. I would return to GW to teach health policy and public health, and I'd work with Fitz to help ensure that his values and legacy were reflected in the new institute's work. As Fitz pointed out, he had been there at the beginning of my career; I would be there at the end of his.

Coming back to teaching and pursuing work that was so personally meaningful was a great blessing, although it was a shock to my system to shift from one hundred miles-per-hour to ten. Suddenly, I had my evenings and weekends free. My calendar changed from fifteen-minute blocks of tightly scheduled meetings to entire days where my only responsibilities were conducting research and mentoring students. I finally had time to give guest lectures at other universities and engage with colleagues around the country. Seeing patients felt completely different, too. I'd worked at the same urgent care clinic for uninsured patients throughout my time as health commissioner and while running Planned Parenthood, but I had always kept an eye on my phone for work emergencies. Now I could focus 100 percent on whatever I was doing. Perhaps the biggest difference was regaining control over what I could say and how and where I said it. It was liberating not to have to parse every word in every conversation and worry about different stakeholders arguing over every tweet. I could speak out on issues I cared about using my true voice: as an advocate for my patients, through the lens of medicine and science.

And I could finally devote time to writing, which I loved. I began contributing regular columns to the *Washington Post*—about drug companies paying hefty settlements for their role in the opioid crisis and making sure the funds went to the people most affected; about Medicare for All as the health-care topic dominating the Democratic primaries, urging voters to consider other crucial health issues such as mental health and the need to fund prevention; about HIV treatment, gun violence, and health disparities. I also gave radio and television commentary on these topics, and began informally advising local, state, and federal legislators and health officials. This, I felt, was how I could continue to make a difference, shaping public opinion and health policy.

I WAS BOARDING A FLIGHT to speak at Duke University when I got a message from my editor, Mike Larabee, at the *Post*.

"I know I need to get back to you on the other one," he wrote, referring to an article I'd pitched. "But thinking about coronavirus this morning—do you see an angle there?"

It was January 2020. I was vaguely familiar with the mysterious respiratory illness that had appeared in Wuhan, China, a yet-unnamed new virus that was part of the coronavirus family. Coronaviruses caused the common cold as well as its much deadlier cousins, SARS and MERS. I knew that this novel coronavirus had sickened more than four hundred people and appeared to be spreading rapidly. The Chinese government had just announced the quarantine of the entire city of Wuhan and its eleven million residents, the largest such effort in modern history. At that moment, there was just one infection from the virus in the United States, a travel-related case of someone returning from Wuhan.

Could this be the next pandemic? That was always a possibility. Thousands of novel viruses appear every year, but for one to infect humans and have pandemic potential, many factors have to align: it must be highly contagious and easily transmitted from person to person, for example. Public health experts monitored for new viruses, something I had seen when I worked at the WHO when I was a global health fellow with Dr. Anthony So. Also, I was in my residency and working in the ER during the H1N1 influenza pandemic, and I had seen how a contagious respiratory illness could tax the health-care system.

Responding to infectious illnesses is the bread and butter of local public health. In Baltimore, we routinely ran through preparedness drills for large-scale disease outbreaks. There was a case of a toddler with suspected measles early in my tenure. Measles is so contagious that one infected person can spread it to an average of eighteen to nineteen people. During the potentially infectious period, this toddler went to a birthday party at a nursing home, then to a Chuck E. Cheese and two hospital ERs—we had to conduct contact tracing in all of these settings. This meant locating everyone who could have been exposed to that toddler, asking them if they'd experienced symptoms, talking through contacts they could have had, and, if necessary, asking them to quarantine from others. For just this one person, there were more than a hundred others who were possibly exposed. My staff were on the phone day and night and traveling to homes and workplaces to investigate exposure and check immunization records.

These experiences revealed the limited capacity of our public health infrastructure even during regular times. Our entire emergency preparedness team consisted of six people, and they were the same individuals who responded to weather crises and helped with our opioid response efforts. When emergencies came up, these staff were pulled off of other priorities, and if we needed additional hands, people would be pulled from wherever we could. School health nurses, senior center operators, and anyone who could help would be redeployed to that emergency. A weather-related event that ended within weeks was manageable, but something like Zika, which required months of preparation and mobilization, meant that other critical health priorities were put on the back burner. These were the trade-offs we were forced to make.

Local health departments around the country suffered from the same lack of resources. Despite the various threats to public health and the huge unmet need for services, these departments lost 28 percent of their combined workforce over the last two decades. The CDC's funding to local government had decreased by half since 2010. We were all stretched to the brink as it was; we had neither the staff nor the resources to respond to a large-scale public health emergency, especially if it required intensive focus over the course of months or years.

In response to Mike's message, I pitched him this idea: that the nation was underprepared to deal with a public health crisis, which was not just a threat to our health but also to national security. Mike thought this was too much like telling people to eat their vegetables. Don't we all know that we need to invest more in prevention? Anyway, nothing much had happened in the United States, and my idea seemed far too theoretical.

We settled on another angle: public health depends on public trust. For any response to be effective, people need to heed government orders, and to do that, they must have faith that their leaders know what they're talking about and have citizens' best interests at heart. A breakdown in that trust means that public health measures fall apart. We saw this happen with Ebola in the Congo, where people suspicious of the government refused to cooperate with medical personnel, going so far as to attack Red Cross volunteers, stop construction of a treatment center, and help others escape their mandatory quarantine. An anti-science, anti-government sentiment was growing in the United States, too, symbolized by the anti-vaccine movement. In 2019, the CDC documented the reemergence of measles with 1,282 cases—a nearly 250 percent increase from 2018 and the highest number of infections since 1993.

Governments shoulder much of the blame for the erosion of trust. It's not surprising that the Congolese harbor deep suspicions of their rulers after many years of civil wars and corrupt regimes; in 2018, there were allegations that the party in power cited Ebola as a reason to exclude opposition strongholds from voting. As I wrote in my *Post* column, Americans were also at risk. Politicians at all levels of government questioned the credibility of their own government experts. Worse yet, science itself had been distrusted, discredited, and demonized. A 2019 report by the Union of Concerned Scientists noted that the Trump administration had levied eighty attacks on science in its first two years. These included disbanding scientific advisory committees, withdrawing funding from research centers, shutting down existing studies, and overruling the federal government's own scientific reports.

Soon after my exchange with Mike, we learned that the Chinese government had betrayed its people's trust by covering up initial reports of the novel virus to the point of forcing doctors who raised the alarm to recant their statements. Li Wenliang, one of the whistleblowers, soon contracted the coronavirus and succumbed to it. Dr. Li's death made him a martyr as Chinese people went on social media to call for transparency and free speech.

The people of the United States would fare no better, but we did not know that at the time.

EVEN AS CASES OF THE new coronavirus accelerated in the United States, the science around the disease was still evolving. But what we already knew was deeply concerning. The virus spread through the respiratory route: if a person coughed or sneezed, and if the large respiratory droplets landed on someone else's nose or mouth; or if that person wiped their nose and then touched a surface that others touched, those others could get infected. Two factors made the virus particularly hard to contain. About half the transmissions seemed to come from asymptomatic people who had no idea they were infected, making it hard to identify those who were contagious. In addition, the virus wasn't spread only by large droplets; microscopic aerosols expelled just through breathing or speaking appeared to carry it, too.

Still, if the novel coronavirus behaved like the four coronaviruses that caused the common cold, it wouldn't be so bad. Unfortunately, though, it was leading to severe illness in many, particularly older people and those with chronic medical conditions. At that time, about 20 percent of COVID-19 patients needed to be hospitalized, and one in four of those became so severely ill with pneumonia that they had to be intubated and put on a ventilator. Hospital systems are not equipped to take care of so many critically ill patients at once. If hospitals are overwhelmed, desperately ill patients might have to be turned away to die at home. It wouldn't only be patients with coronavirus who'd be affected: anyone suffering a heart attack, stroke, or from other conditions wouldn't get care either.

In the early days, health-care workers were able to follow the gold standard of protocols for personal protective equipment (PPE). We knew to don an N95 respiratory mask and put on a gown and goggles before entering the room of a patient with a contagious respiratory illness. And we knew to dispose of the mask and plastic gown after each use. These were CDC guidelines that every hospital followed as part of their procedures. But very quickly, by early March 2020, hospitals were sounding the alarm: they might run out of supplies and be forced to change their protocols. Why? The science hadn't changed, but available supply had. First, providers were told to reuse their N95s for multiple patients. Then they were given only one per week. Doctors and nurses were asked to spray their gowns between rooms rather than change them. Even the basic surgical mask was rationed, to be worn until it was too soggy to stay on. Some hospitals ran out of masks and gowns altogether, and clinicians had to supply their own.

The month before, I had heard stories from China about health-care workers rationing PPE. Hospitals in Wuhan were reporting that doctors and nurses were so short of protective suits that they were wearing diapers to avoid changing out of them. Staff were wearing raincoats and garbage bags and resorted to making their own masks. This was so tragic, I thought, but surely it could never happen in the United States.

But then it did. My Facebook page was filled with pleas from clinicians around the country: "Does anyone have masks left over from home improvement projects?" a friend posted. Someone else said he'd gone to three Lowes and Home Depot stores before he could find a face shield used for welding. The shield didn't cover the bottom of his face, but it was better than nothing. The listserv for my former residency colleagues was a running thread of advice: This Amazon seller had Tyvek suits that could be reused. There's a veterinary supplies website selling gloves. Someone recommended a piercing/tattoo outlet that had masks in stock.

The CDC revised its mask guidance little by little, from reusing masks to recommending bandannas if there were no other option. In Tennessee, a hospital administrator was filmed during a seminar saying that hospital workers out of masks could wear diapers across their faces.

Scarcity wasn't limited to PPE: COVID-19 tests were in such limited supply that patients couldn't get tested even if they had all the symptoms. This made containment impossible. By the time one case was detected, whether in a family or in congregate settings such as nursing homes, jails, and homeless shelters, there were almost always dozens if not hundreds of others. Communities that thought they were infection free had clusters of cases that turned into full-blown outbreaks within days.

The realization was shocking: the United States, the richest country on earth, was vastly unprepared for a pandemic. Despite warnings over the years from prominent scientists that it was only a matter of time, there weren't even sufficient supplies of masks in the federal stockpile. What I had experienced on the local level—that we were prepared for a limited, short-term disaster only—was true for the rest of the country. If a hurricane hit one region, supplies and personnel could be mobilized from other parts. But we had no capability to handle a hurricane that hit every part of the country all at once, especially one that had no end in sight.

As the coronavirus engulfed one region after another, the early intimations of a national systems failure ballooned into a full-on catastrophe: mismanagement, incoherence, and denial at the top; unprecedented subversion of science and truth; and deliberate obfuscation that led to millions of people revolting against public health guidance. Doctors, scientists, and public health experts found themselves in the extraordinary position of serving as a corrective to a pandemic of misinformation and disinformation. In the immediate moment, health-care professionals were called to insist on the truth of science, guide the public to protect themselves, and advise policy makers through challenging decisions—when to implement stay-at-home orders, whether to shut down schools, and how to scale up testing. In the long term, the pandemic exposed as nothing else the need for overdue investment in the public health infrastructure. It unmasked layers of underlying health disparities and brought to light the urgent need to focus on health equity.

For me, it seemed as if everything in my life had led to this moment. I had the training and experience, and the time and capacity, to join the fight against COVID-19 and help address the biggest public health crisis of our lifetime.

THE UNITED STATES FAILED UTTERLY. With our numbers of dead, the verdict is in.

When the history books are written, the bulk of the blame will be assigned to the failure of the Trump administration and its lack of a unified, coherent, and science-based response.

Take the issue of PPE and testing supplies. Producing N95 masks and testing reagents isn't rocket science, but to produce the quantities needed for an emergency on such a scale requires a coordinated, national effort. That didn't happen. Instead, components of tests were produced in large quantities only to hit a roadblock: there weren't enough swabs to collect samples. There was a mad scramble to get more swabs, but just as hospitals received them, various chemical reagents ran out and labs couldn't process the tests. Then, when there was a new supply of reagents, there was a shortage of PPE. Nurses and doctors had to don PPE to perform the tests, and with PPE in such short supply, they were told to conserve PPE and test only those who were severely ill. Instead of anticipating what was ahead, the country was always several steps behind.

The federal government did not supply tests or PPE at the rate that hospitals needed. Individual states were forced to buy them on the open market. Often, they were in competition with one another and with the federal government. Prices skyrocketed, while patients struggled to get tested and frontline health-care workers faced tragic conditions. And because there was inadequate testing, no one knew the true dimensions of the growing epidemic.

The absurdity reached new levels every day. In Maryland, Governor Hogan negotiated with the government of Korea to purchase five hundred thousand tests. Put aside how little sense it makes for individual states to have to turn to foreign governments to ask for help. When the tests arrived, they were placed under 24/7 protection by the Maryland National Guard to prevent the federal government from confiscating them for the federal stockpile. Later it turned out that the tests were defective, an unfortunate result that should have never occurred because there should have been no need to purchase them in this way.

In Massachusetts, the head of a major hospital, a physician, found additional PPE in a different part of the country. He paid five times the going rate and went to the airport to receive it himself, along with tractor-trailers disguised as food-service vehicles. Still, he was intercepted by the FBI, who tried to seize the supplies for use by the federal government.

All the while, I and other public health experts were sounding the alarm: Please, help our health-care workers. We can't send troops into war without armor. The federal government must do its part. The situation is desperate. Today, we're out of masks; tomorrow, we'll be out of doctors and nurses. In New York City, which saw the country's first rampant virus surge, the lack of PPE was a harbinger: scarcity of masks gave way to overcrowded hospitals, severe shortages of intensive care beds, ventilators, and eventually burial grounds.

Often, it felt like a broken record. How many more times would we have to say that tests are essential? Every time the Trump administration made the absurd claim that increased testing led to more infections, I'd go on radio and TV to explain why this was wrong. Tests don't create infections; infections exist regardless of whether you test; and testing, tracing, and quarantine and isolation are how we contain the virus. How many times could we plead with officials to stop justifying the lack of tests and instead figure out how to get what we need? And what about more PPE?

The response from the White House was always the same: "We hope to get more soon." Trump had designated Vice President Mike Pence to lead the administration's coronavirus task force, and when I began giving commentary and providing medical analysis on television, I was often asked to watch the task force press briefings. We heard about this "hope" again and again, as if hope were a strategy, "more" was a quantity, and "soon" was a time line.

What struck me in these briefings was the profound disconnect between the assertions by national political leaders and the reality on the ground. Trump and Pence insisted there was enough testing and PPE, while health professionals working in clinics and hospitals knew this could not be further from the truth. There were only two explanations that I could see: either the administration didn't know and hadn't bothered to learn about the extent of the shortages, or it knew and was trying to cover it up.

In an outlandish bid to deflect responsibility, Trump even suggested there was a nefarious reason why hospitals were running out of masks. "Something's going on, and you oughtta look into it," he said. "Where are the masks going? Are they going out the back door?" The country's president had actually suggested that health-care workers, who were fighting to save lives while risking their own, might be stealing masks. People were dying while the administration muddied the water, and instead of confronting reality, our nation's own president chose to divide the population into those who believed him and those who didn't.

THE LACK OF A UNIFIED federal response resulted in an epic and devastating tsunami of coronavirus. The countries that were able to rein in COVID-19 all deployed a national strategy, unlike the United States. Instead, ours was a piecemeal approach.

States were left to their own devices, without the funding that they needed, to figure out their policies, procedures, and actions. Nowhere was the lack of a cohesive plan more evident than in the different states' divergent stay-at-home orders and then their subsequent reopening. During the first surge of the pandemic, some states issued full stay-at-home orders early on. Others took their time. About half never issued such orders at all, barely adopting even the basic social distancing guidelines that the CDC issued.

In defense of this decentralized approach, some pointed to the size of the country and the difficulty of a one-size-fits-all solution. Why should some places lock down when they had no infections? This argument might have made sense had there been sufficient testing and states could confirm the absence of the infection. That wasn't the case. Indeed, community spread was rapidly occurring throughout the United States. Often, the first case detected was the canary in the mine: one positive diagnosis usually meant that many others were incubating and an outbreak was well underway.

Quite simply, countries that imposed a national lockdown and then quickly ramped up their testing and contact tracing succeeded in containing the virus. They didn't have a magic pill—a secret vaccine or a therapeutic. What they had was a coherent, coordinated approach. Unlike the United States, they implemented consistent restrictions with a clear rationale for their entire population. And also unlike the United States, they maintained unambiguous messaging in which the elected leaders supported the work of public health experts. As a result, many were able to suppress COVID-19 almost entirely. They didn't just bend the curve—they crushed the curve.

There was one hope for the United States: we could have spent the time during the first surge, when many states did curb social activity, to bolster public health infrastructure, build the capacity to find new cases, trace contacts, and quarantine those exposed. But that did not happen.

Hardly a day went by when I wasn't questioned on herd immunity—couldn't we aim for that? Herd immunity is reached when enough people in a community—generally 60 percent to 80 percent—develop antibodies to an illness, either through vaccination or recovery, and the disease stops spreading. I explained again and again that banking on herd immunity without a vaccine was a dangerous proposition: for one thing, it was unclear at the time how long immunity would last after contracting COVID-19. And even if those who recovered did become immune, an infection rate of 60 percent would mean nearly two hundred million infected Americans. With an estimated fatality rate of 1 percent, two million would have been condemned to die for an untested theory.

Others arguing against increased restrictions pointed to the fact that most cases of COVID-19 were mild. We could keep older people at home and allow the young and healthy to go back to school and work, the thinking went. This was problematic for multiple reasons. First, older people weren't the only ones contracting COVID-19. Early reports found that one in five patients requiring hospitalization were aged between twenty and forty-four. We also saw that infected people in their thirties and forties were dying of respiratory failure and, sometimes, strokes. And younger people could be asymptomatic carriers, spreading the virus to an older population; indeed, as we learned, the trajectory of infection did follow this pattern. What started in the young didn't stay in the young.

Moreover, allowing the coronavirus to spread unchecked meant overcrowded hospitals, preventing all patients from getting necessary care. And concerns voiced about the effect of a lockdown on the nation's mental health involved no small degree of hypocrisy—the lawmakers who justified quickly reopening by pointing to children's health, mental health, and addiction rates were the same ones who had not long before voted to reduce funding for these same areas.

IN THE ABSENCE OF FEDERAL leadership, some governors did impose stay-at-home orders, which succeeded in curbing the virus in their states. The federal government, to its credit, issued clear guidelines for gradual reopening that relied on science-based principles. But even this blueprint had major flaws. The most obvious missing piece remained that of testing. A crucial measure for safe reopening was a downward trajectory of infections. But how could one have confidence that this trend was real without mass testing? There also wasn't nearly enough contact tracing. Nationally, there was a need for as many as three hundred thousand additional contact tracers. The work of identifying new cases and then tracing and quarantining every person exposed to those cases is time- and labor-intensive, but it can be done by people with a basic level of public health training. There were various proposals for students and those out of work to be deployed for tracing. Some locales like Boston and New York set up innovative partnerships to increase contact tracers, and Baltimore led an effort with Baltimore Corps and the health department teaming up once again. A national program to recruit, train, and deploy these workers would have been far more efficient than fifty state programs with differing protocols and procedures.

In addition, the federal government declined to invoke any enforcement authority over states that ignored the White House's reopening criteria. The spread of cases had shown that, like other infections, COVID-19 had no respect for state or national borders. Lifting restrictions prematurely in one state would affect neighboring states and spark a second surge of infections that would tear through the country with explosive speed. Yet, many states removed what few restrictions they had—proudly, with impunity—even when they didn't come close to meeting the reopening criteria.

Whereas other countries suppressed their case counts almost to zero before reopening—and even then, were very careful in peeling back restrictions and monitoring the results—the best the United States achieved was holding the rate to below twenty thousand new infections per day. And that was only the number of confirmed cases. The CDC estimated that this could be a dramatic undercount: because for every case detected, there could be up to ten others that had not been diagnosed. The consequences of prematurely reopening were predictable, and public health leaders tried their best to sound the alarm. The science had not changed. Without a vaccine or a cure, the only thing keeping the disease in check was separating people from one another.

We did have one advantage over the initial wave of devastation in March and April. We could see the next surges coming. We had learned from New York's experience. Treatments had gotten better, and we understood the science of the virus much better. Now was the time to implement pandemic preparedness protocols and ensure that there were sufficient supplies.

But instead of doubling down to prepare for the inevitable next surge, the federal government squandered any gains made. There was little investment in strengthening public health infrastructure and no expanded capacity to find new cases, trace contacts, and arrange for quarantine. Individual hospitals did their best to increase their own stockpiles and prepare their own surge plans. Many local and state officials also worked within their limited budgets to increase their staffing. Yet the White House, despite all the warning signs, again failed to put forth a coordinated, nationwide response.

The result was a massive wave, first across the Sun Belt and the South in the summer of 2020, then the entire country over the fall and winter. With numerous outbreaks erupting at once, the nation's ability to respond was severely strained. This time around, many outbreaks occurred in rural communities, which already struggled with a shortage of hospitals and health professionals. They had little capacity to care for critically ill patients, who needed to be transferred to urban hospitals, adding further pressure to places that were also hit hard with their own patients.

By the end of 2020, the coronavirus had killed more than 330,000 Americans. This calamity could have been prevented had there been a national framework from the beginning, or even one established after the first deadly surge.

ALTHOUGH THE TRUMP ADMINISTRATION DID implement some interventions appropriately and well, even these were rife with problems. It imposed travel restrictions on China early on, with the goal of containing the number of cases entering the United States. To his credit, Trump pushed forward these restrictions when many public health experts and the WHO argued against them. However, the restrictions ultimately failed because they were inconsistently applied: more than forty thousand people from China entered, and they did not go through any type of screening. Also, the sole focus on China ignored the fact that coronavirus had spread to other countries, including many parts of Europe. Indeed, the strains predominantly found in the surge that occurred in New York originated not from China but Europe.

The restrictions were also impeded by the lack of testing, compounded by the fact that we didn't yet know about asymptomatic transmission. Thus the virus was circulating in many parts of the country for weeks before it was detected. Not only was the United States poorly and inconsistently monitoring incoming travelers, but we missed that the virus was spreading prolifically right under our noses.

Another potential success was the administration's vaccine development effort. Previously, the fastest development of a vaccine had been four years; many other vaccines took decades to develop, and there are some viruses, such as HIV, that still do not have vaccines. It is a triumph of science and public-private partnership that within a year not one but two vaccines were created and showed remarkable efficacy. Very few in public health could have predicted that a vaccine with such safety and efficacy would have become available so quickly.

However, Trump undermined the vaccine's credibility by tying its federal approval to his reelection prospects. Even the name of the administration's vaccine effort—Operation Warp Speed—raised concerns, a worry that shortcuts were taken in the scientific process. Also, vaccines are not the answer in and of themselves—it's the vaccination that saves lives, and the vaccination hinges on distribution and administration. Local and state health departments that were already shouldering the responsibility of overseeing the rest of pandemic response now needed to lead the most ambitious vaccination effort the United States had ever undertaken. They estimated that they needed at least $8.4 billion to accomplish this. At the time that they got the first allotment of the vaccine, all they had received was about $400 million.

It was no surprise that locales just could not establish the needed infrastructure with this paltry sum. As a result, Operation Warp Speed in drug development failed to translate into any kind of speed for production and distribution. President Trump's promise of one hundred million doses by the end of 2020 barely translated to fourteen million delivered to states and, of those, only four million had been converted to shots in arms. Yet, instead of taking responsibility and identifying urgent solutions, the federal government once again washed its hands of the problem and instead put the blame on local and state health departments. Once again the lack of a national mobilization resulted in a piecemeal approach that left local and state officials in the lurch. They had neither the guidance nor the resources needed to deliver on this critical public health mission, with the appalling result that millions of doses of vaccines sat in freezers while thousands of Americans died every day.

The administration's greatest misstep regarding the vaccine was that it was touted as a cure-all. As the deaths piled up, it was clear that the White House had put all its eggs in the vaccine basket alone, while undermining the lifesaving role of testing, wearing masks, and maintaining social distancing. The vaccine would save the day for many, but so little was done for the people who died in the meantime. It was this denial at the top, and the chaos that flowed from it, that shaped the tragic trajectory of the pandemic.

17

A Pandemic of Misinformation

Of all the factors that caused the calamity of COVID-19 in the United States, the biggest culprit was the deliberate misinformation and active disinformation that came from the White House.

The number of times President Donald Trump contradicted his public health experts is too numerous to count. There were immediate health consequences to his constituents. When Trump, without evidence, extolled the virtues of hydroxychloroquine in combating the virus, there was a run on the drug. Patients who relied on it to treat lupus or rheumatoid arthritis could no longer obtain their daily medication. Others took it, believing the president that hydroxychloroquine was harmless. In Phoenix, Arizona, however, a man died, and his wife ended up in critical care, when they took a form of chloroquine used in aquariums.

During one press conference, Trump talked about the benefit of UV therapy and mused about preventing the virus by drinking bleach and injecting disinfectant. At this point, I was working regularly with CNN. Early in the pandemic, Dr. Sanjay Gupta had recommended that I join him and Anderson Cooper on their coronavirus global town halls. My job was to assist Sanjay with answering viewer questions, and over time

I joined the network as a medical analyst to develop explainers, provide health policy analyses, and contribute to on-air commentary.

After Trump speculated on the value of bleach, I found myself that night on CNN's coronavirus town hall broadcast explaining the extreme danger of these ideas. It could be fatal to drink bleach. For the millions of people who saw President Trump as the most credible messenger, we needed to tell them to listen to medical experts, not the president: please, do not do this.

In the following week, poison control centers fielded calls about bleach ingestion, and for some time afterward I received queries from patients and viewers—including school-age children—about the idea. I even appeared on a surreal CNN *Sesame Street* segment with Sanjay, Big Bird, and Elmo to explain why children shouldn't listen to medical and public health advice from our president.

This deliberate effort to undermine science was particularly harmful in another crucial area: mask-wearing. Early in the pandemic, the scientific guidance was for health-care workers and symptomatic people to use masks but not the general public. When the science evolved, the CDC and WHO changed their instructions to urge everyone to wear a mask. Emerging studies showed that universal use of masks cut transmission by as much as 80 percent. Models were projecting that if 95 percent of Americans wore masks in public, it could save tens of thousands of lives. An analysis by Goldman Sachs estimated that mask-wearing would prevent a drop in the GDP by 5 percent.

The evidence was clear. Yet the federal government continued to resist a national mask-wearing mandate, and Trump himself and many of his top aides routinely attended events without masks. They derided their value, paving the way for state governors to do the same. Some governors forbade local officials from enforcing mask mandates, and the governor of Georgia even sued the mayor of Atlanta for issuing a city-wide masking ordinance.

In this climate, the vital public health intervention of mask-wearing became a political symbol. In June 2020, an Axios-Ipsos poll showed that 65 percent of Democrats reported a wearing a mask while leaving home versus 35 percent of Republicans. Blue state governors and mayors ordered mask-wearing in public places, while many red state leaders railed against it as an infringement of people's liberty. Conspiracy theories of masks being ineffective and COVID-19 being overblown were circulated by right-wing media. When a Republican representative, Louis Gohmert of Texas, contracted COVID-19, he insinuated that wearing a mask was how he got the virus.

Conspiracy theorists would have most likely propagated misinformation regardless of the national leadership. Science skeptics would no doubt have seized on changing guidance as proof that scientists don't know what they're talking about. But when the president amplified misinformation and weaponized it to advance personal political aims, the fringe was given credence. This further undermined public health leaders and doctors, at a time when their credibility was most needed to contain the pandemic.

In some places, local and state public health officials became targets of people's rage and scapegoats for politicians who were under increasing pressure themselves. Dozens were forced out of their roles for providing policy recommendations based on science. Others resigned in the face of protests and threats against their families. Health department employees who tried to conduct contact tracing were harassed, ignored, and turned away, unable to do their jobs to protect the communities they served.

At precisely the time when public health needed to lead and foster public trust, health officials were sidelined. Early on, the CDC held daily media briefings to provide an update on the outbreak and the most recent findings about the novel coronavirus. Clinicians, myself included, tuned in faithfully or read the summary transcripts. The briefings were very helpful in deciphering the complex and quickly evolving disease. Even though much was unknown, it was reassuring to hear expert analysis from those who pored over the hundreds of new studies coming out every day.

Then the briefings abruptly stopped. In their place came daily White House press conferences, spectacles that distracted from the emergency at hand. Instead of the guidance that clinicians and the public desperately needed, the briefings were a jaw-dropping display of contradictory messaging, with the president saying one thing and public health experts having to clean up his misinformation while trying not to contradict their boss.

"Be first, be right, be credible" is the mantra of communicating in a public health emergency. The administration's briefings violated every aspect of crisis communication. More often than not, new information was disseminated to the public by the media rather than presented by top federal scientists. Since traditional media were not trusted by a significant segment of the country, objective and accurate news still did not reach many millions of Americans. The conflicting messages shed serious doubt on the accuracy of the information conveyed.

In addition, the credibility of the nation's foremost scientists, including Dr. Anthony Fauci, one of the most respected infectious diseases experts in the world, came under attack. The belligerence often came from the president himself. Public health experts, scientists, and doctors felt called to step into the void. If the country's leading health officials had been undercut, then those outside government had to speak up and do what our colleagues couldn't do. It was up to us to raise awareness of the threat, present tangible actions to rein in the disease, challenge misinformation, and insist on the following the science.

This was no small challenge in the face of a fierce and concerted effort to damage belief in science itself. Long after a preponderance of evidence debunked the efficacy of hydroxychloroquine, the Senate was still holding hearings on why it wasn't being more widely used. Doctors were invited to testify, citing anecdotes of patients who'd had positive outcomes after receiving the treatment. (Of course, anecdote isn't evidence, and it's possible that the patients could have had the same outcome without taking the medication.) As well as diverting attention from actual therapies and helpful preventive measures, these hearings perpetuated misinformation and distrust of the scientific process.

Even worse, they bolstered an alternate reality where there are no objective facts, only different opinions held by different so-called experts. This was a playbook similar to that used to undermine environmental science, painting climate change as a matter of opinion rather than fact. When the Trump administration brought in a neuroradiologist, Scott Atlas, with fringe views on COVID-19, he became a fixture on conservative news outlets, questioning the use of masks, promoting the discredited herd immunity approach, and making outlandish assertions about how the illness did not sicken children. Many people trusted the rebuttals of public health experts, but many others shrugged them off as a difference in professional opinion.

The White House COVID-19 coordinator, Dr. Deborah Birx, would reveal in time that she would present one set of data to Trump, only to see him use completely different numbers in public. She had no idea where he got this alternate information, but suspected that it was from Atlas and others who wanted to downplay the severity of the pandemic. This active subversion of reality came to a head nearly every day. No one expects policies to be made solely based on scientific guidance; there are numerous other viewpoints that must also be considered, and that's what policy makers the world over consider every day. The danger is when scientific findings are suppressed and facts manipulated to achieve a partisan aim.

THE GOVERNMENT'S AUTHORITATIVE SCIENTIFIC INSTITUTIONS, specifically the CDC and the Food and Drug Administration, were chief targets of this disinformation campaign, which came at the worst possible time. These agencies were instrumental in leading us out of the pandemic, but they were pressured to concede to political demands. This prompted a crisis of trust, and not just by anti-science groups but from among the many who previously trusted these entities.

That there could be an erosion of confidence in the CDC, one of the most revered public health institutions in the world, is something I could never have imagined. Other countries send their scientists to train at the CDC and even name their premier public health entities after it.

I had worked closely with the CDC when I was health commissioner and always appreciated its direct, precise language. Among its many strengths was the ability to synthesize complex scientific information and produce actionable guidelines. No local official has the time or the workforce capacity to wade through thousands of scientific studies. We depended on the CDC to do that review and then formulate national recommendations. City and county health departments could tailor that guidance for their communities and explain it in terms of the local context to help businesses, schools, and other entities. Contrary to constraining them, federal guidelines empowered local agencies to do their work.

So it was striking when the CDC began hedging its guidance and taking actions that were at odds with the scientific consensus. Instead of directing businesses to implement certain safety measures, the statements contained many hedging words such as "if possible" and "if feasible." Many recommendations were so watered down that they lost their meaning. If guidelines to protect the public's health were entirely optional, what was the point of issuing them? After all, we don't simply suggest that people wear seat belts or say that they can follow speed limits if they feel like it.

How the CDC issued new guidelines was also a problem. Once the agency was prevented from giving public updates, changes in guidance appeared on its website without notice or explanation. No one even knew that new information had been posted; often, the changes were discovered only when clinicians went to the website and noticed them days after the edits were made. After the change was reported in the news, there would then be a mad scramble to find out the reason behind it. Had a new study come out and the science had evolved? Was it driven by a logistical need because of limited resources? Or had there been political interference? Much of the time no one knew, and without a scientific rationale the changes fueled speculation and even more confusion.

An especially egregious incident occurred when the CDC quietly changed its guidance to suggest that asymptomatic people did not need to be tested. This came well after studies had unequivocally confirmed the role of asymptomatic spread; indeed, the CDC's own website noted that half of all transmission was due to asymptomatic carriers. The new guidance flew in the face of fact and common sense. There wasn't anything close to sufficient testing at the time, and one had to wonder whether this was a ploy to get around the shortage. Or perhaps it was a gambit by insurance companies that didn't want to pay for testing.

The backlash was swift. Dozens of major medical organizations issued rebukes. Governors held press conferences where they vowed to ignore these guidelines. The former head of the National Institutes of Health and the CEO of the Rockefeller Foundation coauthored an article in the *New York Times* asking the American people to "ignore the CDC." State and local health officials scrambled to issue their own guidance contradicting the CDC. The confusion had a direct impact on patient care, with reports of testing sites turning away asymptomatic people, many of whom were seeking testing because they were exposed to COVID-19.

Reports later confirmed that the change was the result of orders from the White House. Not only did career scientists oppose the change, many were unaware that the directive had been issued. They—and the nation's public health community—were relieved when the guidelines reverted a few weeks later. But much damage had been done. People who had revered the CDC now doubted that its guidance could be impartial and evidence based. Governors increasingly relied on secondary reviews by state experts, reducing the CDC's relevance and reach. And once again, the American people did not know whom to believe.

THE FDA ALSO CAME UNDER political pressure just when the public most needed to trust its seal of safety. First, it appeared to authorize emergency use of hydroxychloroquine after Trump's strong endorsement. It then authorized convalescent plasma therapy despite scant evidence, seeming to have succumbed to direct pressure from the president. After a chorus of consternation from the medical community, the FDA withdrew its approval of hydroxychloroquine and the commissioner walked back his statements on plasma, but not before adding to scientists' concern about the independence of the FDA's decision-making.

This, too, was something unimaginable just a few months before. It is critical to trust that top scientists in the FDA are approving drugs based on science, not political expediency or partisan ideology. Moreover, the need for confidence in the FDA's impartiality took on heightened urgency given the vaccine development underway. The best hope we had of ending the pandemic was to reach herd immunity through vaccination. To get there, the vaccine needed to be not only safe and effective, but also trusted.

Safety is of paramount importance. Unlike a therapeutic that is prescribed to individuals who are ill, a vaccine is given to previously healthy individuals. The bar for adverse reactions must be much higher and the benefit of a therapy that can cause substantial side effects must still be worth the risk. Vaccines are also given to large numbers, so a rare but serious side effect becomes not so rare if the drug has been administered to hundreds of millions. There's also the issue of efficacy: a vaccine that's not truly effective will give false reassurance. If either safety or efficacy are perceived to be compromised, the subsequent distrust will result in millions refusing to take the vaccine, thus prolonging suffering caused by the disease.

The Trump administration's Operation Warp Speed shaved years off the vaccine development process by eliminating bureaucratic red tape and providing a guarantee to drug makers of a ready buyer in the federal government. Production began even before trials were complete so that the moment the vaccines received FDA authorization, there would already be millions of doses ready to be distributed. Importantly, no shortcuts were taken in the scientific studies or during the rigorous approval process. Still, the emphasis on speed sowed doubt in some quarters. The concerns were heightened after Trump began speaking about vaccines needing to be approved before the November 2020 election. A national poll by Pew in May 2020 found that 72 percent of Americans were willing to take a coronavirus vaccine. That number dropped to 51 percent by September.

Politicizing science has consequences. Convincing healthy people to inject a new substance into their bodies is already a major challenge. People have different reasons to distrust vaccines. There are anti-vaxxers who do not vaccinate their children and harbor deep distrust of science. There are also people with real concerns about research due to a history of unethical experimentation and exploitation of their communities. Seeding suspicion of vaccines even among those who

believe in science was yet another distorted message that set back progress and prolonged the devastation caused by COVID-19.

IT IS ALWAYS CHALLENGING TO ask people to change the way they do
things and accept substantial inconvenience in their everyday lives.
Unfortunately, the pandemic of misinformation made the job of health-
care providers that much harder.

One of my patients, Samuel, a man in his forties who worked in
utilities, had to be cleared of the virus before returning to his job after a
coworker tested positive. His exposure had been significant: during the
time that his colleague was infectious, they rode in the same vehicle for
more than five hours. They wore masks but sometimes took them off
to eat and drink. It was raining, and they kept the car windows closed.

Samuel needed to quarantine apart from his family, but that was easier said than done. He lived in a two-bedroom apartment with four
children under the age of ten. His wife had a physical disability that
limited her mobility and required his help. To quarantine himself for
a fourteen-day period was nearly impossible—a challenge for anyone
living in tight quarters. It helped that my patient's work would pay him
during this time, but there were many other Americans in the same
position who might lose their wages or even their job. Other countries
provided quarantine facilities and some U.S. locales did this by con-
verting unused dorms and hotels, but these measures were few and far
between.

Clinicians ask our patients to quarantine when ill or exposed knowing that it's at best a disruption and at worst impossible. It's hard enough
under any circumstances to convince them to do this and help them
find the resources they need. But when people receive contradictory
messages, it's often a lost cause. Some continue to follow their doctors'
guidance, others may not. They may draw on the mixed messaging to
say that doctors don't know what we're talking about. They may hang
on to an alternate view as justification for behaviors that counter public
health guidance.

And they may feel angry at what they see as hypocrisy. As Samuel told me, it's a slap in the face to those who gave up so much to abide by the rules when they see others who don't. (He ended up testing negative that time, though a few months later, he developed coronavirus from another workplace exposure and ended up with severe enough illness that he needed to be hospitalized.)

Among those who didn't abide by the rules was the White House, whose messaging, spoken and unspoken, mattered immensely. When members of Trump's inner circle became infected with coronavirus, the White House proceeded with business as usual. Staff insisted that they were essential workers and continued doing their jobs even though they had substantial exposure. Had it been a school or work site with dozens of individuals who tested positive, the place would have been closed and investigated and protocols would have been put in place before it was allowed to reopen. The opposite happened. The White House continued to host social events where hundreds of people gathered in close proximity and without masks. Staff also held rallies with tens of thousands of participants in parts of the country that were developing into virus hot spots. A reasonable patient could well ask: If the president's team doesn't need to quarantine and isolate, why should I jump through hoops to do so? A business might ask the same: If the White House doesn't have to carry out contact tracing, why should we invest the resources to do it?

CNN often showed footage of Trump rallies and asked me and other experts for our opinion. As a clinician, I would say that the sight gave me a knot in my stomach. I worried for the thousands of maskless people packed closely together. I worried about the families they would go home to, and the second and third generation of infections that could result in their communities. Even if they didn't contract coronavirus at the rally, their behavior suggested that they probably took risks in other aspects of their lives. I worried about the example they set for their neighbors, friends, and children. I worried about hospitals and public health systems that were already at their brink, and how much worse they could be as a result of these individuals' choices.

I also thought, "*What if?*" The president had so much influence. What

if Trump had asked them to wear masks instead of mocking them—
imagine the difference that could have made. What if he'd held drive-in
events and urged people to keep physical distancing, instead of stag-
ing crowded rallies in the midst of a surging pandemic? What if he'd
called on Americans to show their patriotism by caring for one another
instead of dismissing public health measures as a sign of weakness?

Months into the pandemic, veteran journalist Bob Woodward
revealed that Trump knew how contagious COVID-19 was early on
but consciously understated the danger. Trump defended his actions,
saying he did not tell the country in order to avoid frightening Americans. However, fear is made worse by helplessness, and the antidote
to helplessness is agency. There were concrete steps Americans could
have taken to avoid getting sick and spreading the infection. If a hurricane were coming and there was time to take cover, it would be unconscionable to let it rip through communities rather than warn people of
the steps they could take to save their lives. Yet that happened every
day, all around the United States.

When Trump became infected, I hoped he would talk frankly about
his illness and finally help convince his millions of supporters of the
seriousness of COVID-19. U.K. prime minister Boris Johnson did just
this, as did other leaders. I hoped he would say what former New Jersey
governor Chris Christie said after he recovered from COVID-19: that
the virus was no joke, that it was deadly, and that everyone should
protect themselves. Instead, the president doubled down on trivializing
the virus. It wasn't that different from the flu, he said. The media was
exaggerating its gravity. Wear a mask if you want but not if you don't.
You'll be fine if you get it, because there's a cure.

But there wasn't, and great numbers of people were not fine. I saw
the direct impact of Trump's COVID-19 denial on clinical care. At the
time, I was teaching a virtual course on coronavirus management for
practicing health-care professionals. Every Saturday, a colleague and I
presented an overview of the state of the pandemic and then delved
into a particular medical aspect. People from all over the country asked
questions, and these were striking, reflecting as they did the effect of
mixed messaging and disinformation. Each week, multiple clinicians

asked for advice on helping their patients take COVID-19 more seriously. Some even believed the misinformation themselves and challenged our evidence-based presentations about hydroxychloroquine and convalescent plasma.

At one point, a heated exchange erupted when a few providers insisted that the numbers of coronavirus deaths were actually much lower than the official CDC count. They had heard from some media sites that the death count was inflated, and that doctors were falsifying death certificates for profit. The truth is that medical examiners recorded multiple causes of death, a standard practice given that there were often several contributory factors to the tragic outcome of COVID-19. But just because someone also had diabetes doesn't mean that they didn't die from COVID-19; that would be like saying a person who died from a car crash but also had cancer didn't really die because of their accident. It is also true that Congress had granted supplementary funding to hospitals that cared for coronavirus patients, which was needed for such additional resources as PPE, isolation rooms, and extra staffing. However, there was no evidence at all that doctors were somehow faking diagnoses, and to suggest such illegality while those doctors were risking their own lives was obscene.

Most disturbing was that clinicians could think this could be true. Some clung to this notion as well as denying the gravity of the virus, even as their colleagues listened with disbelief and indignation. Such was the extent of the disinformation campaign that even those who cared for patients could doubt scientific facts.

The denial and subversion of truth was so profound that some patients did not accept the reality of the virus even as they died from it. As South Dakota nurse Jodi Doering told CNN, "Their last dying words are, 'This can't be happening. It's not real.' And when they should be FaceTiming their families, they're filled with anger and hatred."

ANOTHER DAMAGING ASPECT OF THE barrage of disinformation was the framing of conflicting choices. Early on, public health was cast as the enemy of the economy. According to a prevailing narrative, Democrats and doctors wanted to shut everything down and destroy the economy; Republicans (led by Trump) wanted to "open up America" and save it. Thus people who lost their jobs had public health to blame, not the virus or the lack of government response to it. There was no nuance in this debate, only two stark choices: everyone should be locked away and isolated for indefinite periods of time, or they should all live their lives as if the pandemic didn't exist.

Pitting public health against the economy was a false choice and a dangerous one. In fact, public health was the only road map to safely reopening society. The economy suffered not because experts had some perverse desire to close everything down but because the virus was out of control. Framing public health measures as the barrier to work and commerce served to further politicize them and sideline the experts.

It simply was not true that there were only two choices, total shutdown or letting the virus spread unabated. The word "shutdown" was applied to restrictions that were nothing like a shutdown, and it was a dangerous misnomer. A true shutdown resembled the measures imposed in Wuhan, where eleven million people were confined to their homes for weeks and neighborhood patrols padlocked doors. A more lenient program was imposed early on in the United States when some parts of the country issued strict stay-at-home orders, but even this was not a "shutdown."

As time went on, we learned that a lockdown wasn't necessary. Being outdoors substantially reduced the risk of transmission, so parks and beaches should remain open. Outdoor exercise was good for physical and mental health, and prevented people from congregating in indoor settings where there was much higher risk. Similarly, strict adherence to mask-wearing and social distancing and improved ventilation meant that many businesses could safely return.

Unfortunately, once the all-or-nothing narrative stuck, it was hard to counter. In that context, reopening was understood as an on-off switch: we closed when things weren't safe, so if we reopened, everything must therefore be safe and we could go back to how things were before. Instead, we needed to see reopening as a dial. Some restrictions could be loosened, to be followed by a period of observation to make sure that cases didn't surge. A spike in infections would mean the dial should be turned back and restrictions reinstated.

Despite my and other experts' best efforts at this, the analogy didn't take, and when states did reopen, people resumed their pre-pandemic activity, leading to a new resurgence in cases. At that point, the headwinds were too strong to reimpose the restrictions widely. Only when hospitals were once again overwhelmed did some limits return, but people often didn't follow them, and the restrictions were often too little and too late to prevent substantial loss of life.

Given that many Americans appeared to return to regular activities regardless of public health guidance, some experts started recommending an approach I knew well: harm reduction. The concept is frequently used in the addiction field: stopping drug use is the ideal outcome, but many people might not yet be able to do that. In such cases, needle exchange reduces the potential harm by limiting the risk of acquiring HIV and hepatitis and transmitting them to others. These programs addressed the reality that if a behavior with harmful consequences was going to happen regardless, steps should be taken to reduce the risk for individuals and others around them.

Harm reduction was not a strategy for eliminating the virus, as other countries had undertaken. But in the absence of a national, science-based effort supported by unity of message, harm reduction could help Americans live with the virus while reducing infectious spread to the extent possible. Additionally, it was a pathway that was not all or nothing. It would avoid seeming to pit public health against the economy, but would rather use a public health approach to help the economy. If employees had to go to work, we could come up with evidence-based practices that could allow them to do so more safely. If people needed to socialize, there were ways to support their emotional well-being without sacrificing infection control.

As states began to reopen in May 2020, I started working with groups that were formulating protocols such as testing regimens, improved ventilation, and guidelines for safe transit. Certain establishments had higher risk, but if people were going to go to them they could still reduce their exposure. Sitting outdoors at a restaurant was much safer than sitting indoors; reducing dining capacity would also do a lot to reduce transmission. Hair salons could cut out their highest risk practices, such as hours-long treatments, just as gyms could stop crowded indoor fitness classes. And mask-wearing had to be mandatory.

Of course, there was a fundamental difference between this iteration of societal harm reduction and the standard public health practice of individual harm reduction. In this case, the risk was being forced on many Americans who would not otherwise have chosen it for themselves and their families.

Still, recognizing that quarantine fatigue was real and there was a substantial negative impact of not having in-person interaction, I changed my own message to help people get back to normal while still keeping safe. Instead of telling them not to get together, I gave advice on how to safely socialize outdoors, keeping groups at least six feet apart, and not sharing food or utensils. I wrote columns and spoke on the radio and TV about different ways to think about risk—coming up with a coronavirus budget, for example: your total budget depends on your health and how far your money goes depends on the level of infection in your community. One of my patients was desperate to get back to the gym. I urged him to go during off-hours, keep far away from others, always wear his mask—and then cut out other risks, such as dining indoors with others.

When the disease shifted to a younger demographic, I urged young people to forgo the highest-risk setting of bars and suggested that they meet in a park or someone's backyard. Dating was upended due to the pandemic, but I gave resources for new approaches, including safe sex practices that looked different from what people were used to. When the country erupted in outrage over the killing of George Floyd and millions took to the streets, I offered advice on how protesters could reduce risk by masking, bringing their own drinks, avoiding the highest-risk concurrent events like indoor gatherings, and quarantining and testing once they return home.

Public health experts came under heavy criticism for appearing to have different standards for racial justice protests and Trump's political rallies. From a purely infection control perspective, neither should be occurring. The difference between them was that most people going to protests recognized the danger and were trying to protect themselves, while, by and large, those going to the rallies and parties were in open defiance of public health guidance. The public health community could have done a better job to spell this out, and to make clear that this virus knows no political affiliations. Our duty, as health professionals and scientists, is to give evidence-based guidance that meets people where they are. If we are not going to dissuade people from going out, we need to pivot to helping people reduce their risk of acquiring and transmitting the disease.

Of course, harm reduction could only accomplish so much in the face of constant attempts to undermine science. The impact of dismantling trust in top medical institutions will reverberate for years to come in further emboldening anti-science conspiracy movements. The pandemic of disinformation will likely worsen as Americans draw from fringe "news" sources and no longer approach problems with a shared reality and a common set of facts.

The consequence on the public's health is all too clear. As infections surged all over the country, I began to see more and more patients who were trying to do everything right but still contracted coronavirus. They were essential workers who came down with COVID-19 at work, despite all the harm reduction practices. They were people who were so careful for months but then attended one family Thanksgiving dinner that sickened multiple generations. One patient told me that all she did was go grocery shopping; she lived alone and hadn't seen anyone else. The level of virus was just so high that activities that were previously low-risk were now much higher risk. The entire country was awash in coronavirus.

The tragedy was that it didn't have to be this way.

18

The Invisible Hand of Public Health

Mary appeared on my computer screen. Like many other patients I saw at the urgent care clinic, this was her first time using her iPhone for a telemedicine appointment.

Her hand holding the phone shook as she spoke. "I'm terrified," she said. "I'm holed up in my house. I don't go anywhere or see anybody." There was no stay-at-home restriction where she lived, but she didn't dare go outside. She was in her sixties, with diabetes and heart disease. As a cancer survivor, she was still on medications that suppressed her immune system.

Mary's grandchildren lived nearby and she ached to see them, but they were in day care and their mother was a nursing aide who worked in wards with COVID-19 patients. The senior center where she saw friends was closed indefinitely. Once a week, a neighbor came by to drop off groceries. Another set of grandchildren lived across the country. There were no plans to visit; it wouldn't be safe for her.

"How long is all of this going to last?" Mary asked. At that point, vaccines seemed to be far off on the horizon. I told her that I didn't know, but it could be many more months. Mary's eyes filled with tears as she talked about how the pandemic had upended her life.

COVID-19 proved the case that those of us in the field have been making for so long, that every aspect of our lives is tied to public health. The calamity of our failed public health systems finally made its invisible hand visible. Also made undeniably clear was the truth that public health measures, if properly implemented, could have changed the trajectory of the pandemic.

We knew what needed to be done. First, contain the outbreak. When that failed and community transmission of the virus was too widespread to contain, the focus should have immediately shifted to mitigation and slowing the spread. The key was to starve the virus of human interaction by keeping people away from each other through the blunt instrument of countrywide stay-at-home orders. Only a national intervention of this magnitude would have flattened the curve.

In its absence, the pandemic infected every facet of American society. The millions of people who lost their jobs suffered because the public health response failed. The children who lost months of education and sustained potentially long-term harm to their social and emotional development were failed by the lack of attention to public health. People who went hungry or lost their homes paid the price of a public health crisis. Their circumstances were themselves public health crises: How could we control a disease when people were homeless and stripped of their basic sustenance?

It wasn't only physical health that was affected. A CDC study found that 40 percent of adult Americans had experienced a mental health or substance use issue. One in ten had considered suicide in the thirty days preceding the study. Overdoses increased throughout the country. All the work to reduce overdoses and treat addiction had been undone. Addiction is a disease of isolation, and recovery depends on relationships. Because of the pandemic, people's physical, social, and emotional safety nets had been ripped away from them. Decades of hard-won progress in other areas like childhood immunizations and lead-poisoning prevention were also being stripped away, with impacts for generations to come.

History has shown that early and aggressive action is key to saving lives. During the 1918 influenza pandemic, Philadelphia held a parade of two hundred thousand people, while St. Louis shut down schools, theaters, and sporting events. The death rate in Philadelphia was double that of St. Louis, a result directly attributable to its city officials' bold, if initially unpopular, actions. Replicating such courageous steps on a national level would have required a coordinated, Herculean effort, against political opposition and in the face of profound economic consequences. Only some local and state leaders had the courage to ask this of their populations, driven by the conviction that each person's survival and well-being was tied to that of everyone else. COVID-19 didn't create this reality, but it did expose it.

Those who had never thought about public health now saw its impact every day. Public health thinking suffused many people's decisions and actions, enlisting ordinary citizens into the public health workforce.

Those of us in the ER always thought of ourselves as the front lines of health care. We see crises as they first emerge. However, in many ways, we were the last line of defense. When hospitals became overwhelmed, there wasn't much we could do in the ER beyond trying to resuscitate patients who were already gravely ill. Sometimes, all we could do was hold the phone for a patient to say goodbye to their loved ones. We couldn't prevent hospitals from filling up with sick patients, and we certainly couldn't prevent patients from contracting the virus in the first place. That work, the work of prevention, had to occur in the community. Individuals were the first line of defense. Public health was our weapon, and all of us were its frontline warriors.

NOTHING REVEALED THE COMPLEX INTERPLAY of public health with every other facet of society more than the outsize impact of the pandemic on communities of color. Studies showed that Latino and African Americans were three times as likely to be infected as their white neighbors. They were twice as likely to die from the virus. A Brookings Institution report found that in some age groups, African Americans had an astonishing mortality rate that was six times higher than whites. Other minority communities were also disproportionately affected, including in New Mexico, where Native American people comprise about 11 percent of the population yet accounted for nearly 60 percent of COVID-19 cases. Because of missing demographic data, we know that these harrowing numbers are only the tip of the iceberg.

These rampant health disparities are attributable to a concept in medicine called "acute on chronic," which refers to a patient with a long-standing medical condition that is exacerbated by an acute illness. This was the case for COVID-19, a new disease that unmasked long-standing health and economic disparities.

The first disparity is in existing health status: COVID-19 caused the most severe illness in people with underlying medical conditions. Racial minorities that experience higher rates of high blood pressure, diabetes, and other diseases, due to a lack of accessible care and contributing environmental conditions, were disproportionately affected by the new virus. In Baltimore, one in three African Americans lives in a food desert, compared to one in twelve whites. It should be no surprise that they bear an unequal burden when it comes to heart disease, obesity, and diabetes, and were therefore predisposed to suffer severe effects of COVID-19. This, indeed, illustrates the problem of amplified disparities, acute conditions made worse by chronic, existing problems.

Then there are economic disparities. Minorities are overrepresented among essential workers; many live in higher density and more crowded conditions; and these factors exacerbate the underlying health disparities. Being unable to shelter at home, and already suffering from disproportionate ill-health, minorities and working-class Americans were predictably condemned to bear the brunt of the infection and death.

The problem of disparities is entrenched and complex, with root causes of structural racism and historical inequities. But there were concrete steps and short-term actions that could have been taken immediately to reduce the disproportionate impact of COVID-19 on communities of color.

I had the opportunity to talk about these steps when I was invited to testify twice on the subject to the U.S. House of Representatives.

The first was getting targeted testing to minority communities. Since testing in the early days of the pandemic was available only to those with a doctor's prescription, people without health care were left in a bind. Testing needed to be accessible to anyone, without precondition, and free of charge. Drive-through testing helped those with cars; walk-in sites had to be made available, too. Local officials needed to map areas populated by vulnerable people and provide testing there, in churches, senior centers, and public housing.

Testing needed to be tracked by demographics. The WHO recommended that the percentage of positive tests done—the test positivity rate—be below 5 percent; above that, and it meant not enough testing was being done to pick up on all those infected. Think of it like a fishing net: if the net picks up fish a high percentage of the time, it means that there are many more fish in the river. Even if the overall test positivity within an area was below 5 percent, there could be urgent work to do if one demographic in that region were testing at 20 percent. A community that was disproportionately suffering from the impact of COVID-19 needed to receive a higher share of resources, but that couldn't be addressed without having the requisite data.

Contact tracers should have been specifically hired from minority communities. Key to an effective public health response is deployment of a credible messenger to find and interview people who may have been exposed to infection. This trusted person should come from within the community, with a shared culture and language. Hiring minority contact tracers would also have helped to reduce the employment disparity, since minorities shouldered disproportionate economic fallout from COVID-19.

Worker protections were another area that was immediately actionable. Some of the worst outbreaks had been in nursing homes and meatpacking plants that had high proportions of minority workers. Infected employees then brought the disease back to their families and communities. The protections were as basic as providing PPE: essential workers such as grocery-store cashiers, bus drivers, and nursing home attendants—all disproportionately people of color—should have had protection, too. From my role in Baltimore, I knew that enforcement in workplaces was crucial to compliance. There was much more that the CDC could do to issue guidelines, and more for federal and state regulatory agencies to do to enforce these protections.

Finally, much more needed to be done to strengthen health insurance coverage. More than forty-five million people lost their jobs during the pandemic, and many lost their health insurance along with those jobs. That was on top of the twenty-seven million who were already uninsured. Lack of insurance leads to delayed treatment of underlying medical problems, which increases the likelihood of severe illness and death from COVID-19. Since minorities constitute a higher percentage of the uninsured, increasing coverage would prevent further amplifying disparities. At a minimum, the Affordable Care Act needed to be protected. On top of that, additional safety-net systems should have been put into place to ensure that no one was priced out of the ability to get care.

THE PROBLEM OF "ACUTE ON chronic" disparities would play out many times during the pandemic. When vaccines first became available, the focus became—rightly so—on increasing speed of distribution. However, there was a cost to solely prioritizing speed. Imagine if hospitals and doctors' offices got all the initial vaccines. The benefit of allocating in this way is that these entities have rosters of existing patients, many of whom would be clamoring to be inoculated. But such a prioritization would leave out the uninsured and people without primary care physicians.

Another way to increase speed initially is to expand eligibility so much that demand for the vaccine will always outstrip supply. That way, no vials of vaccines will sit unused. However, having far more people eligible to receive the vaccine than available doses would run the risk of devolving into a free-for-all. This, in fact, was what happened in some parts of the country. Seniors were having to camp out overnight or enlist relatives to call hotlines dozens of times in desperate attempts to secure an inoculation. In these scenarios, those with connections will almost certainly find a way to jump the queue, while those most vulnerable will be left behind. Access rather than need will end up determining someone's place in line, and an exclusive emphasis on speed could worsen existing disparities.

An exclusive focus on equity ran a different risk. Imagine if the federal government directed vaccine supplies only to areas of the country with substantial minority populations, even if these were areas with lower demand and surrounding areas could have used them faster. Imagine, then, if minorities and lower-income individuals had to be vaccinated before doses were made available to others. Some have championed this as a redress of historical racism and economic inequities, but this type of proposal would run into legal challenges and almost certainly spark a backlash that would further set back progress in achieving equity goals. Fairness at the expense of speed would cost lives, and to many, delaying vaccine rollout for all is as untenable as exacerbating disparities for some.

The trade-off between speed and equity is real, but just as with testing, contact tracing, and worker protections, there are ways to aim for equity that's beneficial to all instead of being perceived as a zero-sum result. Requiring public reporting of demographic information is a key step that would identify gaps in vaccination and guide targeted approaches. Mobile vans, with door-to-door outreach, could be deployed to hard-to-reach areas, and the federal government could set up mass vaccination sites in areas of both greatest need and highest demand. More could be done, too, to prioritize populations that meet the dual criteria of being predominantly low-income communities of color and that are able to be vaccinated quickly. That might include workers in meatpacking plants and inmates in jails and prisons. And every step needs to be taken to remove barriers to obtaining the vaccine, such as cost—there should be no question that getting the vaccine is free of charge.

All of these are commonsense actions that are well within the realm of possibility to implement. What it takes to get them off the ground is intention and a continuing commitment to equity. Without equity as a guiding force, status quo will reign, and the already gaping chasm of health disparities will widen even more. But just as public health is the lens that magnifies and exposes long-standing disparities, it can also be a powerful tool to improve well-being for all and, in the words of the Reverend Dr. Martin Luther King Jr., bend the arc of the moral universe back toward justice.

WE SAW THE CRUCIAL ROLE of public health in another sphere, that of education, inextricably tied as it is to the well-being of children and their ability to learn. I knew this truth firsthand from my time overseeing school health in Baltimore, where students often depended on the schools for asthma treatment, vision care, and mental health services. During the COVID-19 crisis, this intersection of public health and schools produced one of the most complex—and controversial—challenges.

As with every other major decision, the battle of whether to close schools, maintain in-person learning, and reopen after shutting them down became a war of extremes and political tribalism. The reasons for keeping schools open were obvious: being in the classroom was important for children's cognitive development; virtual instruction was not as effective, especially for younger children; many students depended on school for food and safety—one in four cases of child abuse and neglect are first reported by teachers or counselors. Additionally, many thousands of children lacked reliable Internet connection and so could not join virtual instruction. Keeping schools closed exacerbated already gaping educational disparities.

Schools staying open was also crucial to economic activity. All parents were affected by school closures, with women more so, resulting in many of them having to leave the workforce. In addition, there were numerous examples from other countries that were able to open their schools for in-person instruction without substantial outbreaks.

For every data point in favor of school reopening, there were others that made as strong of a case against. The same research could be interpreted two different ways. For example, a study from South Korea found that children under ten were half as likely to spread the coronavirus as adults. While some saw this as justification for allowing in-person schooling for younger children, others pointed to the fact that half of a lot of transmission is still a lot. In addition, even though it was generally true that children did not become as ill as adults, they came home to parents and grandparents and could serve in their communities as vectors for virus spread. The case for closing schools was strengthened when a new associated ailment appeared in children, the multisystem inflammatory syndrome, which led to hospitalization and even death.

To me, the most compelling initial argument against school reopening was that it didn't just affect students whose parents could voluntarily choose to have them there—there were also the teachers, and the societal obligation to protect their health and well-being, as well as that of school nurses, custodians, bus drivers, and other staff. I thought of my mother, who had taught for eight years while undergoing chemotherapy and radiation. She would have understood every reason for children to have in-person learning and would have wanted to be there for them, but would it have been right to compel her to do so if it could cost her her life? Teachers are often older or have chronic conditions; a Kaiser Foundation study found that one in four teachers were at risk for severe disease if infected. Even if it were true that school reopening didn't contribute substantially to increasing community transmission rates, there was still the danger posed to the individual teacher or staff member who had to be in a small enclosed space for hours with potentially infected students. There was an argument to be made that it's not fair to put the burden of society's failures on the people who work in schools, and jeopardize the lives of teachers, staff, and families.

When it came time for the initial lockdown to end, the CDC issued guidance on schools with a list of measures to enhance safety: separating children into pods, reducing classroom capacity, improving ventilation, and wearing masks. All of these were reasonable and, if they were all implemented, would have gone a long way to reduce transmission risk. Unfortunately, just like their other guidance on workplace safety, the CDC documents had many qualifiers like "if feasible" that made them too watered down to be useful. Many schools were unable to afford these measures, and without requirements that they had to before reopening, teachers and students came back to environments that could have been unsafe.

Still, Trump bemoaned the guidelines as "very tough," while Pence, who oversaw the administration's pandemic task force, said that they should not prevent schools from reopening. In this backward logic, the administration failed to grasp that the problem was not the guidelines, but the schools' inability to meet them. The worst part was that the CDC actually succumbed to political pressure and came out with an even more toothless set of guidelines. Instead of emphasizing what to do to make schools safer, the reissued guidance read like a policy justification of why kids need in-person schooling.

Keeping schools safe required enormous amounts of planning—and resources. The challenges were particularly significant for school districts that were already under-resourced. In Baltimore and countless other locales, many schools had cramped classrooms, no air-conditioning or heating, and no way to pay for the necessary improvements without funding from the federal government. There was no money for upgrading ventilation, hiring extra teachers and staff to reduce class size, or purchasing enough PPE for staff—and what about the kids who couldn't afford to buy masks?

Reducing community infection levels, while also investing the resources to improve testing, contact tracing, and school infrastructure, would have allowed children in the classroom much sooner. What was needed were national benchmarks, such as dividing the level of risk into three categories: for a low level of community spread, a checklist of, say, ten items would have to be followed to ensure safe reopening; for a medium level, ten more steps would have to be taken; a high level of infection would necessitate extraordinary mitigation steps. School administrators could still have tailored the guidance to best match local needs, but the overall framework would have provided clarity and coherence across the country.

As with every other aspect of the pandemic, however, rather than acknowledging and tackling the obstacles, the administration downplayed them, went for shortcuts, and resorted to pressure and bullying. Officials threatened to withdraw funding unless schools remained fully open, and some governors, even in the most significant hot spots, followed Trump's lead and mandated full-time in-person instruction.

Following a familiar pattern, states made up their own rules in the absence of trusted national leadership, effectively running an uncontrolled experiment with students, teachers, and their families as guinea pigs. Areas with high rates of transmission often had in-person schooling while places with low rates did not. Schooling itself became divided along partisan lines, with many red states opening their schools and many blue states not. Educators felt like they were expendable, especially after they were not prioritized for vaccines when they became available.

History will judge our country for many elements of our failed response, and the harshest judgment should be reserved for how we have failed our most vulnerable children. Instead of pulling children out of the water and fixing the dam, the nation's leaders threw students and everyone around them into a raging flood.

COVID-19 WAS THE ULTIMATE ILLUSTRATION of why the work of public health is essential, and how it is so closely tied to all aspects of our society. The postal service that many depend on for medications was revealed as a public health issue. During the 2020 elections, voting became a public health issue, as people were forced to choose between their constitutional right to cast their ballot and their ability to safeguard their health.

The pandemic also showed how public health is the key to controlling disease. Scientific advances, important as they are, are not enough. The pandemic response involved many episodes of spectacular science. Sequencing the entire genome of SARS-CoV2, the virus that causes COVID-19, took just three days. Vaccine development broke every record for speed. The efficacy of the vaccines was beyond the wildest expectations of so many experts. The ingenuity, collaboration, and dedication of the global scientific community was on full display.

The United States takes pride in having the most sophisticated medical system in the world. Yet the death count from COVID-19 rivaled that of the 1918 influenza pandemic, and the United States led the death rate. There is a simple explanation. The failure was not that of modern medicine; it was a failure to prioritize public health.

The reality and the limitation of public health is that it's really hard. By definition, it is not one single intervention and doesn't hinge on an isolated, breakthrough scientific advance. Public health measures are multilayered. Containing the virus required many components that we call "non-pharmaceutical interventions." It's not only testing or use of masks; it's the combination of masks, testing, social distancing, hand washing, contact tracing, isolation, and quarantine. These were the tools used to safeguard the public in 1918, and the same tried-and-true measures were still the best protection against a deadly virus more than one hundred years later.

The work of public health is challenging also because it does not occur in a vacuum. It depends on sound policy making and a concerted communications strategy. It is based on science, but relies on winning over hearts and minds to follow evidence-based guidelines. Public health should not be political, and certainly never partisan, but politics are inseparable from policy decisions. Public health needs to balance diverging interests. It's messy and complicated, but the stakes are too high for us to get it wrong.

COVID-19 is a once-in-a-generation public health catastrophe. However, it's a mistake to see it as an isolated event. Every day, there are calamities in communities around the country because we fail to invest in the invisible hand of public health. People pay for the failure with the loss of health, well-being, and years of life. As in the pandemic, those affected the most are always people who already bear the greatest brunt of disparities and inequities.

19

COVID-19 Comes Home

As COVID-19 spread during the winter and spring of 2020, I was living through a major life event: I was pregnant again.

Because of the previous miscarriage, I worried to the point of paranoia. Every cramp was cause for concern. The lightest of spotting sent me rushing to the hospital. I was actually thankful for the severe morning sickness that indicated everything was on track. We were overjoyed when we found out that we were going to have a girl. Sebastian and I already had a name picked out, chosen even before we got married: Isabelle. We couldn't wait for her to join us. As I grew more visibly pregnant, Eli started talking about all the things he'd teach his baby sister.

I was in the third trimester when COVID-19 became a major concern. On my regular prenatal visits, I saw how hospital procedures changed from one week to the next. First, there were questions about travel to China. Then there were temperature screening stations. The following week, visitors were no longer allowed at outpatient appointments, and by late March visitors were barred from the hospital altogether, with the exceptions of end-of-life care and labor and delivery. There was talk that even this could change.

I always advocated for patients to have someone with them in the hospital; now it was possible that I could end up giving birth alone. Of course, I understood the necessity of infection control, but it was hard to fathom not being with my husband for this seismic experience. I was afraid of something going wrong and not having him with me. And if it was frightening for me, a doctor, how much worse must it have been for other patients? I worried whether the circumstances would worsen maternal mortality rates and widen the disparities for Black women.

At the time, we knew very little about the impact of COVID-19 on pregnancy. There were conflicting reports as to whether the virus was transmitted in utero and there was no information at all about its effect in the first or second trimesters. It was an open question as to whether pregnant women were particularly susceptible to COVID-19, as they are to influenza. I was working in the ER during the H1N1 influenza outbreak and saw how quickly pregnant women became severely ill: I remember intubating a woman in her third trimester and treating another pregnant patient who died from complications. Pregnancy compromises one's immune system and pregnant women should be considered medically vulnerable, but how much more vulnerable to COVID-19 were they—were we?

I had other fears. There had been numerous reports of laboring women in China and Italy being turned away from facilities. Julia Belluz, a Vox reporter who lived in Austria, wrote about her decision to induce labor in case of hospital crowding. Was this something I should consider? What if the baby needed special care after birth? And facing potentially months of not being able to see family and friends, I worried about a recurrence of postpartum depression.

I was working on coronavirus during all my waking hours, and at night I had a recurring nightmare: I am in labor, sick with COVID-19, with a high fever and straining to breathe through contractions while wearing a mask. Isabelle is taken away the moment she is born. I cannot touch or nurse her—I have to express my milk and give it to someone else. If I survive, it will be weeks before I'm no longer contagious and can finally hold her. In the dream, I fear I've given her coronavirus and she, too, might die. In other variations, Eli is sick, or Sebastian, and I don't know how to care for them without putting Isabelle in danger.

For me, these were bad dreams, but people were facing these horrors every day. Thirty-three-year old Erika Becerra was excited to welcome her second child. She was more than eight months pregnant when she contracted COVID-19. Her medical condition deteriorated so much that doctors opted to induce the birth. Her baby, Diego, was born healthy, but Erika never got to see him or hold him. She was put on a ventilator during delivery and never regained consciousness; she died eighteen days later.

All around the country, all over the world, people were losing spouses, parents, and children. I prayed every night for my unborn child and my family, and for all the families that were suffering unimaginable terror and tragedy.

IN THE WEEKS BEFORE MY due date, I'd gotten to know Mika Brzezinski, the cohost of MSNBC's *Morning Joe*. I'd long admired Mika for her work to empower women, and we also had a common connection in Elijah Cummings: he was a close friend and the person she and her husband had chosen to perform their wedding ceremony.

Mika suggested that we collaborate to create a video diary of my birth experience. I wasn't sure this was such a good idea. I was coming from a position of privilege in so many ways. I also harbored superstitions and feared that something would go wrong, especially since my past patient advocacy had always involved talking about tragedies, not normal health events.

"A lot of women are having the same anxieties as you," she said. "You can use your privilege to help explain the process and what you're going through to others." The diary would be something of a public service message. Once I saw it in that light, I was persuaded. So during the last days of pregnancy, I began to film one-minute real-time updates on the special contingencies of birth in the time of COVID-19: Should I set a date to induce to be sure of a hospital bed? What would Maryland's new shelter-in-place orders mean for giving birth? What do I pack in my go-bag? And if Sebastian can't come with me, how will we keep in touch?

Isabelle's due date came and went. Every time I appeared on air, I was asked about the baby and why I was still there. One day, contractions began just as I finished an interview and my mic was live when I called Sebastian and told him this could be it. The contractions ended before we were even out the door, but the producers had overheard me and my e-mail was soon flooded with congratulations. Alas, that was not the night. My running joke was that Isabelle was taking social distancing very seriously.

We eventually decided to induce, and Sebastian was able to accompany me to the hospital. The nurse doing my intake looked exhausted. "It's as busy a night as I can remember," she said. The labor ward was flooded with patients and it was short-staffed. A nurse and a doctor had just tested positive for the virus, and six people had been placed on quarantine.

As she took notes, the nurse rubbed her face through her mask. She sighed. "This is my only mask," she said. "The hospital is giving us one a week. I better make it last."

"What day is it for this one?" I asked.

"Day three," she said. I could see that the mask was beginning to fray.

I went into labor just a few hours after the induction started, with Sebastian manning the camera for the final diary commentary. But we soon set the camera aside. Isabelle was born, quickly, and healthy and calm, a characteristic that stayed with her. Along with my relief and joy was a sense of profound gratitude for the staff: the nurse had young children of her own at home; others were older and likely had underlying medical conditions. They took exceptional care of me, even as their exposure endangered them and their families.

When I left the hospital, my nurse joked that she'd see me in the grocery store and want to give me a big hug. "But you won't know who I am," she said. This was another part of medicine that was soon becoming the norm. Patients wouldn't be able to recognize those who had been at their side during intense and fearful times because they never saw the faces of their nurses and doctors.

I WENT BACK ON AIR three days after giving birth to unveil the video diary and offer advice to other pregnant women. After Eli was born, I hadn't felt ready to return to work, but this time not only was I ready, I felt an urgent need to get right back. My role in the media was rooted in my patient advocacy origins and was also a direct extension of my patient care duties and public health research. I was communicating news you can use to the public while interpreting and influencing policy. I was helping my patients with their needs and bringing light to societal shortcomings. I felt desperately driven to get back to this mission.

Throughout the spring and summer, in the CNN town halls, Anderson Cooper and Sanjay Gupta interviewed people who had volunteered for the vaccine clinical trials. They were everyday individuals who talked about their sense of powerlessness in the face of the pandemic, and they had signed up for the trials because it was something tangible they could do in this fight. Particularly compelling were the people from minority groups who had chosen to volunteer to ensure their communities were adequately represented. Their participation was a mark of trust in a medical establishment that had caused their community great harm in the past, and it was an effective way to push back against vaccine hesitancy.

Their example inspired me to volunteer, but none of the trials were enrolling pregnant or breastfeeding women. By the time I stopped nursing, Pfizer and Moderna had both released preliminary data that looked very promising. The FDA had yet to authorize the vaccines, but it seemed all but certain. As a health-care worker, I would have been in the first group inoculated, but I still wanted to enter a trial given the pressing need to develop more vaccines. The initial two vaccines wouldn't be enough to satisfy demand globally. In addition, other vaccines could possibly impart longer-lasting immunity or better suit certain populations. More scientific studies were necessary, which meant a need for more volunteers.

The vaccine candidate that most excited me was being developed by Johnson & Johnson. It was a single-dose vaccine, which gave it a considerable advantage over most other vaccines that required two doses. It can be stored at standard refrigerator temperatures, making distribution easier, especially in lower-income countries. As it happened, a health center in the Baltimore region was enrolling patients for this trial. I signed up online and then went in person to take part in the study.

My intake, which took about two hours to complete, involved a questionnaire that assessed my exposure risk. My responses were fairly unexciting. Sebastian and I followed all the precautions I talked about daily to my patients and in the media. We saw no family members or friends indoors; we only got together outdoors, with households spaced at least six feet apart. The only visitor we had was my sister Angela, who quarantined prior to travel and stayed with us for a month. Our family was in a pod with our nanny's, and she and her husband and children were also very careful. Sebastian was working almost entirely from home. In my clinical practice, everyone followed stringent infection control protocols.

The vaccine study was randomized and blinded, so neither I nor the person giving the shot knew whether I got the vaccine or the placebo. As I have a history of severe allergic reactions (to penicillin and peanuts), I stayed for observation for thirty minutes. I was fine and left the center with nothing more than a sore arm.

WITHIN A FEW WEEKS, MY immunity was put to the test.

Sebastian had been putting in long hours getting a new company off the ground. He had started an IT consultancy just before the pandemic hit and felt responsible for the engineers and developers he had recruited. They were pulling all-nighters to deliver on a particularly complex project, so he made little of the fact that he felt tired and developed a dull headache. One day, after a long stretch without a break, he was so weary he had to take a nap and missed a meeting. He still wasn't terribly concerned. Years ago in South Africa, he'd been diagnosed with tick-bite fever. Occasionally, the symptoms recurred, including fatigue, headache, and muscle aches. That probably explained it, he reasoned.

It wasn't until five days into his symptoms that it occurred to either of us that something else might be going on. That morning, Sebastian woke up feeling feverish and achy all over. Suddenly he lost his sense of taste and smell, a very specific sign of COVID-19.

I couldn't believe that I, who spent almost all my waking hours thinking about COVID-19, had missed the clues. How had I failed to spot coronavirus in my husband? Since we hadn't considered that he might have a contagious illness, Sebastian hadn't been isolating. We'd slept in the same room. He'd held baby Isabelle, then eight months old, and played with three-year-old Eli.

Sebastian went to get tested, and the result came back positive. By that point, he was running continuously high temperatures above 102°F and having shaking chills. His headache and muscle aches were worse. The only thing that helped him was around-the-clock ibuprofen and lying in a warm bath. He was so fatigued that he could barely eat, which wasn't helped by the fact that everything tasted like cardboard.

Just as we learned that Sebastian had coronavirus, Eli and Isabelle both started having runny noses. Isabelle developed a fever and diarrhea. This time there was no question that the children were infected with COVID-19, too.

Once it was clear that everyone was sick, I knew that it wasn't an option for me to quarantine. Sebastian was in no position to care for himself and both children. I figured there were three possibilities for me: I was already infected and just hadn't tested positive; I'd received the vaccine rather than the placebo and had immunity; I wasn't yet infected but still could be if I remained exposed to everyone else.

Had I been consulting a patient in my situation, I would have advised them to try to stay away from others. Household contacts are very high-risk, and preventing someone from contracting the virus is the first priority. However, as I knew well from my clinical work, the real world is different from the ideal. In the real world, my family needed me. People everywhere were making the same choice to put their families first, knowing that they risked infection.

Sebastian continued to spike high temperatures for days. He developed a cough and started having trouble breathing. The pulse oximeter we used several times a day showed that his oxygen level was dropping, and I could hear through my stethoscope that he probably had pneumonia. Isabelle's diarrhea got much worse and I worried about keeping her hydrated. Night after night, I set my alarm to wake me every hour to change her diaper and feed her. It was a relief that Eli's symptoms didn't slow him down. Scooby Doo, Winnie the Pooh, and Big Bird kept him occupied while I tended to everyone else and tried to keep working—I figured that screen time was a small price to pay to get us through this.

In the early days of the pandemic, Sebastian and I had made a will and talked through the different possibilities of what might happen: What if one of us died or if one of the children became gravely ill? Still, we thought we were safe. We were following every precaution. We knew other people were doing the same and still got ill, but it surely couldn't happen to us. Surely, with all our caution, we'd make it through the few months until vaccination became available. Now, when he was awake and had the energy to talk, Sebastian and I reprised those conversations and revisited our will.

Like many Americans, we never figured out where our family contracted the coronavirus.

Given my exposure, I was the most likely source, although I had been regularly tested and the results were negative. In the weeks preceding his sickness, Sebastian had been grocery shopping once and had two outdoor meetings with clients. No one with whom we had had recent contact experienced symptoms and they all tested negative, including our nanny, who was uppermost in our concern because she helped care for her elderly parents. We were so vigilant and still COVID-19 came into our home, which confirmed yet again the power of this pernicious virus.

The next days were a blur. Isabelle's fever persisted. She developed a large rash over her belly and was less playful than her usual cheery self. I looked up every case study I could find on COVID-19 in babies and landed on tragic reports of infants her age who had initially had mild symptoms but progressed to multi-organ failure and death. I dug into their stories in search of details that distinguished those babies from Isabelle: Were their fevers higher or their diarrhea worse? Did they have preexisting illnesses? I felt guilty for trying to find nuggets of hope that my child was different and would be spared an unthinkable fate.

Sebastian seemed to be improving, but I knew it was too soon to feel relieved. I had seen patients like him, otherwise healthy, with odds strongly in their favor for a good outcome, until they became very ill. Sometimes the deterioration was precipitous, and it often occurred after the patient initially seemed to get better. Sebastian and the baby had switched rooms so that I could closely care for Isabelle, and I'd peek in multiple times at night to check that he was still breathing. I feared I was living the tormented nightmares of my pregnancy. I prayed and then went on, hour after hour, tending to our family.

We were among the lucky ones. Sebastian's breathing never deteriorated to the point that he needed to go to the hospital. Recovery was slow, but each day he got a little stronger. After a rocky week, Isabelle's diarrhea stopped, and her fever and rash subsided. Eli never missed a step. I feared that I'd develop coronavirus after all the exposure and kept taking my temperature, but I never developed a fever and had three subsequent negative tests. But for the grace of God go I. We escaped a tragedy that so many others did not.

MY FAMILY'S BOUT WITH CORONAVIRUS gave me a new understanding of the hardships my patients were facing. So many of them wanted to do the right thing and follow the medical advice, but the barriers to doing so were steep.

One patient, a woman in her forties, confided that she and her husband contracted COVID-19 but kept going to work. She was a cashier at a gas station and her husband worked in landscaping. Her hours had already been cut back, and she feared being laid off. Her husband didn't dare stop working for the same reason. Their actions were a public health hazard, but it was hard not to sympathize with their situation. It is society's failure that patients need to choose between their job security and the risk of harming others.

A man in his thirties, another patient, had lost his job as a line cook in a restaurant. Unemployment benefits were tiding him over for the time being, but he was terribly anxious about the future. His wife had been laid off, too. How would he provide for his wife and three children? They had no savings and were also under pressure from their landlord. At some point, their parents moved in with them. There was no possibility of social distancing in their house, and everyone contracted coronavirus. His mother died. They held a small funeral but his siblings, who lived across the country, couldn't be there. "COVID robbed us of years together," he said. "Now it's going to rob our children of their futures."

On the day that a patient had scheduled a telemedicine appointment, she showed up in person. She couldn't afford to pay her phone bill, nor did she have the money for the bus fare. She had walked nearly two miles, in cold weather and with hip pain. Her son had helped her financially, but he couldn't carry on any longer. He was one of the many who had owned a restaurant that went out of business.

Some of my patients recovered from COVID-19, but became what were known as long-haulers, people with lasting consequences to their health. A former pro athlete said he woke up every morning feeling as if every bone in his body were broken. He was on disability because he was in so much pain and felt so fatigued. One woman suffered continual headaches and still hadn't regained her sense of taste or smell—a major professional liability in her work as a chef. She was among the fortunate ones, she said, even as she'd suffered unbearable loss: both of her parents had caught the coronavirus and died.

At the same time, my colleagues on the front lines were running on empty. They had nothing more to give. Many were quitting. A friend, a respiratory therapist married to a nurse, had decided that either she or her husband would have to stop working so that their children wouldn't be left as orphans. Another friend, a paramedic whose wife was pregnant at the time, brought a mattress to the garage and slept there for months. When the baby was born, he decided he couldn't continue working and risk infecting his family. Their concern was real, and the danger existential. Tens of thousands of health-care workers had died—including two ER physicians I knew personally and the head of the ICU at Mercy, where I gave birth to Isabelle. Others had brought COVID-19 back to their families: one firefighter contracted coronavirus and passed it on to his infant daughter, who later died.

The loss was intolerable and continual suffering was all around us.

What made the experience so much harder was that none of it was inevitable.

By the end of 2020, the United States had set an unenviable record. We were number one in just about every metric for coronavirus. Only 4 percent of the world's population, we constituted 25 percent of its infections. Other countries suffered multiple waves of coronavirus, too, but none to the degree we experienced in the United States. There were also countries that successfully contained the virus, saving countless lives.

What did these countries do differently? First, they had strong, competent, and courageous leaders who recognized the gravity of the situation and were willing to use their political capital to control the crisis. The effort was nationally driven and centrally coordinated. Political leaders sent a clear and coherent message that was in lockstep with scientists and doctors.

Second, they prioritized data and testing, which allowed them to pull ahead of the infection curve while the United States was constantly behind. South Korea had the first case of coronavirus on the same day as the United States, but from there, the trajectories diverged completely. We were flying blind while they relied on aggressive testing and exceptional contact tracing. By the winter of 2020, South Korea had suffered a few hundred deaths and life was essentially back to normal.

In another critical difference, these countries let public health lead their response and fought the damaging argument that public health measures are antithetical to freedom. All societies impose restrictions to protect health—laws against drunk driving are one example. We accept that people cannot choose freedom for themselves while committing others to a sacrifice they didn't elect to make. In a free society, individual liberty does not take precedence over the health and well-being of everyone else.

There is a way to approach public health that leads with empathy. Many people may be ignoring public health guidance because they simply don't understand it. Confusing messages lead to rebellion; if rules appear to be arbitrary, then why follow them? There were many examples during the pandemic of how one person's actions affected others: a wedding of fifty-five guests in Maine resulted in at least 177 infections, for example. Seven people died, none of whom attended the wedding. I don't believe that most people would knowingly cause such harm to others, but they must be made aware of that risk. They must be provided credible data, through trusted messengers, with a clear, consistent message.

Public health is about a collective approach to well-being. Leaders elsewhere avoided using the pandemic to divide and polarize their people; they rallied their citizens to come together against a common enemy: the virus. They did not take the opportunity to deny people of their constitutional right to vote or be counted in the census. They did not choose inflammatory language, calling COVID-19 a "China virus" or "kung flu," which stigmatized whole groups of people and made them the target of racist attacks. Mask-wearing was framed not as a matter of enforcement but as an appeal to people's better selves, as an act of respect and patriotism. They led with empathy and called on their constituents to see their common humanity.

We could have done this, too. I believe in the inherent goodness of the American people. If the United States had set out with that assumption rather than one that presumes all people are looking out for themselves, we could have had a very different outcome. Instead, the United States missed many opportunities. While some localities made exceptional efforts, the grave abdication by many of our leaders left the country firing blind at a moving target, barely able to fend off the catastrophic effect of overwhelming our health-care systems and exhausting doctors, nurses, and essential workers on the front line.

Just as the pandemic laid bare key systemic failures within our society, it has given us renewed impetus to address them. It is now abundantly clear why science must remain beyond politics and why public health must be understood as nonpartisan to be effective. Public health experts may engage in advocacy, but that is not political in nature—it exists to educate and protect. Public health professionals should be aware of the politics involved in formulating policy, but the recommendations from public health can never be perceived as having partisan aims.

The appalling health disparities and neglect in public health infrastructure are critically important to address, but it will take time and requires practical, short-term answers on the way to long-term, systemic change. There should also be a hard look at the American reliance on simple solutions. Our culture of instant gratification rejects the difficult, sustained work of public health and instead looks for the easy way out. It dismisses prevention while glorifying specialized medical treatment. This is a culture of a "pill for every pain." Science is the superhero we expect to come to our rescue. This time it did, but what about the next time?

I AM HOPEFUL AS I look into the future. The election of Joe Biden in November 2020 brought substantial changes to the pandemic response. Top scientific experts were once again allowed to speak and to lead. Equity became embedded in metrics and goals. There were commitments to strengthen public health infrastructure and to address the social determinants of health. President Biden and his team seemed to understand that COVID-19 served as a tragic validation of how public health is the foundation of our society and how our collective fates are intertwined.

Some changes are here to stay, such as the rise in telehealth and at-home diagnostics. Fault lines that were made undeniably visible will require resources to redress with concrete action. For example, the confirmation of systemic racism in health care could lead to more intentional efforts to recruit people from underrepresented backgrounds into the field. Also, with so many millions of unemployed Americans having lost their health insurance, perhaps we might finally see momentum to reimagine our employer-based insurance system and, indeed, our entire way of delivering accessible, affordable, and high-quality care.

COVID-19 will not be the last pandemic we will face. We cannot be caught off guard again without safety rails for our individual and societal health, and that requires addressing the chronic underinvestment in our public health infrastructure. We cannot forget that public health is the lifeline for so many people. It is key to our national security and prosperity, and to our very survival.

As a country, we must create a future where public health is understood as the glue that holds all the other parts of society together. Local, state, and federal public health must be funded in a way that recognizes its centrality to all other issues. Public health should be required training for everyone, no matter their field, given its foundational role in every sphere. Public health is about the practical, recognizing that perfect solutions will do little if few follow the guidance. And it is about empathy. It's a field that can bridge some of the most challenging divides in our country to transcend partisanship and unite people in a shared vision of doing what's right for all.

Public health could save your life today; now we all know it.

Epilogue:
Life Lessons

When I started writing this book, I thought the biggest challenge would be to illustrate the crucial impact of public health on our everyday lives. Tragically, COVID-19 made that task easier, while also inflicting on this country a public health crisis of unimaginable scale.

It has been a privilege to serve on the front lines of medicine and to play a part in navigating this and other public health challenges. My path to acquiring the tools to do so involved the support of incredible mentors. The examples they set are a beacon that lights the way, and I offer their wisdom here.

"Turn your pain into your passion, your passion into your purpose," Congressman Elijah Cummings would say. When I first heard him talk about using one's pain to guide one's purpose, it spoke to me deeply. So much of my life involved doing exactly that—facing adversity and finding strength in struggle. My childhood as an immigrant, growing up in poverty, and battling with stuttering were my greatest sources of shame, but they also formed the core of my identity and gave me deep empathy for the obstacles my patients face. The extraordinary pain of my mother's illness led me to patient advocacy and the calling to reform a broken system.

My passion and purpose found their ideal field in public health, a discipline which, by its very nature, strives to improve lives, reduce inequities, and make real, practical changes in the service of people and communities. It ties together all other disciplines and is a powerful tool in the fight for social justice.

I believe strongly that we are not defined by the circumstances of our past but by how we choose to respond. Sir Winston Churchill said that "Success is not final, failure is not fatal; it's the courage to persist that counts." To me, that courage entails falling down, standing up, and trying again. Bold visions do not always turn into reality, but the risk of failure is worth taking for the possibility of what could be.

Find your voice and the best way that you can effect change. In the course of my advocacy, I learned that people make an impact in different ways, and what works for one person may not for another. It's taken me both time and trial and error to identify how I might best advocate for change. I've been the activist rallying on the outside; I've been the person pushing from within. Finding the way to make the biggest difference can depend on the position you hold at any given moment. There's a need both for loud voices that push at the boundaries and for those who strive for inclusivity and building bridges.

I have great respect and admiration for people who use their voices in different ways. It takes all of us to strive for change. Our society needs rabble-rousers to keep us on our toes, idealists to keep us grounded in our values, and pragmatists who will get things done. We need the visionaries who aim for the stars and the compromisers who move us closer, one step at a time. There is a role for everyone in our march toward progress.

Lead with empathy. Societal progress hinges on having empathy for those who are not like us, but events in the country over the past several years have only intensified a tendency to quickly dismiss people who are different or hold different views. Extremes can dominate the national conversation and leave many feeling as if they don't belong. Being progressive or conservative doesn't have to connote divisiveness, just as being moderate shouldn't equate to a lack of courage or imagination.

We can begin by recognizing each other's humanity and listening to one another. The world is filled with complexities and nuance. Solutions don't easily fit into neat, ideological categories, and we can approach our shared challenges with humility and compassion. I believe that most of us share a common goal: a society in which we have stable jobs, affordable health care, decent schools, safe communities, and a better future for our children. A requisite for reaching that goal is the ability to have honest and open conversations about the hard issues.

Don't just dwell on the problems: do something. The problems in public health are complex, with every aspect of our well-being dependent on every other aspect. Understanding the challenges is a necessary but insufficient part of the work; there needs to be a quick pivot to action, with the recognition that "good enough" now beats solutions that look great on paper but will never happen in reality.

The effort to combat opioid overdoses in Baltimore had to start wherever it could. Naloxone alone was not sufficient, but we couldn't wait for every system to be in place before we began saving lives. Similarly, the response to COVID-19 was slowed by the effort to find a perfectly accurate test, when scaling up a cheap and speedy test could have detected far more infection. It might have missed 20 percent of positive cases, but the alternative was to miss 100 percent while no testing was done.

Progress takes time, and incrementalism makes a difference. Systemic, long-term change is the ideal, but that should not prevent us from doing what is possible in the moment. Our goal may be to prevent families from falling into poverty, but those in difficult situations need our help right now, and we must offer them lifelines and safety nets—the same ones my family was able to receive.

Paradoxically, the desire to work on many things at once can hold back progress. Just as maintaining an equal level of outrage on all matters can diminish the impact of protest, prioritizing too many projects can lead to underperforming at best and paralysis at worst. The inability to do everything shouldn't stop us from starting with something. Better is the goal; perfect is not on the menu.

Heed the lessons of people on the front lines. In many fields, there is a chasm between the people making the decisions and those working on the ground. I've seen this gulf between national policy makers and local leaders, elected officials and community members, and hospital administrators and health-care workers. The local people on the front lines often have less power and a diminished voice. Yet they are the first to see a problem, and they know what their communities need. If the national discourse and decision-making is to reflect people's lived experiences, those working on the ground need to be heard.

Getting involved at the local level is also an effective but overlooked way to make a difference. People often think about running for office because achieving policy change is commonly equated with being an elected official. This is one mechanism, and we need far more citizen engagement in politics, but there are also other ways to bring about change. In every community, there are people and organizations working on issues that matter, and they depend on the time and skills of volunteers.

In Baltimore, the health department often worked with local community groups to find residents who would testify before the city council and state legislature and tell their stories to the media and public outreach campaigns. Their voices helped mobilize others. There is a great need for volunteers with diverse skills ranging from accounting to marketing—their help can add much value to local organizations.

Someone out there is looking up to you. I was blessed with people to look up to. My family's sacrifice to *chi ku* had everything to do with who I was able to become. So did the generous guidance of the mentors I was lucky to meet along the way. If not for Dr. Garcia's faith in me, I might never have thought I could become a doctor. If not for the alumni I met through him and Dr. Paulson, I would never have learned the unwritten rules of applying for medical school; without them, I almost certainly would not be a doctor today.

In late 2019, two of my dearest mentors, Elijah Cummings and Fitzhugh Mullan, died a month apart. Both were champions for social justice who had remarkable careers and touched countless others with their work. It was striking that at both funerals, so many in attendance considered the man we had come to mourn as their own personal mentor and source of inspiration. To pay tribute to Fitz, doctors of all ages, myself included, spoke about how we, too, wore our white coats with fists clenched, forever imbued with the "fire in the belly" from the spark he lit in us.

At Congressman Cummings's service, I recounted what ended up being our last conversation. I knew he was very ill. I told him how blessed I had been to have his mentorship.

"I am the one who is blessed," he said, "because you are part of my destiny as I am a part of yours."

Those who mentored, taught, and cared for us will forever be part of us. Their legacy lives on as we carry the torch to the next generation and fulfill our shared mission to fight for the world as it should be.

ACKNOWLEDGMENTS

The acknowledgments section is the last to write and, in some ways, the hardest. Throughout my education and career, I have been blessed to have known exceptionally dedicated and superbly competent colleagues, from whom I draw daily inspiration.

Below is but a partial list of the many individuals I have had the great honor and privilege of learning from and working with.

In the book, I refer often to how much I looked to mentors including Elijah Cummings, Barbara Mikulski, and Fitzhugh Mullan, and how much my life is changed because of Raymond Garcia, Donald Paulson, William Peck, and Stephanie Rawlings-Blake. I'd also like to thank David Brown, Michael Cannon, Douglas Char, Koong-Nah Chung, Robert Graham, Sanjay Gupta, Jim Johnson, Leslie Kahl, Josh Kosowsky, Nick Kristof, Michael Larabee, Bernard Lown, Lenny Marcus, Mark McClellan, Avner Offer, Ali Raja, Anthony So, Kimo Takayesu, and Stephen Trachtenberg for their mentorship and guidance.

During medical training in St. Louis and Boston, I got to know many wonderful future physician-leaders. Kao-Ping Chua and Chris McCoy were partners in countless endeavors, and I am also grateful to Chioma Agbo, Erik Antonsen, Bernard Chang, Katy Li, Griffin Myers,

Shannon O'Mahar, Justin Pittman, and Jonathan Rogg for their friendship. Thank you also to my colleagues at George Washington University, in particular Lynn Goldman, who, along with Fitz, brought me back to GW, and Robert Shesser, who recruited me the first time. I am grateful to work with the entire team of the Fitzhugh Mullan Institute for Health Workforce Equity under the direction of Polly Pittman. Polly, Fitz would be so proud of how you are leading the institute to live out his vision and embody your shared values.

I often wake up and wish that I were going into work at the Baltimore City Health Department, in large part because I miss the extraordinary team we assembled. What a talented, passionate, and superbly competent group of public servants! Thank you to Jeff Amoros, Jacki Anderson, Shelly Choo, Olivia Farrow, Mike Fried, Mary Beth Haller, Jennifer Martin, Michelle Mendes, Perry Myers, Sean Naron, D'Paul Nibber, Dawn O'Neill, Darcy Phelan-Emrick, Mona Rock, Jose Rodriguez, Greg Sileo, Matthew Stefanko, Cassandra Stewart, and Heang Tan. Kristin Rzeczkowski has been my right hand throughout our time in Baltimore and subsequently; I will always be grateful to you, Kristin.

Thanks also to Melody Bailey, Aisha Burgess, Camille Burke, Patrick Chaulk, Francine Childs, Sharon Colburn, Cathy Costa, Shonda DeShields, Rebecca Dineen, Kimberly Eschleman, Nathan Fields, Adena Greenbaum, Malcolm Green-Haynes, Jonathan Gross, Ryan Hemminger, Derrick Hunt, William Kellibrew, Joneigh Khaldun, Amanda Latimore, Jeffrey Long, Molly Martin, Elouise Mayne, Andrew Niklas, Mark O'Brien, Glen Olthoff, Paul Overly, Lisa Parker, Sonia Sarkar, Margaret Schnitzer, Stacy Tuck, James Timpson, Tammy Vines, Cathy Watson, and Mary Grace White. Dante Barksdale, may you rest in peace.

I'm very grateful to, and extremely proud of, the outstanding special assistants who have worked with me: Gabriel Auteri, Evan Behrle, Cameron Clarke, Kelleigh Eastman, Kathleen Goodwin, Anisha Gururaj, William Henagan, Leah Hill, Cooper Lloyd, Narintohn Luangrath, Emily Mediate, Kate Mullersman, Nakisa Sadeghi, Shirli Tay, and Katherine Warren. One of my most cherished collaborations was with Fagan Harris and the Baltimore Corps, which brought us terrific, mission-driven fellows including many of the special assistants above (and Amy Burke, David Fakunle, Anja Fries, Ava Richardson, Anisha Thomas, Lizzy Unger, Janice Williams, among others) who are continuing to make a difference in our city and around the world.

Baltimore is filled with inspiring leaders who are so committed to the city we love. I wish to express my heartfelt thanks to some of the leaders I've had the opportunity to work closely with: Helen Amos, Celeste Amato, Franklyn Baker, Christopher Bedford, Peter Beilenson, Diane Bell-McKoy, Rick Bennett, Ben Cardin, Rudy Chow, Bill Cole, Michael Cryor, Heidi Daniel, Ron Daniels, Kevin Davis, Vinny DeMarco, Bob Embry, Bill Ferguson, Niles Ford, Brian Frosh, Don Fry, Mark Furst, Matt Gallagher, Tom Geddes, Hank Greenberg, Pete Hammen, Carlos Hardy, Al Hathaway, Carla Hayden, Sarah Hemminger, J. Howard Henderson, Debra Hickman, Tomi Hiers, Sandy Hillman, Jan Houbolt, Ben Jealous, Joe Jones, Mark and Patricia Joseph, Charlotte Kerr, Traci Kodeck, Jon Laria, Lainy Lebow-Sachs, Mark and Traci Lerner, Robbyn Lewis, Brooke Lierman, Annette March-Grier, Bill McCarthy, Patrick McCarthy, Douglas Miles, Demaune Millard, Redonda Miller, Rachel Monroe, Diana Morris, Shirley Nathan-Puliam, Gena O'Keefe, Yngvild Olsen, Marla Oros, Jocelyn Pena-Melnyck, Jay Perman, Dennis Pullin, Al Reece, Karen Reese, Jan Rivitz, Nancy Rosen-Cohen, Sam Ross, Faye Royale-Larkin, Dutch Ruppersberger, Boyd Rutherford, John Sarbanes, Shanaysha Sauls, Brandon Scott, Clair Segal, Kurt Schmoke, Josh Sharfstein, Mohan Suntha, Crista Taylor, Christopher Thomascutty, Chuck and Maria Tildon, Chris Van Hollen, Vickie Walters, David Warnock, Kathy Westcoat, Mitchell Whiteman, Edgar Wiggins, Tom Wilcox, David Wilson, Tony Wright, Christy Wyskiel, and Jack Young.

Then there are the many in medicine, public health, and public policy whom I'm proud to have as my colleagues and friends. This, again, is but a long but still nowhere close to complete list: Stephanie Aaronson, Shantanu Agrawal, John Allen, John Auerbach, Mary Bassett, Georges Benjamin, Janice Blanchard, Michael Botticelli, Mika Brzezinski, Robert Califf, Elizabeth Carpenter, Candice Chen, Lincoln Chen, Dave Chokshi, Amy Christensen, Patrick Conway, Karen DeSalvo, Malika Fair, Judy Feder, Jonathan Fielding, Harvey Fineberg, Julio Frenk, Julia Frifield, Philip Fung, Elliot Gerson, Merle Gordon, Peggy Hamburg,

Patty Hayes, Rain Henderson, Jay Higham, Ed Hunter, Chris Jennings, Mitch Katz, Jennifer Lee, Vivian Lee, Amy Liu, Davis Liu, George Lundberg, Peter Lurie, Boris Lushniak, Helen Milby, Kristi Mitchell, David Nash, Bob Phillips, Leslie Pollner, Karen Remley, Anthony Romero, Jon Samuels, Darshak Sanghavi, Nirav Shah, Umair Shah, Steve Shannon, Vivian Sisskin, Pierre Vigilance, Kara Odom Walker, Jim Wallis, and Lee Wallis.

Lyric Chen, Kao-Ping Chua, and Aaron Mertz have been my closest friends for many years, as have Venashri Pillay and Matthew Wright. Sebastian and I are also so grateful to be surrounded by a community of kindhearted people. You all mean the world to us. Thank you, Rick Berndt and Marie-Camille Havard, Maya Rockeymoore Cummings, Elizabeth Embry, Tom Hall and Linell Smith, Fagan Harris and Meryam Bouadjemi, Ellen Heller and Shale Stiller, Bel Leong-Hong and Ken Hong, Kevin and Melisa Lindamood, Maggie McIntosh and Diane Stollenwerk, Aaron Merki and Paul Pineau, Dawn and Wes Moore, Irene Dankwa Mullan, Vivek Murthy and Alice Chen, Lissa Muscatine and Bradley Graham, Peter Neffenger and Gail Staba, Guy Raz and Hannah Stott-Bumsted, Steve and Margaret Sharfstein, and David Watts and Lynn Arnaiz.

This book would not have been possible without my agent, Jessica Papin, and editor, Riva Hocherman. Thank you to the entire team at Henry Holt and Metropolitan. And to the people who read early drafts—Kevin Lindamood, Aaron Mertz, Lissa Muscatine, and Sean Naron—and to the two people who read many versions of very, very early drafts, Nakisa Sadeghi and Angela Wen.

My book begins and ends with family. It's dedicated to Sebastian, and our children, Eli and Isabelle. We thank my father, Xiaolu, and Sebastian's mother, Veronica, along with Angela, Alastair, and Caryn. Flor and Joe Farrell, you are our family, too, and Anthony, Jack, and Neil.

Finally, not a day passes when I don't think about my mother, Sandy Ying Zhang. These are the words I wish I could have said to you: I miss you and I love you.

INDEX

ABCs of Safe Sleep, 179, 196–98
ABC TV, 237
Abell Foundation, 199–201
"acute-on-chronic" situations, 152, 290, 292–93
addiction, 60, 100–101, 106, 108–42, 170, 181. *See also specific substances*
  attitudes toward, 141–42
  children and, 152, 193
  COVID-19 and, 266, 288
  ER and, 131
  harm reduction and, 284
  medical system and, 110, 113, 141
  mental health and, 125, 131
  opioid overprescribing and, 113, 141
  public health and, 118, 137, 158
  racial disparities and, 158
  seniors and, 108–9
  stigma around, 109, 228
  ties to other issues, 108
  trauma and, 194
addiction treatment
  access to, 124–25
  attitudes toward, 141–42
  benefits of, 112
  call center for, 124–27, 149
  COVID-19 and, 288

  ER and, 131
  families and, 125–26
  funding for, 142, 153
  hospitals and, 112–14, 131–34
  hub and spoke model and, 134
  incarceration vs., 141
  medication-assisted, 114
  naloxone and, 116–24
  need for, 108–12
  NIMBYism and, 111–12
  publicity about, 121–22
  Pugh and, 136, 138–41
  Stabilization Center and, 131–33
adverse childhood experiences (ACEs), 193–94
Aedes mosquito, 169
Affordable Care Act (2010), 54, 61, 214–15, 230, 247, 292
African Americans, 95, 100, 156–57
  COVID-19 and, 289
  food deserts and, 290
  infant mortality and, 195, 198
  maternal mortality and, 159, 230
  opioid crisis and, 158–59
air quality, 3–4
alcohol, powdered, 204–5
alcohol dependence, 227–28

American Academy of Pediatrics, 205
American Medical Association, 242
American Medical Student Association
      (AMSA), 37, 40–42, 47–55, 58, 61,
      63, 93, 140, 247
American Public Health Association, 168
Amoros, Jeff, 207
Anderson, Jacki, 221
Angell, Marcia, 50–52
animal control, 99
Annie E. Casey Foundation, 201
anti-vaccine movement, 258, 278–79
anxiety, 125
Armanpour, Christiane, 237
asthma, 1–4, 12–13, 29, 35, 45, 62, 65,
      129, 172, 203, 294
at-home diagnostics, 311
Atkinson, John, 39, 43, 55–56
Atlanta, 272
Atlas, Scott, 275
Auteri, Gabriel, 106, 128, 149–50, 201, 218

Bad Batch (app), 129–30
Baltimarket programs, 171
Baltimore, 3
   assistance and, 160–61
   lawsuit on teen pregnancy funding
      cuts, 215
   as majority-minority city, 9
   mayoralty race of 2016 and, 135–37
   median incomes in, 152
   neighborhood forums and, 10
   population decline and, 10
   St. Louis and, 94–95
Baltimore City Council, 98, 102–4, 119,
      132, 163, 170, 181, 205–7, 222, 316
Baltimore City Health Department. *See
      also specific issues and programs*
   ACA repeal and, 214–15
   achievements of, 168–69
   addiction and, 106, 111–30, 141, 153,
      170, 173
   advocacy and, 247
   awards and honors and, 168
   Bad Batch app and, 129–30
   business community and, 153–54
   care for most vulnerable and, 107, 170
   CDC and, 275
   child health and, 107, 190–208
   community groups and, 154–55,
      172–74, 316

COVID-19 and, 267
cross-agency agreements and, 128
data vs. story-telling and, 101, 171–72
Day of Service at, 178–79
dogfighting laws and, 170
Eastern clinic break-ins and, 175–80
elderly and, 171–72
emergency response protocols and,
      146
funding battles and, 99, 103, 154–55,
      168–69, 185–88, 204
goals and successes at, 170–73
Gray unrest and, 143–52, 154–56, 159
healthy babies program and, 204
hired to head, 5–6, 93–104
HIV/AIDS and, 166
hub and spoke model and, 134
inequities addressed by, 152–53
infant mortality and, 194–98
leadership lessons at, 160–69
Levels of Care and, 133–34
measles immunization and, 170
mental health services and, 106,
      153–54, 170
newsletter and podcasts by, 155
pace of work at, 164–65
powdered alcohol and synthetic
      marijuana and, 170, 204–5
pregnancy and birth of Eli while
      heading, 216–22, 227–28
Pugh as mayor and, 136–40, 209
racism and Healthy Baltimore plan
      and, 156–58
reproductive health and, 210–11
Safe Streets program and, 183–89, 204,
      214
school-based programs and, 203–4
Stabilization Center and, 131–33
sugar-sweetened beverages battle and,
      205–7
team at, 103–7, 140, 146–50, 165
TECHealth and, 173
teen pregnancy prevention and, 210,
      215
Title X and, 210–11, 229
trauma-informed care and, 154–55,
      179–81
visibility of public health as goal of,
      170–76
Zika and, 169
Baltimore City Human Services Agency, 9

Baltimore Corps, 106, 126, 201, 207, 267
Baltimore Emergency Operations Center
    (EOC), 144–46, 149–50
Baltimore Fire Department, 128
Baltimore Police Department, 11, 128
    addiction treatment and, 141, 181
    Gray death and, 143
    homeless and, 180–81
    mental health and, 180
    naloxone training and, 119–20, 122
    Safe Streets and, 185
    trauma and violence training and, 180
Baltimore Public Library, 145
Baltimore Sun, 138, 186
Batts, Anthony, 119–20
Becerra, Diego, 301
Becerra, Erika, 301
begging as child, 31–32, 96
Behavioral Health System Baltimore, 129
Behrle, Evan, 126–29, 133–34
Beilenson, Peter, 98–99, 124–25, 195
Belluz, Julia, 300
beverage industry, 206–7
Biden, Joe, 311
Billion Steps challenge, 173
birth control, 210–11, 229, 243–44
Birx, Deborah, 275
bleach, 271–72
blood pressure, 62, 193, 205, 290
B'More for Health Babies program,
    195–99, 204, 219, 228
Boston, 70–71, 87, 96–97, 153, 183, 216,
    267
    Marathon bombing, 86–87
Botticelli, Michael, 153
Brazil, 169
breast cancer, 229
    mother's illness with, 75–84, 88–89,
    313
breastfeeding, 197, 220, 222, 227
Brigham & Women's Hospital, 70, 82–83
Brookings Institution, 289
Browne, Francois, 190
Brzezinski, Mika, 301
buprenorphine (Suboxone), 113–14, 133
Burundi, 64
Business Advisory Group on Health, 153

Califf, Robert, 153
California State University, Los Angeles
    AMSA and, 37, 40–42

premed advising and, 36, 38
undergraduate education at, 30,
    33–38
Canada, 27–28, 53
cancer screenings, 6, 243
cancer survivors, 287
cardiovascular disease, 4, 65, 101, 156–57,
    171, 193, 287
cars, child heat deaths in, 190–92
Carter, Leasia, 190–92
Carter, Wilbert, 190
Catholic Charities, 137, 184
Catholic Church, 173–74, 247
census, 7
Centers for Disease Control (CDC)
    COVID-19 and, 261, 265, 267, 272–77,
    282, 288, 292, 294
    erosion of confidence in, 273–77
    local funding cuts and, 258
    measles and, 258
    opioid prescriptions and, 141
    school safety and, 295
    Zika and, 169
cervical cancer, 49, 96, 216
Chen, Lyric, 85, 246
chi ku (eat bitter), 11, 14, 28, 41, 77, 316
Child Fatality Review (CFR) Committee,
    191–96, 220
children's health, 107, 173. *See also* infant
    mortality; schools
    abuse and neglect and, 100, 190–92,
    294
    asthma and, 1–4, 29, 65, 129, 173, 203,
    294
    COVID-19 and, 266, 272, 288, 294–95
    elections of 2016 and, 210
    eyeglasses and, 199–203
    heat deaths in cars and, 190–92
    hunger and, 4
    immunizations and, 212, 215
    obesity and, 205–7
    substance exposure in utero, 193
    trauma and, 4–5, 193–95, 199
China, 30, 88
    childhood in, 11–18, 57, 59
    co-sleeping and, 196
    COVID-19 and, 259, 268, 300
    emigration from, 2–3, 18–19
    Tiananmen Square uprisings and,
    63–64
    travel restrictions and, 268

Choo, Shelly, 132, 134
Christie, Chris, 281
Chua, Kao-Ping, 54, 71, 248
Churchill, Winston, 314
Citizens for Patient Safety, 88
civil rights movement, 48
climate change, 274
Clinton, Bill, 66–67
Clinton, Hillary, 209
CNN, 237–38, 271–72, 280, 282, 303
Code in the Schools, 129
code traumas, 182
Columbia University, 218
community health centers, 211
complement-deficiency disorders, 43
Comprehensive Addiction Resources
    Emergency (CARE) Act (2019),
    142
Congo, Democratic Republic of, 64–65,
    258–59
"conscience clause," 212
conspiracy theorists, 273
contact tracing, 265–67, 273, 291, 298,
    309
convalescent plasma, 277, 282
Cooper, Anderson, 271, 303
Cooper, Carnell, 183
co-sleeping, 196, 198
counter-detailing, 51
COVID-19, 4–7, 170, 256–313, 315
    "acute on chronic" disparities and,
        292–93
    aerosol transmission of, 259–60
    asymptomatic transmission of, 259,
        269, 276–77
    Biden and, 311
    budget and, 285
    CDC guidances and, 276–77
    contact tracing and, 265–67, 273, 291,
        298, 309
    deaths from, 260, 266, 268, 282,
        297–98, 308–9
    demographic tracking and, 291, 293
    economic impact of, 272, 282–83, 294,
        307–8
    essential workers and, 286, 291–92
    failure to prioritize public health and,
        4–7, 261–63, 287–89, 294–98, 313
    FDA and, 277–78
    government failures and, 261–70,
        277–78, 288–89

    harm reduction and, 284–85
    health care workers and, 308
    health insurance and, 292
    hospitalizations and, 260, 266
    lessons of, 311–12
    long haulers and, 308
    mask-wearing and, 270, 272–73,
        280–81, 283, 298
    mental health and, 288
    misinformation and, 262, 266
    outdoor vs. indoor activities and,
        283–85
    overdoses and, 288
    pregnancy and, 299–301
    quarantine and, 266–67, 279–80
    racial and economic disparities and,
        289–91
    reopening and, 266–67, 283–85, 288,
        294–96
    restaurants and, 284–85
    schools and, 288, 294–96
    social distancing and, 270, 283, 298
    testing and, 261–67, 269–70, 276–77,
        284, 290–91, 298, 309, 315
    test positivity rate, 291
    transit and, 284
    travel restrictions and, 268
    treatments and, 267
    Trump and, 271–86
    vaccine development and, 269–70,
        277–79, 297
    vaccine distribution and, 269–70,
        292–94, 303–4
    vaccine trials and, 303–7
    ventilation and, 283–84
    weddings and, 310
    younger demographic and, 285
cribs, free, 197–98
crime, 108, 112, 136
criminal justice reform, 247
Crisis Line, 126–27, 129
Cultural Revolution, 12, 14, 16
Cummings, Elijah, 4, 83, 142, 151,
    165–68, 181, 188, 219–20, 223, 251,
    301, 313, 316–17
Cure Violence, 183, 186

Daily Record, 187
Daniels, Ron, 200
Dating Matters program, 181
Davis, Kevin, 181

Democratic National Committee, 102, 209–10

Democratic Party, 49, 247, 256, 272, 282–83

dental care, 30, 175

depression, 125

Detroit, 105

diabetes, 4, 62, 114, 148, 193, 205, 287, 290
    gestational, 195

diagnosis, 83–84

dialysis, 65

disinfectant injections, 271

Doering, Jodi, 282

dogfighting, 170, 175

domestic violence, 182, 193, 195

"Don't Die" campaign, 121–22, 126, 197

Dreamers, 75

Drug Enforcement Administration (DEA), 128

drug reps, 50–51

drunk driving laws, 309

Duke University, 63, 256

Eastern health center break-ins, 175–79
    Day of Service after, 178–79

Eastman, Kelleigh, 207

Ebola, 175, 258–59

educational attainment, 4–5, 101, 294. See also schools

Eileen, dialysis patient, 62

elections
    of 2004, 49
    of 2016, 135–37, 209–10
    of 2020, 249, 269, 278, 297, 311

Elijah Cummings Healing City Act (2020), 181

Embry, Bob, 199–200

emergency medicine (working in ER), 103
    "acute-on-chronic" conditions and, 152
    addiction and, 109–11, 114, 125, 128, 131–33
    child deaths and, 190–91
    COVID-19 and, 289
    decision to specialize in, 4, 36, 61–62, 85–86, 146–47
    health-care system and, 4, 63
    heart attacks and, 84–85
    neurology clinical work and, 43–45
    residency in, 70–71, 80, 82, 161
    social factors and, 65–66
    violence interruption and, 182–83

Empowered Patient Coalition, 87–88

English, as second language, 21–23, 34

environmentalism, 247, 274

epilepsy, 45

Europe, 268–69

Facebook, 261

Farrow, Olivia, 99, 105, 132–33, 218

Fauci, Anthony, 274

Federal Bureau of Investigation (FBI), 263

fentanyl, 127–30, 173

Florida, 182

Floyd, George, 285–86

Food and Drug Administration (FDA), 153, 275, 277–78, 303

food assistance, 4, 7, 22, 129, 150, 152, 203, 211–12, 294

food deserts, 4, 157, 171, 290

food poisoning, 168

free speech, 64

Fried, Mike, 126, 128–29, 201

Frifield, Julia, 246

Fry, Don, 137–38, 173

Fulbright Scholars, 106

Gandhi, Mahatma, 55

Garcia, Raymond, 35–38, 40, 56, 235, 316

Geiger, Jack, 47

George Washington University, 48, 105
    ER at, 87–88, 93, 96
    Fitzhugh Mullan Institute for Health Workforce Equity, 255–56

Georgia, Republic of, 88

Girl Scouts, 146

Gohmert, Louis, 273

Goldberg, Whoopi, 237–38

Goldman Sachs, 272

Goodman, Bob, 50–51

Goodwin, Kathleen, 218

Governing magazine, 168

grassroots activism, 52, 55

Gray, Freddie, 143–56, 160–61, 164, 184, 200

Gray, Zaray, 190–91, 193

Greater Baltimore Committee, 137

gun lobby, 189, 245

gun violence, 5, 100, 101, 182–85, 189, 256

Gupta, Sanjay, 271–72, 303

Gutierrez, Carlos, 39

Hallisay, Julia, 87–88
Hallisay, Katherine Eileen, 88
Hammen, Pete, 131–32, 139
harm reduction, 284–86
Hayden, Carla, 145
health care. *See also* racial and economic
    disparities
  access to, 6, 22, 29–30, 49, 215
  as human right, 47, 54, 59, 215
  social factors and, 63, 65–66
  as system, 4, 45–48, 61–63, 87
  universal, 47, 49, 53–54
health-care professionals. *See also*
    physicians
  conscience clause and, 212
  COVID-19 and, 281–82, 308–10
  diversity and, 37–38, 55, 311
  Gray unrest and, 152–53
  pharmaceutical industry and, 50
health insurance, 47, 121, 124–25,
    200–201, 214–17, 229, 292, 311
  lack of, 4, 53
Healthy Baltimore 2020 plan, 156–57,
    171, 173
Healthy Holly (Pugh), 136
Healthy Moms, Healthy Babies, 240
heart attacks, 29, 84–85, 148. *See also*
    cardiovascular disease
herd immunity, 265–66, 278
heroin, 109, 127, 152. *See also* addiction;
    opioid epidemic
Hickman, Debra, 96–97
Hillcrest Elementary School (Logan,
    Utah), 21–23
HIV/AIDS, 6, 49, 60, 63, 96–98, 142, 166,
    175, 240, 256, 284
Hogan, Larry, 185–88, 204, 222, 263
Holliday, Fred, 88
Holliday, Regina, 88
homelessness, 3, 7, 25–26, 60, 96, 180,
    203, 288
homicide rates, 5
hospitals, 10
  addiction and, 112–14, 121, 128, 133
  advisory boards and, 85
  B'More for Healthy Babies, 196
  COVID-19 and, 260–61, 263, 266, 282,
    289, 299–300
  Gray unrest and, 144
  hub and spoke models and, 134
  Levels of Care and, 133–34, 141

  patient-centered care and, 84–85
  mortality and morbidity reviews and,
    191–92
  premature infants and, 217
  residents' work rules and, 54
  Title X and, 211
housing, 4, 7, 22, 136
housing discrimination, 157
hunger, 4, 21–22, 100, 178–80, 203, 288.
    See also food assistance
hydroxychloroquine, 271, 274, 277, 282

IBM, 98, 216
immigrants, 1–4, 7, 26–30, 211–12, 222
  political asylum and, 7, 27–28, 75, 212
immune suppression, 287
immunization, 170, 175
infant mortality, 5, 101, 156, 194–98, 240
influenza
  H1N1 pandemic, 257, 300
  pandemic of 1918, 288–89, 297–98
insulin, 62, 114, 148
International Overdose Awareness Day,
    122
Internet, 294
Iowa primaries of 2004, 49
Italy, 300

Jack Rutledge Fellowship, 54
jobs, 10, 136
Johns Hopkins University, 94, 185, 200, 201
  Hospital, 96
Johnson, Boris, 281
Johnson & Johnson vaccine, 303–4

Kaiser Foundation, 295
Kaplan MCAT test prep program, 36
Khaldun, Joneigh, 105, 113–14, 132
King, Martin Luther, Jr., 294
Kosowsky, Josh, 83–84
Kristof, Nicholas, 63–64

Lacks, Henrietta, 96
Larabee, Mike, 256, 258
Latinos, 289
Law Enforcement Assisted Diversion
    (LEAD), 141, 181, 189
leadership, 102–3
  advocacy and, 314
  Cummings on lifting people up and,
    165–68

empathy and, 314–15
highlighting achievements of team and, 168–69
ideological purity and, 140–41, 158–59
incremental change and, 52–53, 314–16
learning from people on front lines and, 316–17
mentoring and, 316–17
Mikulski on pacing and, 163–65
motherhood and, 222
pain, passion, and purpose and, 313–14
positioning and, 139–41
Rawlings-Blake on authenticity and, 160–63
women and, 97–98, 161–63
lead poisoning, 99, 152, 179, 195, 205
Legionnaire's disease, 175
Lehman Brothers, 69
leukemia, 37
Levels of Care, 133–34, 141
LGBTQ rights, 49, 212, 247
life expectancy, 5, 7, 66, 95, 101, 152, 156, 171
Li Wenliang, Dr., 259
Lloyd, Cooper, 153
lobbying, 206
Los Angeles, childhood in, 23–26, 29–30
Los Angeles Arboretum, 81, 88
low-birth-weight babies, 217
Lugar, Dick, 68
lupus, 271

Malaysian Americans, 105
malnutrition, 64–65
mammograms, 215
Maraldo, Pam J., 252–53
marijuana, synthetic, 170, 205
Marshall Scholars, 106
Martin, Jennifer, 145
Maryland
    child homicide law and, 192–93
    COVID-19 and, 263
Maryland Chief Medical Examiners Office, 127
Maryland General Assembly, 117–18
Maryland National Guard, 263
Maryland Shock Trauma Hospital, 183
Maryland State Legislature, 132, 136, 173, 185–86, 204–5, 221–22

Massachusetts General Hospital, 70, 86–87
McCarthy, Bill, 137–38
McCoy, Chris, 54–55
measles, 147, 170, 257–58
meatpacking plants, 291, 293
Mediate, Emily, 240, 246
Medicaid, 62, 240
    child vision screenings and, 199, 201
    immigrants and, 211
    naloxone and, 7, 22
    pregnant women and, 216–17
Medical College Admissions Test, 36–38
medical error reduction, 49
medical school. *See also* Washington University Medical School
    advocacy and, 46–47
    AMSA and, 55
    application to, 36–39
    clinical training and, 46
    cost of, 38–39, 51, 55
    pharmaceutical industry and, 50–52
    preclinical training and, 40, 46
    speech disorders and disabilities and, 59
Medicare for All, 256
medications
    access and affordability of, 44–46, 50, 62–63, 148–50, 297
    COVID-19 misinformation and, 271–72, 274, 277, 282
    prescription access program and, 151
Medley, Lamont, 184
meningitis, 44
Mental Health and Trauma Response Plan, 150, 154–55
mental health needs, 60, 97, 100, 106, 125, 131, 150, 153–54, 166, 170, 174, 180, 193–94, 203, 240, 247, 256, 294
    COVID-19 and, 266, 288
    stigma and, 228, 233
MERS, 256
Mertz, Aaron, 67–69, 71
methadone clinics, 111–14
Michigan, 105
Mikulski, Barbara, 163–65, 171, 235, 246
Minnesota, 241–42
miscarriage, 250–51, 299
misdiagnoses, 78–79, 83–84
Moderna vaccine, 303
Mormonism, 20–21

Morning Joe (TV show), 301
motherhood, combining career and,
    215–22, 227–28, 248–49, 299–303
mothers. *See also* breastfeeding;
    postpartum depression; pregnancy
    maternal health and, 210
    maternal mortality and, 159, 230, 240,
        243, 300
    prenatal care and, 216–18
    support for new, 197–98
MSNBC, 301
Mullan, Fitzhugh "Fitz," 47–48, 55, 87, 96,
    255, 316–17
multisystem inflammatory syndrome, 295
Murthy, Vivek, 153
My Life (Clinton), 66

Nai Nai (paternal grandmother), 11–16,
    18–19, 22, 27, 32, 59, 81
naloxone, 110–11, 115–19, 121–23,
    128–30, 136–37, 141, 179, 181, 189,
    197, 315
Naron, Sean, 106
National Association of City and County
    Health Officials, 168
National Institute on Drug Abuse, 153
National Institutes of Health, 277
Nation Health Service Corps, 48
Native Americans, 290
needle exchange programs, 98, 116,
    118–19, 127, 129, 284
New England Journal of Medicine, 50
New Mexico, 290
New Mexico State Health Department, 48
New York City, 263, 267, 269
New York Times, 63, 235–36, 252–53,
    277
NIMBYism, 111–12, 114, 124, 136
Nixon, Richard M., 210
No Free Lunch, 50–51
non-pharmaceutical interventions, 298
nursing homes, 291

Obama, Barack, 54, 105, 153–54, 169, 188
obesity, 290
O'Brien, Mark, 126–29
Offer, Avner, 68
Office of Management and Budget, 105
Olsen, Yngvild, 131–32
O'Neill, Dawn, 99, 105, 176–77, 218
Operation Warp Speed, 269, 278

opioid epidemic, 5, 109, 113, 115, 132,
    134, 141–42, 147, 153, 158–59,
    193, 210, 241, 256, 315. *See also*
    addiction; addiction treatment
overdoses, 5, 10, 108–11, 124, 127, 156
    naloxone and, 114–20
    stigma and, 141
    survivors program, 133
Oxford University, 66–72, 94, 126, 246

paid family and sick leave, 173, 221–22
pain management, 113
pandemics. *See also* COVID-19; influenza
    early and aggressive action and, 288–89
    factors creating, 257
    public health and, 297–98
Pap smears, 210, 217, 229, 240
patient advocacy, 6, 49, 87–88, 96, 159
patient-centered care, 83–88, 93, 247
Paulson, Donald, 35–36, 38–40, 43, 56,
    316
PBS NewsHour, 201–2
Peace Corps, 88
Peck, William, 56
pediatricians, 182
Pence, Mike, 264, 296
personal protective equipment (PPE),
    260–65, 282
Pfizer vaccine, 303
pharmaceutical industry, 50–54, 113, 141,
    256
pharmacies
    Gray unrest and, 148–49
    naloxone and, 120–21, 129
PharmFree movement, 50–52, 54
Philadelphia, 288–89
Physicians for Social Responsibility, 47
physicians. *See also* health-care
    professionals; medical school;
    misdiagnoses
    advocacy and, 49
    conscience clause and, 212–14
    doctor-patient relationship and,
        80–84
    early desire to become, 29–30, 35–36
    pain management and, 113
Physician Sunshine Act (2012), 52
piano and violin playing, 30–32, 73
Planned Parenthood, 6, 211, 228–54
    federated model of, and affiliates,
        231–32, 240–43, 245–46

repositioning attempted at, 230–31,
237–40, 242–45, 252–53
This is Health Care initiative and, 243,
249
pneumonia, 29
poison-control centers, 272
police. See Baltimore Police Department
police brutality, 143. See also specific
cases
reform and, 188–89
postpartum depression, 228, 233, 300
poverty, 3–5, 7, 29, 48, 96–97, 101, 108,
157, 194
preeclampsia, 195
preexisting conditions, 45, 62, 215
pregnancy. See also miscarriage; mothers
cost of, 216–17
screening and, 195
premature infants, 152, 217
prisons and jails
COVID-19 and, 293
incarceration rates, 5, 101, 157
medical transfers and, 212–13
promotores, 241
public assistance. See also food assistance;
Medicaid; and other specific
programs
childhood in Utah and, 22–23
public charge rule and, 211–12
public health. See also COVID-19; and
specific diseases, health issues, and
policies
attacks on, 273
"be first, be right, be credible" and,
274
Biden and, 311
CDC and, 275–76
community and, 7–8
credible messengers and, 120, 291,
309–10
disparities and inequities and, 156–58,
293–94
economy and, 283
education and, 4, 7, 136, 294–97
empathy and, 309–10, 314–15
going upstream and, 194
harm reduction and, 128, 284–86
incremental change and, 315
invisibility of, and need to maintain,
4–7, 168–76, 223, 257–58, 266,
269–70, 287–89, 297–98, 309–14

lessons from front lines of, 170–74,
316–17
meeting people where they are and,
115
metrics and, 171
misinformation and, 271
multilayered nature of, 298
Oxford studies in, 68–69
passion and purpose in, 314
politics and, 6, 213–14, 309–11
public trust and, 258–59, 276–78
simple solutions vs., 311
social factors and, 66, 289
Public Health Medical College, 55
Pugh, Catherine, 136–41, 209, 217–18,
221

quarantine, 257–58, 266–67, 279–80, 285,
298

racial and economic disparities, 3–6,
101–2, 143, 152, 166, 247, 256
COVID-19 and, 262, 289–94, 298,
311
denial of care and conscience clause
and, 212
health insurance and, 292
health metrics and, 156–58
infant mortality and, 198
maternal mortality and, 159, 230
opioid treatment and, 158–59
public health infrastructure and, 107,
311
social factors of health and, 65–66
upstream model and, 194, 208
women's health care and, 49
racism, structural, 143, 156–58, 290, 311
Rawlings-Blake, Stephanie, 93, 102–4,
106, 119, 128, 130–31, 134–35, 139,
144, 154, 160–62, 174, 187, 197
Red Cross, 258
redlining, 157
reproductive health, 49, 173, 175, 210–11,
228, 229–31, 234–35, 236, 238–45,
247–48, 249. See also mothers;
pregnancy; and specific issues
Reproductive Options Education, 47
Republican National Committee, 210
Republican Party, 214, 247, 272–73
Reuters, 70
rheumatoid arthritis, 271

Rhode Island, 133
Rhodes Scholarship, 66–68, 71
Rhodes Scholars network, 103, 106, 126, 147, 240
Richards, Cecile, 228–29, 232–33, 245
right-wing media, 273
Rockefeller Foundation, 277
Rodriguez, José, 120, 127
Roe v. Wade, 47
Rwanda, 63–64, 96–97
Ryan White Act (2009), 142
Rzeczkowski, Kristin, 105, 156, 175–77, 218, 220, 236, 246

Safe Streets, 183–85, 214
same-sex parents, 212
San Gabriel Valley, 32–33
Sarbanes, Paul, 68
SARS, 256
SARS-CoV2 virus, genome sequenced, 297
Saudi Arabia, 171
Schmoke, Kurt, 103
schools, 5, 10, 22–23, 199–204
    asthma and, 172, 294
    COVID-19 and, 294–97
    economy and, 294
    eyeglasses and, 199–202, 294
    free lunch program and, 21–22, 180, 203
    mental health counseling and, 150, 154, 294
    missing, as child, 31–32
    sex education and, 9, 210, 215
    trauma and resilience programs in, 180–81
    vaccinations and, 170
science
    COVID-19 misinformation and, 272–75, 286
    erosion of public trust in, 5, 259, 286
    politicization of, 278–79
Seattle, 141
seizure medications, 44–46, 62
senior centers, 5, 99–100, 108–9, 197
seniors, 109, 150
    fall prevention and, 171–72
Sesame Street, 272
sexually transmitted infections (STIs), 100, 243
Sharfstein, Josh, 98–99, 131, 195
Shock Trauma Hospital, 94

ShopRite, 171
Sidel, Victor, 47
SIDS (sudden infant death syndrome), 195–96
Singapore, 141
single-payer system, 47, 53
Sisskin, Vivian, 58–60
Sisters Together and Reaching (STAR), 96–97
Skolnik, Michael, 88
Skolnik, Patty, 88
sleep-related infant deaths, 195–98
Smith, Joseph, 22
smoking, 100, 205
So, Anthony, 63, 257
Souter, David, 68
South Africa, 69–71
South Dakota, 241–42
South Korea, 263, 294, 309
speech disorders, 57–60
speech therapist, 58–60
Stabilization Center, 131–33, 136, 141
state governors, COVID-19 and, 272–73, 277, 296–97
"State of Health in Baltimore City" (white paper), 135–36
Stefanko, Matthew, 127
steroid medication, 3, 30
St. Louis, 94–95. *See also* Washington University Medical School
    Baltimore and, 94–95
    ER in, 65
    influenza pandemic of 1918 and, 289
    medical school and, 39–40
Student Health Organization, 48
student loans, 38–39, 51, 55
stuttering, 57–60, 67
substance use disorders, 108, 125, 131, 193, 288. *See also* addiction; addiction treatment programs; *and specific substances*
Sugar Free Kids Maryland, 205
sugar-sweetened beverages, 205–7
suicide, 182, 193, 288
Swiss cheese model, 192, 194

Tan, Heang, 218
Tay, Shirli, 105, 146–48, 165, 218
teen pregnancy prevention, 210, 215
telemedicine, 203, 287, 311
telepsychiatry program, 154

Texas, 243
"This is Health Care" initiative, 243, 249
Thomson Reuters, 216
Tiananmen Square uprising, 63–64
tick-bite fever, 304
Title X, 210–11, 229–30
Transforming Engineering for Civic
    Health (TECHealth), 129, 173
transgender people, 212
trauma, 100, 154, 157, 179–89, 193–94,
    204
trauma-informed care training, 179–81,
    189
Trump, Donald J., 142, 209–15, 246–47
    ACA repeal and, 214–17
    attacks on science and, 259
    COVID-19 and, 262–64, 268–75, 278,
        280–81, 285–86, 295–97
    immigrants and, 211–12
    Medicaid and, 216–17
    public health and, 210
    reproductive health and, 209–11
    Title X and, 229

unemployment, 108, 152, 307–8, 311
Unidos US, 233
Union of Concerned Scientists, 259
United States
    citizenship application and, 95
    immigration to, 17–24
    simple solutions vs. public health and,
        311
U.S. Conference of Mayors, 102
U.S. Congress, 52, 54, 99, 132, 141–42,
    154, 169, 282
U.S. House of Representatives, 290–91
U.S. Postal Service, 7, 297
U.S. Senate, 105, 163, 274
U.S. Supreme Court, 68
U.S. surgeon general, 47, 108, 153
University of Illinois, 17
University of Maryland, 58–59, 94
University of Southern California, 88
University of Witwatersrand, 70
Utah, childhood in, 17–24
Utah State University, 17, 19–24

vaccines
    ACA and, 215
    COVID-19, 269–70, 277–79, 292–94,
        297, 303–7

efficacy and, 170, 278
opposition to, 258
safety and, 136, 170, 278
vasectomies, 243
ventilator, 44–45
Vermont, 134
veterans, 180
Vietnamese immigrants, 29
View, The (TV show), 237, 238
violence, 4, 7, 157, 173, 179–89. See also
    domestic violence; gun violence;
    trauma
violence interruption program, 182–88
vision care, 199–202, 294
Vision for Baltimore, 201–2
Vision to Learn, 201
Volkow, Nora, 153
voting, 7, 297

Wai Po (maternal grandmother), 12, 15
Walker, Alastair, 71
Walker, Eli (son), 216–22, 227, 232,
    234–35, 248–51, 300, 302, 305–7
Walker, Isabelle (daughter), 299–303,
    305–8
Walker, Sebastian (husband)
    birth of Eli and, 215–16, 219–20
    birth of Isabelle and, 299–302, 305
    career support and, 97–98, 164
    COVID-19 and, 304–7
    marriage to, 70–72, 81, 89
Walker, Veronica, 71
"Walking Gallery" (Holliday), 88
Warby Parker, 201
Warren, Elizabeth, 142
Warren, Katherine, 147–48, 156, 218
Washington, D.C., 87–88
Washington Post, 184, 256–57, 259
Washington University School of
    Medicine, 39–43, 46–47, 56–58, 65,
        67, 75, 105
    AMSA and, 47
    commencement speech at, 56
    ER rotation at, 61–62
    graduation from, 52, 63
    mother's breast cancer during, 76–79
    neurology rotation at, 43–46
    PhD research at, 43, 46, 55–56
Wen, Angela (sister), 28, 30, 33, 40, 71,
    74–75, 77–78, 81–83, 88–89, 222,
        304

Wen, Louis Xiaolu (father), 7, 59, 74–75, 211–12
  early life in China and, 11–16
  free speech and, 64
  immigration to U.S. and, 2–3, 18–34
  political asylum and, 7, 27–28, 75, 212
When Doctors Don't Listen (Kosowsky and Wen), 83–84, 87, 105
White Coat, Clenched Fist (Mullan), 48
WIC program, 144, 197
women's health care, 234. *See also* reproductive health
  conscience clause and, 212
  domestic violence and, 182
  racial disparities and, 49
Woodward, Bob, 281
Workgroup on Drug Treatment Access and Neighborhood Relations, 137–38
workplaces
  accommodations for parents and, 221–22
  worker protections and, 291–92
World Bank, 171
World Health Organization (WHO), 63, 169, 257, 268, 272
WuDunn, Sheryl, 63
Wuhan, China, 256–57, 260, 283

Ye Ye (paternal grandfather), 11–12, 14–15, 18–19, 21–22, 27, 32–34, 81
Yellowstone National Park, 24
"you but not me" phenomenon, 50
Young, Quentin, 47
youth health, 170, 185

Zhang, Sandy Ying (mother), 7, 211–12
  breast cancer and death of, 75–84, 88–89, 313
  Canada and, 26–28
  childhood asthma and, 12–14
  daughter Angela and, 28, 33, 81, 217
  education in China, 11–12
  free speech and, 64
  immigration by, to study at Utah State, 2–3, 16–17, 19–23, 41
  Los Angeles and, 24–26, 29–33, 41
  marriage of, 14–15
  relationship with, 39–40, 42, 73–75
  as school teacher, 30, 32–34, 41
  stuttering and, 59
  thoughts of, with birth of son, 217, 221–22
Zika epidemic, 168–69, 258

ABOUT THE AUTHOR

Dr. Leana Wen is an emergency physician, public health professor at George Washington University, and nonresident senior fellow at the Brookings Institution. She is also a contributing columnist for the *Washington Post* and a CNN medical analyst. Previously, she served as Baltimore's health commissioner, where she led the nation's oldest continuously operating public health department. She is the author of the patient advocacy book *When Doctors Don't Listen: How to Avoid Misdiagnoses and Unnecessary Tests.* Dr. Wen lives with her husband and their two young children in Baltimore.